GAY AGENDA 21
By
Nemanja Ljubojevic

GAY AGENDA 21

ISBN: 9781088502877

Contents of the book:

GAY AGENDA 21

CHAPTER 1 "INTRODUCTION"

Alvin Toffler: *"The illiterate of the 21st century will not be those who cannot read and write, but those who cannot unlearn the many lies that they have been conditioned to believe."*

Intelligence is not knowing everything but questioning everything you think you know.

The gay (LGBT) movement is presented as a movement for tolerance, acceptance, and equality, but in truth, this "civil rights" movement is being pushed to destroy the nuclear family and end society as we know it.

Even though the movement is best known as the gay movement this term does not adequately describe the agenda behind it. A more precise name for such a movement would be "The androgynous agenda" since it not only involves sexuality but also sexual identity, but an even more accurate description of this movement would be "The sexual liberation movement".

Like all civil rights movements even though it preaches equality, equality is never the end goal, prior examples include the feminist movement (where women, in contemporary western civilization, are not satisfied even though they are legally, socially and economically equal to men, while continually presenting themselves as perpetual victims of made-up societal oppression), the African-American movement where some black people (members of the Black Lives Matter movement funded by George Soros) are not happy being equal to white people but rather want supremacy. The same principle applies when it comes to the LGBT movement, which has several stages: don't kill us (done), tolerate us (done), give us equal rights (done), recognize our out-of-wedlock cohabitation (done), give us the right to marry – on the basis that out-of-wedlock cohabitation is equal to marriage (done), give us the right to adopt children (done), give us legal protection to shield us against anyone who dares to use free speech to disagree with us or prove us wrong (done), and after all this they still have gay parades and want more rights even though every single one of their demands has been met. Why do they still hold pride parades in countries in which they have equal marriage rights? When will it stop if it is intended to stop at all?

One has to wonder for how long are these gay rights movements going to go on. If they get more rights after achieving equality that means they will inevitably enjoy supremacy over those who are not members of their movement.

The gay movement is not about equality, so this means it has alternative motives, and that is to normalize and legalize pedophilia in the same way gay marriage was legalized. This will occur once people become more "open-minded" and tolerant of this kind of lifestyle. Using human empathy against the people.

The topic of the gay movement is far broader than most people can possibly fathom.

GAY AGENDA 21

CHAPTER 2: "HISTORY"

George Santayana: *"Those who cannot remember the past are condemned to repeat it"*

Aldous Huxley, preface to the 1946 edition of Brave New World: *"As political and economic freedom diminishes, sexual freedom tends compensatingly to increase"*

People arguing homosexuality is normal and should be accepted often say that this behavior has been present throughout the entire human history. Pedophilia, incest, and rape have also existed for a very long time, should we accept them as well based on that argument? First of all, there is no way of knowing if homosexuality existed for as long as humanity since there are no historical records of homosexuality prior to 2000 B.C. (that's for male homosexuality, female homosexuality doesn't go that far back in history), but what we can be sure is that heterosexuality existed from the dawn of mankind since if it didn't we would not be alive right now.

When you look at history every civilization (including those that precede Christianity and any other monotheistic religion) is based on the nuclear family, marriage between a man and a woman (Celts had a form of marriage way before Christianity appeared). Meaning that the heterosexual monogamous relationship was established as a norm in nearly every culture around the world before religion "forced" it on everyone. Marriage (union between one man and one woman) also precedes the state. Meaning that the state cannot define marriage since marriage in a traditional sense existed before the state was conceived. If the state was to dictate what constitutes a marriage that would be contradictory to laws of nature since it was the traditional family that created the state in the first place and not vice-versa.

Ben Shapiro argues that the state should not be able to define marriage because it will abuse this power. The government should be out of the business of marriage. If it doesn't, it will end in a scenario in which the state will force churches, synagogues, mosques to conduct gay weddings by threatening to revoke their tax-exemption status (classic civil rights chess move, give somebody rights by taking someone else's away).

Historically speaking homosexuality was present where women and men were segregated. The more segregated men and women become the more likely sexual deviancy would manifest (modern examples include non-secular Islamic world and prisons). From the historical point of view, homosexuality existed in some rare circumstances. Some of these cases were a result of sexual abuse in early childhood, but most are a result of a numerical deficiency of one of the genders. In Greece (ancient times) and the Islamic world (in the Middle Ages) homosexuality appeared when there was a shortage of men or women. When there is a disproportionate number of one of the two sexes, the members of the sex that is greater in number cannot find a mate of the opposite sex so they turn to their own sex, especially when it comes to men since men due to their naturally higher testosterone level have a stronger sex drive. Historically this happened during wars (Spartans, Crusaders) when men would leave their wives to fight the enemy who knows how many miles away. In some cases they would not see a female body for years either because they would kill the women of conquered lands, or the women would commit suicide knowing all too well that if they got captured they would end up in slavery. The same principle applies to monks in monasteries that would not see a woman for decades at a time.

American soldiers were shocked when they entered Afghanistan and witnessed acts of homosexuality between men and reported numerous accounts of men raping boys.

Another thing that contributes to the rise of homosexual behavior is polygamy. Polygamy also gives rise to incest. The Islamic world used to be way more advanced in comparison to their European counterparts when it comes to math, astrology, art, architecture back in the first few centuries of its inception (7,8,9th century). But due to incest, it's quality fell off drastically in no small part due to the fact that children with less IQ result from incest (there is a direct scientific correlation which proves that the aftermath of incest is lower IQ in resulting progeny). This is why in the Middle East people have a lesser IQ than those in Europe, North America, Japan which unlike Islamic countries do not practice incest or polygamy. Both incest and homosexuality tend to rise in societies that practice polygamy since there is a disproportionate ratio of men to women in the sexual market.

Are human beings monogamous or polygamous? (both and neither), out of 1100 known cultures throughout the history around 900 had cases of polygamy, better yet some members of these 900 cultures practiced polygamy (mostly the elites), not all members of said cultures were involved with the polygamous lifestyle. Not surprisingly those who didn't practice polygamy created a civilization worth mentioning (every notable civilization is based on the nuclear family, the traditional monogamous marriage is a bedrock for every great civilization). Human beings are neither monogamous nor polygamous but monogamy, unlike polygamy, has been proven to work.

All around the world there are examples of human life in tribes that have a form of marriage, a bond between one man and one woman, and these tribes have not changed their family arrangement for thousands of years and have not been touched by Christianity, furthermore showing that heterosexual monogamy wasn't forced by religious teachings. Before monotheism, pagans had a form of marriage, meaning that marriage is not a religious construct since people have opted for this type of family arrangement regardless of religious influence. No civilization prospered in a non-monogamous arrangement.

Polygamy is only manageable with wealthy men since having multiple wives and who knows how many children requires an extraordinary amount of monetary resources. This is proven in the Islamic world where men are able to marry multiple wives. Since polygamy can be sustained only by economically powerful men, this means that the vast majority of men (low and medium income men) will be left without a woman. This results in higher rates of rapes committed against women since there is a disproportionate number of men to women and higher rates of homosexual activity between men since there are not enough women to go around. So polygamy influences the rise of incest resulting in the drop of average IQ and in the rise of homosexuality (example: non-secular Islamic world).

Many would be surprised to hear that the Middle East is ripe with pederasty, pedophilia, and homosexuality. The reason is segregation of the sexes. When western troops bombed and entered Afghanistan they were shocked to discover that Bacha Bazi was making a comeback after the Taliban was overthrown. Bacha Bazi is a form of sexual abuse where young boys and adolescent men are forced into sexual slavery by older men who train them to dance, sing and dress like women. They are sold to the highest bidder and sexually abused. The boys can be as young as 5 and by

19 they are discarded because they are no longer desirable. Here we see a historical link between homosexuality and pedophilia, just keep this in mind during the upcoming chapters. In the second part of the 20th century, these (and other) problems in the Islamic world were slowly but steadily shrinking thanks to their modernization, including the implementation and promotion of monogamy. This is one of many reasons why I was against any military "humanitarian" intervention by the west in the Middle East. The Islamic world by default, by nature strives to become less radical and more secular or more modern (as all religions do, Christianity did this in the beginning of the 17 century by excluding it's more radical parts, the reason why the Islamic world took longer is simple – Islam is the youngest one of the 5 big monotheistic religions thus it needed more time to deradicalize itself). Since parts of the Islamic world were bombed to oblivion and sent back to the Stone age polygamy, pedophilia, and homosexuality are now on the rise.

Look at modern day prisons (and to a lesser extent the army) where homosexual activity is rampant. One of the following is true: either a large number of convicts are gay people or people who are not gay (haven't been gay before they entered prison) start indulging in homosexual activities (this is true in both male and female prisons). The reason, as history is pointing out, is because there are is an absence of members of the opposite sex. In the U.S.A. if you count prisons the largest number of rape victims are men and those rapes are perpetrated by other men, mostly in prisons.

The pro-gay marriage brigade argues that gay marriage should be legalized hinging on the claim that homosexuality was normal in ancient times (predominantly Ancient Greece and Rome). I would like to point out counter-arguments. First of all, was gay marriage legal in Ancient Greece and Rome? No. If the ancient world was so open and tolerant to homosexuality, as some leftists claim, then they would allow gay marriage. No society (for religious reasons or otherwise) ever in the history of mankind (up until recently) allowed gay marriage. If Ancient Greeks were so tolerant towards homosexuality why were their gods not homosexual? Greeks based their gods on themselves they gave them the same characteristics as mortal humans (because they believed that gods created humans in their own benevolent image), if Greeks were so gay-friendly there would be accounts of Greek gods being homosexuals, but there aren't any. The Greeks didn't describe one of their gods as a homosexual. In the ancient world (every culture, from the Aztecs to Persia) there are no

accounts of gods being homosexual. This means that the ancient world didn't look kindly upon homosexuality otherwise they would imagine their gods as being homosexuals. The conclusion is that the ancient world didn't deem homosexuality (if it was at all present) as a worthy enough characteristic for their gods. It's interesting to note that throughout millennia almost every polytheistic religion gave family and children related characteristics to female gods. Whether it's Sumeria, Persia, Incas, Mayans, Aztecs, Europe or China, godly traits of "family protection", "marriage", "fertility", "childbirth and child-rearing" and anything else related to these topics were almost exclusively attributed to goddesses. It's like the ancient world saw that the default state of a woman is being a mother, again, rebutting the homosexual argument.

Camille Paglia (transgender person herself) in her work "Sexual Personae" points out that in history every time transgenderism rose as a phenomena social collapse follows. Sexual deviancy correlates with the collapse of society. Her research proves that as a culture begins to decline what we see is a rise in the transgender phenomena, which, according to her, is a symptom of cultural collapse.

Where does that leave our society and what sexual deviances can we expect to emerge as the civilized world implodes and falls in the ashes of history? All throughout human history in the decadent stages of society transsexual-like behavior has risen exponentially. Camille Paglia is a big critic of the modern transsexual movement saying it is blown out of proportion when it comes to numbers and variety. She voiced her concern that the rise and popularization of transsexuality in the USA is a sign that the western civilization is heading towards a collapse. Is the collapse of a society a result of the rise of sexual deviancy or is the rise of sexual deviancy a result of a society that is in decline? Whatever the case they obviously complement each other – the correlation is indisputable. We can say with certainty that the same applies to homosexuality.

What happens to civilizations that go down this road? The Greek-city states and the Roman Empire (predominantly Western) collapsed after straying from traditional family values. Rome fell because of its weak leaders who were more engulfed with organizing orgies than saving the empire. In the later stages of the Roman Empire, their morally depraved family-elites started practicing incest. This resulted in weak-minded leaders (such as Nero-an emotionally unstable psychopath, Caligula-an emperor who married his horse and had a sexual relationship with his sister). This is how the beginning of the end started. The Roman aristocracy wanted to keep hold of the power, to keep everything in the family so to say, this was done through inbreeding which resulted in mentally challenged offspring and low IQ emperors. Afterward, they were not foreign to all manners of sexual depravity (other examples of people first accepting incest and them later on moving to other sexual depravities such as orgies and homosexuality are the Habsburgs and the British royal family, and we all know how the Habsburgs and their Austro-Hungarian Empire ended). The same ingredients that ultimately destroyed the Roman Empire are now being promoted in the western world.

On the other side we have civilizations that outlasted Rome, coincidentally they did not approve and encourage this destructive behavior. The German and other barbarian tribes did not advocate sexual freedom on the level of their "civilized" counterparts from the Mediterranean. This is true across the board: Alemanii, Lombardi, Burgandii all promoted the nuclear family (while they were still pagans and Christianity still wasn't implemented), they were disgusted with the Romans "free" lifestyle and in the end defeated the "progressive" and liberal Rome whose leaders were engulfed in their sexual perversion.

Nowadays people say that Germany has a proud history when it comes to the adult industry. This is not true. Germanic tribes were not liberal like the Romans. Many barbarians across Europe did not condone prostitution. It is only in relatively recent history that this change occurred in Germany. According to the Swiss journalist and historian Ahmed Huber, this change took place in the second part of the 19th century. He says: *"they have introduced in German art, culture, theater and movies decadence, immorality, the first homosexual theatres, and plays were made in Berlin in the 1920s, the first adultery theater plays were made in the 1880s and 1890s, adultery, then sexual perversions of all sorts, sadism, masochism, a lot of homosexuality, all these things and then decadent art, an art that is absolutely ridiculous so-called modern art, and this created among the German people a big revolt. The Nazis, of course, benefited from it and this is why Hitler came to power."*

If we look at Germany after WW1 history is merely repeating itself. After its defeat, Germany had not only economic but social problems. The country was devastated and that reflected on its citizens. Promiscuity was on an all-time high, alcohol, and drug (mostly opium) abuse was common and homosexual, bisexual and transgender deviancy were on the rise and in some upper circles it was even normalized, unemployment was at a record high, around 8 million people were unemployed.

The people were obsessed with mindless, hedonistic sexual perversions. Berlin earned names such as "Whore of Babylon", "World's most immoral city" because it surpassed Paris (another sexually liberated city) when it came to the practice of sexual deviancy. So who controlled Germany at this time – the liberals did. This took place during the Weimar Republic up until 1933 (Hitler's inauguration). Many have rightfully referred to the Weimar Republic as the Weimar Soviet Republic, due to the similarities of social and moral sickness found in both Russia and Germany after the Great War. The degeneracy, that infested Germany post-World War 1, represented nothing more than fertile ground for an ideology like Nazism to gain roots and amass a following.

According to Hitler's so-called "Second book" (Translated as "My world order" or "Hitler's anti-world order") after the Bolshevik revolution "*after the revolution, came the collapse of morality, customs, the abolition of marriage and instead of that the institution of sexual freedom was proclaimed.*" After the Bolsheviks seized power in Russia in 1917 incest, bigamy and adultery were all dropped for the list of official crimes. Divorce was made easier (which is a symptom of Socialism) than ever before and prostitution (including child prostitution) rose up.

The things that are now being pushed by liberals in regards to the sexual revolution are the same things that were rampant in the Weimar (Soviet) Republic. During this relatively short but nevertheless detrimental period, Germany as a nation and its citizens stagnated. And who has the majority of power in today's Europe and America – the liberal left (the so-called progressives). I would not call the advocacy for social collapse as progressive.

What we can clearly see in Europe and North America, ever since World War 2 ended, is the revival of the Weimar Republic.

Where does this leave our civilization, is the contemporary gay and trans mania a sign that Europe and North America (Western civilization) are coming to its end?

GAY AGENDA 21

CHAPTER 3: "THE BORN THIS WAY MYTH"

The entire gay normalization and subsequent gay marriage legalization is based on the notion that gay people are born that way, one of the sub-theories being that there is a gay-gene which would mean that gay people can't help it being born this way, furthermore anyone who disagrees with their lifestyle is on par with a racist (since it's not black peoples fault for being black) and would automatically make these people homophobes and bigots. But what if gay people are not born gay, should they still retain the rights that they have obtained under the false pretence of homosexuality being innate?

If homosexuality is biological, why is there no biological reason to be gay?

Nicholas Andrew Cummings is an American psychologist, author and former president of the American Psychologist Association. In an interview, he said some interesting things. According to him, in the 1970s the feminist and gay movements were almost one and the same as things got more political rather than scientific. When it came to the gay movement the Leona Tyler principle (principle that says that a psychologists opinion should be based on scientific, unbiased, objective data) did not apply, in the late 1990s the Leona Tyler principle was forgotten (it was in the 80's that the gay gene myth was born), political stances override any scientific results. The gay movement captured the A.P.A. (American Psychologist Association). It became a movement for diversity. He continued by saying that there is a need to form an organization that would recruit straight white males which are underrepresented now in the A.P.A. According to Nicholas, The American Psychologist Association was run by around 200 people who were ultra liberal and questioning gay, lesbian rights was not accepted. It became the civil-rights issue rather than a scientific issue. What we need to have is an open dialogue, said Nicholas. Certain research does not get founded, the founding agencies cherry-pick what they find. In 1975 he made a resolution that stated that homosexuality is not a mental illness but open unbiased research was never done, he said. According to the Leona Tyler principle, the A.P.A. would never take a position publicly

that wasn't supported by scientific evidence. As things became more political than scientific the Leona Tyler principle, which was never withdrawn, simply disappeared. Nicholas conclusion is that the A.P.A. (which declared that homosexuality is not a mental illness) has become politically correct, political correctness rules not science. On his own accounts, Nicholas Andrew Cummings claims that he had noticeable result in his own words "curing" gay men.

Homosexuality was never scientifically declassified as a mental illness. If you are asking yourself why was it classified as a mental illness in the first place, I recommend watching a documentary "The gift" from 2003 which depicts the homosexual lifestyle in America. This documentary is one of the last unbiased documentaries on the dangers of the homosexual lifestyle. Not long after it came out, political correctness took over, and now people are forbidden from objectively talking about such a lifestyle.

Identical twins and homosexuality. If people are born gay, if there is such a thing as the gay-gene then the identical twins (since they share the identical genetic make-up, they have identical DNA) should have the same sexuality, either neither is gay or both are gay.

According to research done by Dr. J. Michael Bailey on identical twins in Australia - if one twin identifies as gay the likelihood of the other having the same sexual identity is 11 percent.

Peter Bearman from Columbia University and Hannah Brückner from Yale discovered that when it comes to male identical twins concordance rate were 6,7 percent and female identical twins were 5,3 percent, meaning in over 90 percent cases for both male and female twins if one was homosexual the other was not.

The concordance rate should be 100 percent (if one identical twin "has the gay gene" the other one should as well, meaning both should identify as homosexuals since they share the same genetic makeup) and not 11/ 6,7/ 5,3 percent. Even if you factor any kind of anomalies with twins this number should not be as low as it is if the "born this way" theory was to have any credence.

8 other studies done across the US, Scandinavia all came to the same conclusion-gays are not born that way. The results of all of these studies were duplicated on triplets.

An interview between Joe Rogan and Milo Yiannopoulos (a gay man) during a radio talk-show. Milo stated that the 'born this way' theory is an invention of the gay lobby and that there is no scientific basis for the born this way argument. In the 1980s the gay lobby came up with the 'born this way' theory with the sole purpose of defaming anyone who disagrees with the gay lifestyle since if homosexuality is innate (according to the gay lobby) no one could criticize homosexuals since they never chose to be gay. Milo concluded by saying that the 'born this way' theory is a lie.

In another interview, Milo said that he would choose not to be gay and that everyone should as well. He said he would like to have kids but is unsure if he wants to bring them up in a gay household because so much of sexual orientation is based on nurture.

During a conference at University of California Santa Barbara as he was answering questions inquired by a gay woman he told her that she would be happier with a boyfriend, he claims that there no real lesbians. For most women, gay activity is a form of reaction or response says, Milo.

In 2015 the US government spent 3 million tax-payer dollars investigating why gay women are obese. The research didn't find the reason but they found something else. If you are a woman that chooses a gay lifestyle you are much more likely to get:

- hit by your gay woman partner (there is a lesbian domestic violence epidemic which no one is talking about)
- incarcerated
- get obese
- get poor

Epigenetics-Eugenics:

Eugenics (population control) is an ideology that rose popularity in California between two World Wars, promoted by Margret Sanger (a feminist, an advocate for birth control and one of the founders of Planned Parenthood, remember her name since she will be mentioned in later chapters) and was perfected in Hitler's Germany. It's a form of selective breeding with the aim of improving the genetic pool and overall genetic quality of people through the generations. The goal is creating the übermensch (superhuman). This is done by breeding in desirable characteristics and breeding out undesirable characteristics in society.

Epigenetics is a brand new field of science that revolves around hereditary changes in gene expression, eugenics is changing genes through selective, wanted breeding and epigenetics is changing genes in already living beings.

Epigenetics claims that homosexual tendencies in most cases appear in early childhood or sometimes in rare cases in the womb. The conclusion -

homosexuality in at least the vast majority of cases appears after birth meaning it's not innate.

Those who defend homosexuality often quote American scientists who claim that there is a gay gene (what about those American scientists that say that no one is born a homosexual?). What about, for example, Russian scientists who still treat homosexuality as a mental illness? Why are Russian scientists blaming America for spreading homosexuality? Why haven't Russian scientists found the gay gene? What makes American scientists more credible than Russian ones? Is it because people are biased when it comes to this topic so they use the information that coincides with their view, ignoring that which contradicts them?

To this day, if you exclude Youtube videos and social media posts, there has not been any concrete and unfalsifiable evidence that someone is born gay from a biological or psychological point of view.

GAY AGENDA 21

CHAPTER 4: "SCIENTIFIC FALLACIES AND LOGICAL INCONSISTENCIES"

Hypothetically speaking if homosexuality was genetic, innate, natural, then this phenomenon ought to stay in relatively same numbers and not change drastically in a small period of time. But this is not the case.

Homosexual, transsexual and other similar behaviors are on the rise and have been for some time. People defending homosexuality say that it is normal and that people can't become gay since homosexuality is not some kind of disease. They say other people should accept homosexuality since they can't themselves get "sick" and become gay. According to them, homosexuality cannot be transferred from one person to the other through birth. Here lies one of many flaws in the LGBT logic and their so-called science. On the one hand, they claim that homosexuality is genetic, one of those theories being the mythical gay gene, and on the other hand, they say homosexuality cannot be transferred to other people, for example to children (if a gay person gives birth). They completely neglect the fact that children inherit their parents DNA. So according to them, children inherit DNA from their biological parents just not the gay gene (even though the children's genetic structure is completely built on the parent's one). So the LGBT science ends up contradicting itself, using the gay gene theory when it is convenient but ignoring the science of how genetic reproduction takes place when it benefits their cause. If a gay woman gives birth then the gay gene should be present in her children. The child should inherit the gay gene but this is not the case since the gay gene does not exist.

This is what psychologists call cognitive dissonance, or "doublethink" in Orwell's '1984' – simultaneously believing in two completely contradicting things, believing that there is a gay gene (meaning it should be transferred to children of gay parents) yet at the same time not believing that gay gene can be transferred to offspring.

Gay activists say that the only difference between heterosexuals and homosexuals is DNA, the gay gene. If there is a gay gene and homosexuality is genetic then what about other types of sexualities (infinite amount of sexual orientations to be more precise)? It used to be gay rights, then it included transsexuals, then bisexuals and so on. First, it was LGB, LGBT, LGBTQ and now it has more acronyms than there are letters in the English alphabet. All of these letters represent either sexual orientation or gender identity. When it comes to sexual orientation does this mean all of them have different genetic codes? If gays have a different gene structure compared to heterosexuals, what about bisexuals, pansexuals, omnisexuals and all other sexual orientations under the sky? Do all of them have different genes from one another? Is there an infinite number of gene types for the ever-growing number of sexual orientations?

The advocates of gay marriage claim that the LGBT community is a small portion of society (most studies show that in western countries the LGBT community is around 3-5 percent of the total population). The majority of the LGBT population are bisexual, bisexuality has risen dramatically in the last few decades. It is no secret that the gay movement has not only gotten larger and more influential but also gained a lot of new members (gay or not) and it is increasingly getting added support. As I have previously stated the rise of transsexual, homosexual, bisexual behaviors correlates with the decline and demise of a society (nowadays it's western society: North America and Europe). Then it should be no surprise that there is an ever-increasing presence of sexual liberation movements as our contemporary civilized world comes closer to its parapet. The western civilization is on the brink of economic, moral, cultural (thanks to forced immigration, forced multiculturalization and sexual liberation) downfall. The gay movement not only grew in members, but it also gained an infinite number of sub-movements (largely focusing on sexual orientation or gender identity) including ones that are even more destructive: bestiality, pedophilia, polygamy.

According to countless studies and reports, homosexuality and the rest of sexual paraphilias are on the rise and have been for several decades now. On the one hand, you have the rise of homosexuality and on the other, fewer and fewer people identify as heterosexual. According to research in North America and Europe year in year out there are more and more homosexuals, there are now more homosexuals than ever before. One might argue that the reason for the increase of homosexuals is a result of them being more accepted in society, that their numbers have always been the same but now they are able to come out without fear of anything. I would like to make a counter-argument: how come then that in Holland, a country where gay marriage is legalized, homosexuality is still on the rise?

No wonder parents across Europe have voted Amsterdam the worst city in Europe to raise children, too much liberal ideology perhaps? The same thing is evident in Canada and the USA. Regardless of when gay marriage is legalized, homosexuality and other similar behavioral patterns increase in numbers. According to a recent study in Australia nearly 50 percent of women have had or want to have a homosexual experience. In Great Britain in the nineties, the percentage of people identifying as exclusively heterosexual was 95 percent, a subsequent study in 2015 shows that only between 40 and 50 percent of the population identify as exclusively heterosexual. In this age of sexual experimentation and exploration more and more people identify on some level with the LGBT spectrum, meaning fewer people identify as heterosexual. Without a sign of this stopping or even slowing down I do think we have a problem in our society when heterosexual people are slowly becoming the minority. I'm not saying that the human race will become extinct because everybody will become homosexual but I do think we have a problem when more and more people, especially the younger generations and women, are more likely to identify as homosexual or bisexual rather than heterosexual. The homosexual spectrum has become a trend, something cool and it's being pushed as the new normal, not just the alternative to heterosexuality like back when it all started. I do think that all these things prove that we are living in a mentally sick society, not because of individual lifestyles and acts but because we live in a world where homosexuality is deemed not only normal and something that should be accepted but also something that should be encouraged while heterosexuality, traditional marriage, monogamy and biological, natural, healthy procreation (all the things our and every other civilization is based on) is looked down upon.

Queer theory: is one of the newest oxymoronic new age sciences which says that sexuality and sexual identity are fluid and can change throughout a person's life. Again flaw in their theory, first they claimed that one is born gay and cannot change that, now they say that sexuality is a "sliding scale" or is "malleable" and that one can change their sexuality at will. So which one is it? – the one that suits their purpose at any given time. This theory, which has no basis in science, only in the minds of deluded people, hinges its claims on situations when people have homosexual experiences, or when people after 20 years of marriage to the opposite sex get a divorce and start a relationship with a person of the same sex. This theory tries to separate sex and gender. It says that sex is the biological sex (reproductive organ) that we were "assigned" arbitrarily at birth by the doctor and gender is what you identify as male or female (or anything else) regardless of what reproductive organ you were born with. This thesis is the basis for transsexual teachings, that gender does not exist and that men and women are a social construct, a person can become male or female or both or neither regardless of their biological sex because everything is a social construct.

Science does not recognize this as a legitimate theory, science does not accept the "the nurture over nature theory" or "blank sheet of paper theory" (Tabula rasa). The blank sheet of paper theory says that our behaviors, preferences, actions completely depend on the environment and our surroundings. Meaning everything and I do mean everything can be considered a social construct. Sadly for the proponents of this pseudo-scientific theory, this is not the case. When it comes to men and women the way we act, what we like, what we do depends on our biological sex. Sex is not a social construct, there are numerous differences between men and women from the day we are born and even in the womb. These differences follow us our entire lives, men and women are not and should not ever be biologically equal. Sex is not only determined by our reproductive organs, for almost all people the sex (penis or vagina) they were born with represents their gender identity, almost all of us that identify as gender we were born (not "assigned"), we have a male or female brain corresponding with our biological reproductive organ. For almost all people on this planet if you have a male reproductive organ you have a male brain and if you have a female reproductive organ you have a female brain. These two brains are inherently different and follow their biological sex. These differences are hard-wired in our brain and predetermined from the time of conception. One is not superior to the other, they are just different, tasked with different things. This is why men are better than women in some things and women are better than men in other things. This makes our society work, regardless if it's our contemporary society or the hunter-gatherer tribes. Since the dawn of time, human beings relied on this principle to survive and evolve. Take away women or men out of the equation and our society and our race would cease to exist. This is especially true when it comes to raising children.

Studies estimate that up to 60 percent of personalities children inherit from their parents. Children's IQ is mostly dependent on the IQ of their parents (in most cases the IQ of the child won't deviate too much from their parents IQ). Children's IQ is determined more by the mother's IQ than the father's. This correlates perfectly with what I have said years ago "if you want to destroy a society destroy the women." Something I will get to later on.

The LGBT movement says that gender is a social construct which we were arbitrarily assigned at birth. Let's put their theory to the test. The story of David Peter Reimer: born as a boy but due to a medical error while he was very young he was reassigned as a girl and was raised as a girl by his parents. His life was hard due to this. Though he was raised as a girl his behavior suggested he was a boy.

Doctor John Money-a sociologist that had a theory that gender is a social construct. According to him, gender was not something you were born into but something you learn thanks to socialization and upbringing. He was the doctor that operated on David Peter Reimer and turned him into a "girl". Today this is known as the nurture-not–nature theory, a theory that says that gender is not biological but rather learned or taught. David Peter Reimer, a born boy, was raised as a girl by the parents. The experiment by this Mengele-like doctor had proven to be an utter failure. The boy exhibited boy-like behavior from early years all the way to teenage years. Even though he was told he was a girl and was raised like one he acted, played like a boy and was eventually relieved to find out that he was one.

A born boy, who was raised as a girl and spent his entire childhood thinking he was a girl, started identifying as a boy, exhibiting the behavior of a typical boy, found happiness when he found out he was a boy and yet these gender ideologues claim gender is a social construct.

When it comes to hermaphrodites (people who have both male and female genital parts) they always have only one functioning reproductive organ (this is why doctors advise that they should wait till they are mature to decide which gender are they). Doctor John Money, while trying to prove his theory that gender is a social construct, treated hermaphrodites where he failed to accurately identify the gender of his patients which resulted in suicides committed by those people he operated on. Even though his theory that gender is a social construct failed completely, thus failing to prove the nurture-over-nature theory, his theories are now at the forefront of the gay/trans movement.

When it comes to transsexual people the suicide rate does not change before and after surgery and/or hormone therapy. Transsexual people are as likely to be unhappy and commit suicide before the operation as they are after it (depending on the study it's around 40 percent). The suicide

rate in the transsexual community doesn't go down after sex-change operations.

The same theory, about gender fluidity, is now implemented when it comes to sexual orientation. The theory suggests that people can change their sexuality in the course of their life. Yet more cognitive dissonance (doublethink) by the gay movement. In the beginning, they said that homosexuality is innate and people are born that way and that nothing and nobody can change that since it's rooted in biology. They are now contradicting themselves to serve their purpose further. So now gender and sexuality are not innate and unchangeable anymore but are in fact interchangeable by free will. People can change their gender and sexual orientation on a daily basis, or they can even mix multiple ones at the same time. When it comes to sexuality there is an ever more prevailing theory that says that the person you have sex does not reflect your sexuality, in other words, you can have sex with one gender and still not have the sexuality that corresponds with your actions (example: if a man has a sexual relationship with a woman this does not mean he is a heterosexual). This is probably because everything is a social construct including your gender and sexuality thus the person you have sex with might not be what they seem to be (I.E. man or woman), they might be both or neither. This completely refutes their previous theory about the born this way myth and the gay gene. They are changing theories to suit their agenda and people are completely oblivious.

Another one of these newer theories says that everyone has the potential to be a homosexual. In essence, the theory says that every human being has a gay gene present in their body and that external chemical influences can activate that gene and anyone can become homosexual. The main problem with this theory is the very notion that the gay gene exists. Since the gay gene doesn't exist, chemicals can't make us homosexual through the activation of this gay gene as the theory suggests, rendering it false. When it comes to the actual influences and consequences chemicals have of human gender-identity and sexuality I will cover it later down the track.

Once the pro-gay marriage crowd loses the scientific debate based on provable facts and objective reality, they will always resort to the last argument in their arsenal, one based not of fact and proof but rather on emotions and feelings – love. You can often hear them say things like "they love each other". If this narcissistic and vapid interpretation of "love" were to have any weight, one ought to be able to apply it universally. The love argument automatically falls short when you take into consideration incest. If we use the love argument to justify the marriage between 2 consenting adults of the same sex, what about incestual relationships then? We can have two consenting adult siblings demanding marital rights based on this "love" argument. If we let gay people marry based on this argument, why not let a grown brother and sister marry? The perils of incest relationships and progeny resulting from those arrangements need no addressing. Thus the "love" argument falls flat-footed as soon as you include incest.

Even though beauty definitely has a subjective element there are universally accepted and proven beauty traits that men seek in women and that women seek in men. These traits are commonly said to be social constructs like everything else but this again is simply not the case. From the dawn of humanity, men have sought young (20 – 30-year-old), long hair, hourglass figure, hip-to-waist ratio, child-bearing hips, fertile women. All these things are indicators of health and that the woman is able to carry and give birth to children. Women have universally sought men who are taller, reverse pyramid shape, muscular, financially able to support her and their offspring. Now the gay and feminist alliance is trying to categorize all of these and many other scientifically proven facts as social constructs.

These quasi-intellectual pseudo-scientific theories derived from the LGBT movement are nothing more than sophistry. If things do not change and this continues to increase both in numbers and variants, what else can we expect?

GAY AGENDA 21

CHAPTER 5: "INEVITABLE ATTACK ON HETEROSEXUALS AND THE FAMILY"

Anti-discrimination is discrimination.

As I stated before almost every "civil rights movement" is not a movement for equal rights but a movement for supremacy. The Feminist movement went from women getting equal rights, a right to get educated and get a job to being nothing more than a movement of misandry. The black rights movement went from black people having equal opportunities as whites to a movement that blames white people for everything (Black Lives Matter movement is nothing more than a black version of the KKK).

This by default means that the gay movement and its supporters, regardless of whether they are gay or not, will knowingly or unknowingly eventually attack heterosexuals and the nuclear, traditional family, or have they already?

Since the nuclear family consists of two elements: monogamy and heterosexuality both need to be attacked and destroyed in order for the Gay agenda to achieve its goal.

MONOGAMY OR POLYGAMY?:

From a financial point of view, polygamy is only manageable if a man (husband) is wealthy since all those multiple wives and their children need an abundance of resources, especially in a financial sense. So for mid and low-income males polygamy is not logical since they would not have the means to financially support all of them. Just look at the present Islamic world, polygamy is present but most of it is present with men who are rich. Since the vast majority of men are not filthy rich where does this leave them and society as a whole? In a normal world where the number of men and women is almost the same in proportion (50:50 just like in our world), there is a woman for every man and vice versa. In a polygamous environment, wealthy men who seek polygamy would have multiple wives and leave men that are not rich with a smaller chance of finding a wife since there would be a smaller pool of women to draw from. Naturally, in this scenario, some men would be left without a mate of the opposite sex. Where does this leave men with no wives? As history has shown us (including present-day Islamic world) when there is an unequal number of women and men we as a society get a problem. Men who are unable to get a female mate by conventional means result to the rape of women or even men (Middle East and prisons). Rape is the lowest kind of mating strategy, most commonly committed by lower than average IQ men, financially unsecured, low self-esteem who have no other way of procreating. Just look at the Middle East where the women are "monopolized" by wealthy men which leaves a proportion of the remaining male population with two options, either to rape or indulge in homosexuality (Bacha Bazi) to satisfy their sexual drive since there are not enough women to go around. The key of sex is procreation, the continuance of our species for both men and women (orgasm is one of the ways nature has tricked us into having sex in order to have offspring). If you need historic proof, find me one civilization that was built on polygamy. Exactly, not a single one managed to survive and progress in a polygamous environment. The Islamic world stagnated for more than 1000 years due to polygamy.

Another bad side to polygamy is the raising of the children or better yet lack of it. In a polygamous family, the children would effectively be left without a father, since the father would not be able to care for all of his children equally. In a polygamous environment a man having multiple wives and who knows how many children cannot possibly devote the needed time, attention and affection to all of his children. So what, I can hear the feminists scream, the children have a mother that will nurturer them, they don't need a father. Or do they?

Contrary to gender studies and third wave feminist ideology children need both a mother and a father. Feminists, gender ideologues, and other pseudoscience supporters argue that there is no need for a father in a children's life. This is yet another form of misandry and a plan not only to break up marriage and the family but also to destroy any healthy relationship between a man and a woman. Study after study irrefutably shows that children equally need a father and a mother. Children need a feminine figure (mother) and masculine figure (father) in their life. This is why monogamy works the best because children get a mom and a dad, they get traits from both biological parents. Because women and men are not biologically equal they help each other in raising the kids in different ways, and the kids need both parents in order to fully develop.

What happens when this is not the case when a child does not have a feminine figure in the shape of a mother or a masculine figure in the shape of a father?

New age feminism argues that single mothers are good for society and that children don't need a father figure.

In Anne Coulter's book "Demonic": she cites numerous studies on the topic of single mothers and children that they raise. Around 70 percent of juvenile delinquency, teenage pregnancy, teenage runaways are committed by children that were raised by single mothers. The same percentage comes into play when it comes to rape, murder, drug addiction 70 percent of which are done by kids that were raised by single mothers without a father in their life.

Single motherhood in the black community in the USA jumped from 20 percent to 70 percent in the last few decades. In white households, the percentage is not that bad but still has grown tremendously since the 70s, ever since feminists starting glorifying single motherhood. We are now living in a society that it is so sick that it promotes single motherhood thus depriving children of their fathers.

Look up any research and you will find that kids need a father as well as a mother for the best development possible. Human beings (like most mammals) don't abandon their offspring after birth but rather stay and raise them (both parents). In the animal kingdom, there are of course species where one or both parents leave their offspring to fend for themselves, sometimes even before they are born (eggs). Humans and most mammals are not like that. Human babies need the help of their parents (both ones) to survive in the world, and this help, without which children would not survive, is needed for a long time (years, much longer than with any other species in the animal kingdom). There are certain traits and benefits a child gets from growing up with both parents, some traits they get from the father, some from the mother. All of these traits are welcomed and needed. According to studies mothers provide empathy, stability, nurture, they are natural caregivers, fathers, on the other hand, provide security (I don't only mean financial), protection. Contrary to popular belief married men tend to live longer than unmarried ones on average. There are harmful side effects to kids who don't grow up with a mom or a dad since they only get one set of traits either feminine or masculine depriving them of the other. So what are the effects on a child growing without one parent (mom or dad)? This is a compilation of data from both sides of the political spectrum :

-less school/academic success

-children in fatherless homes are much more likely to be poor

-more drug addiction, alcohol abuse, smoke, suicide attempts, mental illnesses, health problems

-child abuse (especially when it comes to single moms, women are now more likely than ever to be perpetrators of domestic violence, mostly on children, close to 50 percent of all child abuses in the USA are committed by mothers, and that's not even including abortion and murder after childbirth)

-when it comes to daughters who were raised by single moms, without a father figure, they are much more likely to be promiscuous (science says it's because they didn't have a father so they seek validation from other men, more often older men which they see as a father figure)

-daughters grown up without a father tend to have an irrational hatred towards all men, though this could also be attributed to the influence of feminism

-growing up without a mom negatively impacts boys as well, on the other hand, it is interesting to note that men who were raised by single moms often are incapable of having a decent meaningful relationship with women

-numerous studies have shown that the ideal setting for raising a child is a heterosexual monogamous relationship when it comes to success in education, levels of fulfillment and happiness, success in their own relationships (kids are more likely to get divorced in their own marriage if they come from a family where the parents are divorced, and kids of still married parents are less likely to get divorced themselves). The positive traits which kids receive are amplified even more if the parents are married rather than merely living together, thus refuting the notion that marriage is just an insignificant sheet of paper

-children coming from single-parent homes are more likely to have children outside of marriage and outside any partnership thus ensuring this process is likely to continue onto their children and grandchildren

-research indicates that there is no better way to raise children than in a home where the biological mother and father are married. There is not a single area, on average, where children raised by their biological mother and father do not outperform children from other "alternative" family demographics

-other studies show that the children coming from single-parent homes are at a disadvantage compared to children living with their mother and father

I am not trying to undermine the importance of a mother when it comes to raising children. In no shape or form am I saying that children don't need a mother or that the mother is not as important as a father for the development of a child. I am not implying that fathers are more important than mothers. There are countless studies that show the numerous negative effects of the absence of a female figure (a mother) has on children (boys and girls). The main reason I have devoted a portion of this chapter to the importance of fathers in children's lives is to prove the widely popular feminist notion that children don't need fathers as false and a sign of misandry.

Human beings are programmed to procreate like all other living things on this planet. For that procreation, we, like most of the animal kingdom, need both a female and a male. Unlike some living things, human babies need both parents not only to survive but also to get the necessary traits and skills to thrive. It is a biological right of parents to have kids and raise them and it is a biological, natural and logical right of a child to be born due to fornication between its future mother and father. Thus it's a normal right of a child to be raised by its biological parents. This is why heterosexual monogamy has been proven to work (unlike polygamy, polyandry, polyamory) and has persisted throughout the millennia. This keeps the family together, parents close so that they are able to provide the care their child needs. And for the child, it brings stability and assurance that it will be raised in the best possible environment for its development. In a polygamous environment the man who has more wives and multiple kids with each wife will not be able, due to logistical reasons, to give all those kids the necessary time and love needed for their proper growth and development, leaving some or all of the children essentially fatherless or in the "best" case scenario (choosing the lesser of two evils) the kids will receive only a partial involvement of the father in their life. The father will not be able to give all of his kids the required attention which is obviously bad for the kids and society later down the track.

Children need a father and a mother, better yet a masculine (male) and feminine (female) figure in their life for full development. No matter how masculine, butch and man-like a lesbian married couple may be they will not and cannot replace a father figure, no matter how feminine gay men are they can never supplant a child's need for a biological mother. Men are good at being men, women are good at being women, we are bad at being the opposite sex. For a child, there is no substitution to being raised by its biological parents. Anything else is an attack on the natural rights of a child.

ATTACK ON MARRIAGE:

As I have previously stated all civilizations have been, or are based on a monogamous relationship between members of the opposite sex. Heterosexual monogamy is the bedrock of any and all human civilizations. There is no other formula that works as good as this one. That is not all. This two-way equation (heterosexual/monogamy) is best for the children. Science has proven that for raising kids two parents (biological) are the best. Studies on single-parent households prove this, kids need both parents.

People naturally associate, we all yearn to belong to a group. This can be done through religion, ethnic origin, nationality, but there is no greater bond than that created between a child and its biological parents. The goal of certain people is exactly the opposite - to break this bond.

Anti-family ideologues argue that the family needs to be destroyed because it is unsustainable. Usually, they point out that the proof for this is the ever-increasing divorce rates. If divorce rates are so high than marriage as an institution needs to be abolished. They often quote the 50 percent divorce rate as evidence. Most of the people advocating the end of marriage as an institution are people from LGBT and feminist groups (no surprise there since these two movements are practically one and the same - something Nicholas Andrew Cummings said was visible even back in the 70s). But the 50 percents divorce rate is a myth. Anti-marriage activists came to this number by comparing the number of divorces in one year and the number of people getting married in that same year. This is called the divorce-to-marriage ratio. This is how they got to the notion that 50 percent of marriages end in divorce. The trouble is that it is inaccurate to compare the divorce rate to the marriage rate since this excludes people that are already married (people that have been married for more than one year). This ratio only shows that the number of new marriages in relation to divorces is 50 percent but this does not include the overall married population. Another problem with this method of calculating divorce rates is that in the number of divorces they included marriages that ended due to the fact that one of the spouses died, thus raising the number of divorces unrelated to divorce. For example, divorce rates in the UK have been steadily declining since the peak in the 70s. People whose parents were divorced have a higher chance of getting divorced themselves, people who were once divorced are more likely to do so again. Even though this 50 percent divorce rate is exaggerated there is still a divorce problem in our society. Anti-marriage ideologues will use this to try and dismantle the family claiming that marriage is a failed institution so it needs to be abolished. But this is not the case, it's not marriage that is failing (there is no better setup for the kids and society) but it's the relationships between men and women in general that are failing. Anti-marriage ideologues will point out that this is proof that marriage needs to be forgotten in the sands of time. They are forgetting one thing, marriage and relationships between men and women are not failing on their own or because men and women have somehow become incompatible, but rather because this has been done deliberately. If marriage was left alone it would not have found itself in this crisis. But it was not left alone, it was and still is attacked from all angles, both men and women are being targeted but it's the kids that suffer the most. Continuing the trend from the 20th century, certain groups are pushing for the destruction of marriage, the nuclear family and the relationship between a man and a woman and their children. One of the loudest advocates for the annihilation of marriage in the last few decades comes from the LGBT community.

As was said the feminist and gay movements are practically the same, they have an aligned goal – destroying the nuclear family. Women who have been indoctrinated by the far left ideology that is feminism were taught that they don't need a man and that the family is a sign of oppression. Men aren't the only ones negatively affected by this ideology.
According to research, feminism has made women miserable and unhappy. There are equally unintelligent movements with men, such as MGTOW (Men Going Their Own Way - a men's movement that suggests that men should not get married and give up on women for good). What feminism is for women, MGTOW is for men. It's these and many other dangerous ideologies that are harming the relationships between men and women. In the end, it's the kids that suffer the most.

This war on men and women is not a sign that marriage and the family are failed institutions since it has been done systematically by those who have a vested interest in splitting the sexes and destroying the nuclear family (divide and conquer).

Quotes by prominent feminists icons:

-Andrea Dworkin: *"Marriage is an institution developed from rape as a practice."*

-Linda Gordon: *"The nuclear family needs to be destroyed.......the break up of families now is an objectively revolutionary process."* Notice the word 'revolutionary'. Most feminists, at least the prominent ones, are Marxists. This is not surprising since feminism is a Marxist movement. Even today left-wing pro-feminist women tend to vote for Socialist policies.

-Dr. Mary Jo Bane: *"In order to raise children with equality, we must take them away from families and communally raise them."* (communally raise them, you mean like in Communism comrade? Do kids belong to the state now?)

In Holland, there is a movement to legalize polygamy on the basis of human rights. What about the rights of children that I have discussed earlier in this chapter, the right to be raised by their biological mother and father.

Natalie Bennett, a British politician and a member of the green party, publicly stated that she is *"open to three people being legally capable of marriage."* This Gay revolution will not stop at legalizing gay marriage. After gay marriage, there will be a push for polyamory, polygamy, polyandry and other similar lifestyles. The changing of the definition of marriage is not intended to stay at a binary level, they will push for a three-party marriage (first bigamy) after that four people will be able to get married, and so on. They want to destroy the institution of marriage not only in perspective to who can get married but also how many people can get married until they reach a situation where the definition of marriage can include anyone (any sexual identity or sexual orientation) and any number of people. Will people be able to marry kids once they lower the age of consent (which they are pushing for anyway), will people be able to marry animals, inanimate objects, or even themselves? They will change the definition of marriage so that it becomes so random and so all-inclusive that the definition of marriage doesn't need to exist since any arrangement will be defined as marriage. Marriage will be all-encompassing, anything and anyone with an unregulated number of participants will be classified as marriage, thus the meaning of marriage will become void, meaningless and obsolete. They are turning traditional marriage into a sexual free-for-all farce.

This is why people like Ben Shapiro and anarchists/libertarians quite rightly argue that the state/government should never be allowed to define marriage. The state will define marriage in the way it suits its own personal goal (which I will get to later). The state will abuse the power that it is vested with. One of these definitions is that out-of-wedlock cohabitation is equal to marriage / out-of-wedlock children are equal to children born to married parents. On the surface, this is done to protect children born out-of-wedlock. In reality, it denigrates marriage. This way people can have the benefits that marriage brings but without actually being married. One problem though, according to every research out there kids raised by married parents outperform children raised by non-married parents (even ones that are cohabitating). They outperform them it various regards: education, financially, emotionally etc. So kids are not equal – depending on what circumstances they are raised in, yet they are encouraging out-of-wedlock co-habitation at the expense of marriage. Parents who are not married (just cohabitating) are more likely to get separated than married parents which is obviously bad for kids. The state will redefine marriage and family not to protect the children but to achieve its own goal.

Even libertarians/anarchists are advocating against the state/ government defining marriage (since the state would abuse the power vested to it by the people). One may think that libertarians would accept pretty much anything but this is not the case. Anarchists are not advocating for the collapse of society but rather the collapse of the oppressive state. Society can survive without the state/government, the state doesn't and can't exist without society. Society is not codependent on the state. Anarchist, like all, should have an interest in preserving society/human race. They know that society can only continue to advance if future generations advance. They also know that the best environment for raising kids is the mother-father duo parental structure.

Another tragic thing is that more and more people get married because of pregnancy (it used to be that first people get married and then plan a family – which has proven to be good for the kids, now it's the complete opposite). Usually, this ends in divorce while the child is young which has negative repercussions on the child. Even though both women and men are to blame for this tragic phenomenon, this goes side by side with the rise of female promiscuity. As to how female promiscuity has an unfavorable impact on society I will cover it in a later chapter.

If you look at the gay movement from the 50s and up to this point it is clear that most of those who were and still are advocating the abolition of marriage without proposing an alternative (note: there is no such thing as a substitution for a heterosexual monogamous marriage, history proves this, so any alternative to this is a downgrade from the traditional/nuclear family at the cost for kids and society) are members of the LGBT movement.

Masha Gessen (gay woman, LGBT activist), in 2014 while speaking at a gay and lesbian event said "*I agree that we should have the right to marry, but I also think equally that it is a no-brainer that the institution of marriage should not exist, fighting for gay marriage generally involves lying about what are we going to do with marriage when we get there because we lie that the institution of marriage is not going to change and that is a lie, the institution of marriage is going to change and it should change and again I don't think it should exist.*" After this speech, she was met with a raptures applause from the audience.

One of the arguments for gay marriage used by gay activists is referred to as tax-exemption or tax-breaks. They claim that since gay couples are forbidden from marriage, are at an unjustified disadvantage compared to heterosexuals. This I would say is a false argument. First, we need to establish why tax-exemption (and other similar monetary benefits for married couples) exist. They exist because of children. Since children require high parental and monetary investment for their full development and the fact that society as a whole benefits from well-brought-up children it's easy to see that tax-breaks are used to help heterosexual married parents when it comes to child rearing since it alleviates some of the strain child-raising has in a monetary sense. Gay couples don't have this "issue" (I don't want it to seem as though I am insinuating that children are an issue). Tax-exemption is given to those who can conceive naturally – heterosexuals, gay couples don't need this added right (which they would get through the right to marry) since they can't conceive by natural means. Since tax-exemption is meant for those who can conceive and help them raise their kids if gay couples get tax-break rights they would enjoy rights that don't belong to them since they can't have kids. They will end up with the same rights as heterosexual married couples but without the added responsibility of child rearing which is the main reason tax-exemption rights were given to married heterosexual couples in the first place. In a sense, gay couples – by having the right to marry (get tax-exemption laws applied to them) and not having the added responsibility of raising children since they can't have their own will end up with more rights than heterosexual couples who are married and have kids.

There are countries in the west where gay couples have equal rights as married heterosexual couples apart from the fact that they can't say that they are married, thanks to civil partnerships which grant them those rights. Yet that is not good enough, they want more rights.

Remember when I said that the gay movement is not about equal rights but rather supremacy? For who knows how many years of human existence the only (and best) family setup that has proven to work always was and still is a marriage between a woman and a man. For some reason there are those that think that for society there is something better than this, it doesn't take a genius to see that whatever alternative they propose has failed previously in history.

Ann Coulter: *"if you were in a womb right now and you can choose to be black, white, rich, poor the one thing you should hope for is that your parents are married"* according to the research from both Right wing and Left wing organizations noted in her book.

Like it or hate it, agree or disagree, the best possible environment for raising kids is for them to be raised by their biological parents who are cohabitating, preferably married.

Liberal-leftist ideology knows no boundaries. Their hypocrisy follows their insanity. The push for gay rights, for gay marriage, is not a push for equality. In our contemporary, society there is a push to demonize heterosexual marriage and relationships, on the other hand, gay marriage is being celebrated. Just look at popular culture (movies, books, TV-shows), they are pushing the notion that straight marriage is bad and boring but gay marriage is being presented as the best thing in the world. The institution of marriage is being trampled when it includes members of the opposite sex, but in the case of gay couples, it's being raised on a pedestal. This is pure hypocrisy. Heterosexual monogamous relationship (including marriage) is being portrayed as unsustainable while the gay lifestyle (including gay marriage) is presented as a paradise. Why is heterosexual marriage being demonized from all angles and homosexual marriage being pushed, promoted and celebrated by today's culture and the media?

ATTACK ON THE PARENTS (MOTHER AND FATHER, HUSBAND AND WIFE):

The terms mother and father, husband and wife are now deemed offensive to the LGBT community.

Kathleen O'Day Wynne is a Canadian politician and the 25th Premier of Ontario. She is the first female premier of Ontario and the first openly gay head of government in Canada. In 2016 her administration brought "BILL 28 All Families Are Equal Act", an Act to amend the "Children's Law Reform Act, the Vital Statistics Act" and various other acts.

The aim is to erase mothers and fathers from the picture. This document uses 1984-style "newspeak" to push the gay/androgynous agenda. According to this act:

-*"a birth means a complete extraction of a fetus from a person"*
They replaced the word child or baby with the word "fetus" (this is done to belittle the miracle of birth, to make it less human, prior the word fetus was used to describe a baby that has been aborted and now they are using the same term for a child that is all but born, this is also done to push the complete liberalization of abortion), and the word mother is replaced with the word "person" as if anyone except a woman can give birth (this is a continuation of the androgynous plan, making men and women biologically equal, what is next? Will men be able to give birth?)

-throughout the entire act, the terms mother and father has been replaced with "parent"

-the bill removes presumption in law that a child has only two parents, it allows up to 4 unmarried, unrelated adults to agree to be parents by contract to a yet unborn child

There is a war on motherhood and fatherhood, mothers and fathers. They are bombarding us with this gender neutral notion that there is no biological sex.

Students in one University of Florida course have been banned from using words such as "husband," "wife," "mom," or dad" in the classroom and risk losing points off their grade if they don't comply. This was done by their professor. The students were also ordered to replace the words like "boyfriend", "girlfriend" with the more inclusive ones like "partner" or "significant other". Saying "husband" or "wife" was forbidden.

In 2012, France proposed banning the words “mother” and “father”. Justice Minister Christiane Taubira told France's Catholic newspaper La Croix: "*Who is to say that a heterosexual couple will bring a child up better than a homosexual couple, that they will guarantee the best conditions for the child's development*?" The plan was to ban the words “mother” and “father” from all legal documents. The official explanation from the court in France was so not to discriminate against the gay population. So now the mere words like “mother, father, husband, wife” are offensive?

The UK is also contemplating the removal of the words of “husband” and “wife” under the government's plans to legalize same-sex marriage.

Germany wants to ban the words “mother” and “father”. Germany is planning to pave the way for gender-neutral ideology and get rid of words like “mother” and “father” and instead replace them with terms like “parent 1 and parent 2”

In 2014 California has banned words like “wife” and “husband” from its Marriage law. They have proposed to exclude the words “husband” and “wife” for more inclusive words like “spouse” and “married persons”. They say the words “husband” and “wife” are anti-gay terms.

BMA (British Medical Association): told its doctors that pregnant women should not be called “expected mothers” as it could offend transgender people. Instead of that, they should call them “pregnant people”. This comes from a 14-page booklet titled “A Guide to Effective Communication: Inclusive Language In The Workplace”. They say this is done so not to offend intersexual and transsexual men. This book also describes the terms being born male and born female as offensive since according to the liberal-social justice warrior brainwashing everything is a social construct and there is no biological sex.

ATTACK ON GENDERS:

For as long the English language existed the words “sex” and “gender” were synonyms.

In 1995 Beijing, the United Nations world conference took place. There they divided “sex” and “gender” into two separate words. Anyone who has a brain will tell you that these two words are the same. This is where the whole transgender concepts started being pushed. To these gender ideologues the word “sex” represents the reproductive organ (penis,

vagina) that you were born with and the word "gender" is what you identify as (male, female). So you can be born with parts of one gender but yet be the other. They say gender is fluid, you can change it from one day to the next and back again. You can be whatever you want regardless of nature. This concept completely negates biological sex.
Women and men are not equal, we are not the same.

Gender ideologues (gender neutral /gender non-binary theory, queer theory), social justice warriors, gender study members claim that amongst other things, gender is a social construct, that the way we act, what we like, how we dress, talk, think has nothing to do with biological sex. Essentially their theory suggests that there is no gender and that the only reason men and women act the way they do is a result of social norms, oppression, patriarchy. They say that people are not female or male and should decide for themselves what they want to be. A man can choose to be a woman (regardless of the fact that not only he has a male reproductive organ but also has a male brain) and the other way around. According to these social Marxists, the rest of society should accept you for whom you claim to be irrespective of objective biology. Their theories are based on emotion and feelings, not facts.

According to them, men and women are the same/equal. Let's see what science, research, studies, and evidence have to say:

-According to the LGBT commies, there is a false stereotype when it comes to the colors we choose claiming that the reason women pick pink and men blue is a result of social pressure and prejudice. Research on kids shows that little girls prefer warm colors (red, pink, orange, yellow) and boys prefer cold colors (blue, green, purple). Kids know nothing about social conventions and norms thus the argument is invalid.

-Women are better at hearing, the reason being that they have about 11 percent more neurons in the part of the brain responsible for hearing and distinguishing sound.

-Females express their emotions better than males, MRA (Magnetic Resonance Angiography) scans prove this. Men tend to be less skilled when it comes to verbal expression which is why they compensate by using hands to express themselves when words fail them.

-Boys and girls play differently. Boys: larger play in groups, focus on the game, competitive, rough and tumble, confrontational, establish dominance. Girls: focus on relationship building, while playing they focus on caregiving and relationships (there is an evolutionary explanation as to why women are naturally better caregivers). The transgender movement blames this on social norms. But these male-female differences have been around from the beginning of hunter-gatherer times, there are not a result of some man-made constructs. They are close to universal across the mammal kingdom. Studies on primates, monkeys, rats show that male members are more likely to engage in physical conflict with one another for dominance, while the female members often care for the youngest of the bunch. Unless you are naive enough to think that there is a social construct imposed on half of the animal kingdom you will see the scientific evidence that proves that men and women are differently wired from birth.

-Boys and girls play with different toys. A study on 1.5-year-old kids has shown that girls prefer to play with toys, and boys have a strong preference for trucks. These results were duplicated on 9-month-old babies. Even when teachers and parents encourage gender-neutral play (translation: gender opposite) the girls chose dolls over trucks as soon as they were given the choice. In a study, girls were given to play with trucks. They ended up playing with trucks as though they were babies. When boys were given only girl toys they played with dolls as though they were swords. In another study male monkeys preferred to play with toy cars while female monkeys preferred to play with dolls. This is true for nearly all mammals, they play differently depending on their sex.

-Males are more likely to exhibit aggression physically and females are more likely to do so verbally. This difference has been documented in almost all other mammals.

-Men prefer women with high pitched voices, women prefer men with deep pitched voices. This has been proven time after time. Some may argue that this is a social construct. A research in an African tribe shows that in the middle of nowhere, in the middle of the desert completely cut out from contemporary "gender norms" men preferred women with high pitched voices, while women preferred men with deep voices and rated men with high pitched voices as unattractive.

-There is a difference in IQ distribution. When it comes to males it tends to go towards one end of the spectrum or the other, men tend to have either a higher than average or lower than average IQ more often than women, while women tend to be around average when it comes to IQ. For example, if the average IQ is 100, women tend to gravitate around that number, while men are more likely to either be noticeably higher or lower than the average IQ, meaning on average half of the men are going to be smarter than the average woman and half of the male population is going to be dumber than the average woman.

-Women and men complement each other. Mothers create stability, comfort, nurture. Fathers roughhouse, challenge, tease.

These are but a few innate biological and psychological differences between women and men. This list is by no means complete. Our species and civilization evolved and survived thanks to these differences. Note that a large portion of these and many other scientific studies have been conducted on animals (mostly mammals) and human tribes that have been living the same way for literally thousands of years and have not been touched by the supposed "gender norms" of the civilized western world, and little kids or babies who have no idea about gender or gender roles but are only acting a certain way because their brain is hard-wired from birth.

These social justice warriors special snowflakes actually claim that one is arbitrarily assigned a gender at birth by a doctor thus making gender (male or female) a social construct.

If you are still brainwashed that biological sex does not exist and that gender is a social construct remember the story of David Peter Reimer and the study of Doctor John Money who tried and miserably failed to prove that gender is a social construct and that there are no innate differences between men and women.

The elite are pushing to make the two genders (male and female) biologically equal. This has nothing to do with the right to get educated, join the workforce, or the right to vote. Once they achieve their goal of making men and women biologically the same we will find ourselves in the nightmare that is Brave New World, a world where everybody is equal in every sense of that word (Communism), equal in the way we act, think (or better yet the inability to think). The goal is to destroy true individualism in the name of collective uniformity (collectivism). The goal of every dictator throughout history is to achieve uniformity through conformity. The human race survived on the premise that women and men are not equal, biologically speaking they brink different unique things to the "table" but above everything else, the most important reason men and women are not equal is so they can ensure the best development for their children. If someone were to change this - make women and men equal, there would not be women and men, but rather one gender (if you can call it that) and our civilization and race would cease to exist as we know it. But how is this being done? The key is androgyny.

Women and men are not biologically and psychologically equal and hopefully they never will be, since that would represent a crime against nature and biology (one gender is not superior to the other, they are simply different). Men and women are not the same, we are physically and mentally different, we input, process and deliver information differently, we evolved with different priorities. This knowledge comes from brain scans, controlled studies, evolutionary psychology, and anthropology. An end to one or both sexes will mean an end to our species as we know it and I would classify that as a crime against human nature and biology. There are universal traits that men find desirable in women and there are different traits that women find desirable in men. Men represent masculinity which women find attractive, women personify femininity which men desire, this men=masculinity and women=femininity as I have said earlier is not a social construct but a biological fact. Who we are (man or woman) is not only defined by our reproductive organ but also by our brain that in almost all cases (excluding hermaphrodites) corresponds to the sex that we were born as. Men need women and women need men, masculinity seeks femininity and vice-versa, this is why we cohabitate.

There is an agenda to destroy the natural way of things, to turn men into something more like women and to turn women into men. The agenda is to create a world where all humans are both genders or neither of the genders (depending on the way you look at it). They are trying to bridge the biological gap between the two sexes, to make men more like women and the other way around. The plan is for men to adopt feminine traits and for women to adopt masculine traits. The attack on masculinity, femininity and objective biology has begun, they are trying to bridge the gap between innate differences amongst men and women.

-Caster Semenya (identifies as female) – born a male with only male reproductive organs, went through the mutilating procedure of removing fully functioning male genitals, won the 800-meter final victory in the Rio Olympics by beating every opponent with ease. It's worth mentioning that this race was a female only event and the winner was Caster Semenya, a born male. Caster Semenya also has three times the testosterone level of an average woman.
-Fallon Fox (born a man, identifies as a woman) – competes as a transgender post operation (male to female) MMA fighter in women's

categories and in the process decimating opponents like Tamika Brent who suffered a concussion and a broken eye socket. Ronda Rousey (born a female, identifies as a female) is an MMA fighter who criticized Fallon Fox for having an unfair advantage because he went through puberty as a male. Even though Fallon Fox had a sex change and went through hormone treatment he still has a bone density and muscle structure of a man (men are biologically and evolutionarily designed to perform on a physical level higher than women, men are physically stronger than women and their bodies reflect that). A man has a male body, male bones, and male muscle structure, but because he identifies as a woman he is able to compete in a women's only event. This is a downright unfair advantage and in my opinion discrimination towards women.
-Laura Hubbard (born a man, identifies as a woman) – won the women's over 90 kg division weightlifting competition in Australia, setting 4 records in the process.

All of these and many more (expect to see this kind of stuff more regularly) examples of men who identify as women (transsexuals) will result in men competing in women's sport categories and will leave women at a serious disadvantage in any area where victory is dependent on strength, speed, vigor or any trait that men are by nature better than women. No matter how many sex changes and hormone injections, you cannot change this, a man cannot become a woman and the other way around. Just because a born male identifies as a female does not mean his male body will suddenly become weaker and less masculine to accommodate his feelings. He is still in a male body which is better equipped for tasks where strength is needed. Even though he identifies as a female his body is still that of a male which leaves actual women in their female bodies at a disadvantage in any competition that requires strength (men are stronger than women, that is a biological and evolutionary fact, of course, there are things where women excel and are by default better than men). A man who identifies as a woman still has the muscle mass, stamina, bone density of a man which gives him a serious advantage over women in competitions that require physical endurance. When you put women alongside men in a competition that requires strength women will get physically hurt. If you think this is equality than you are delusional. Rather than this being classified as equality, tolerance or acceptance, I would rather define it as outright discrimination against women, this is true violence against women. These are the same geniuses that say that women and men are biologically equal (including when it comes to strength), but if, God forbid, a man hits a woman (in a mixed-sex boxing match, or injures her non-maliciously in a sports game) those same people would shout "discrimination", "men can't hit women" or "violence against women." Men and women are equal they say, no one says anything if a woman hits a man, but if that man retaliates he is labeled a "woman beater" because then those same people use the argument that men are stronger – equality. The hypocrisy of the Liberal-left knows no boundaries. I'm not against women playing sports, but female and male sports should stay separated. What is next, same-sex bathrooms and locker rooms (more on this later)?

Of course, there are things in which women are by nature better than men (on both a physical and psychological level). Just one example, women are innately better at long distance and endurance swimming than men. The reason again being biological predispositions, women have higher levels of body fat thus making them more buoyant. I had to cover this topic because to these gender ideologues gender is malleable or interchangeable, this is the prelude for transsexual teachings. These Socialists, who are still gullible enough to believe in the "blank sheet of paper" theory (which has been debunked countless times) when it comes to genders believe they can mold humans into whatever gender they desire regardless of biological sex and objective reality.

There is a two-pronged attack:

-the push to turn men into women (emasculation of men / feminization of men), the plan to make men more like women, for them to adopt traits and behavioral patterns that are feminine

-the push to turn women into men (masculinization of women), the plan to make women act, dress, talk and behave more like men

Today you can see an ever increasing trend of men acting like women, wearing women's clothing, being more feminine and out of touch with their masculine side. This results in women not having an interest in those kinds of men since they don't resonate masculine traits that women find desirable. On the other hand, women are becoming more masculine, they are taught to act like men and the result of that is that men don't find masculine women attractive since men are biologically programmed to seek out feminine women.

Women and men are not equal (biologically and psychologically speaking, we are different, one sex is not better than the other just different in their own way). This I hope will not change. Men are bad at being women and women are bad at being men.

Transsexuality is still recognized as a mental illness (gender identity disorder). More and more men are becoming, at an increasing rate, more like women, their appearance and mannerism is becoming so feminine that women don't find them appealing. Men don't act anymore in a way (masculine traits) that women subconsciously prefer. Society cannot and will not survive without one of the two genders and it will not survive without masculine and feminine traits. Men are bearers of masculinity and women of femininity.

When it comes to transsexuality or transgenderism I will cover this in greater depth at a later chapter.

Let me put this plain and simple, women from a biological and psychological standpoint are programmed to seek masculinity (men) and do not find feminine men attractive. Men have an innate preference for feminine women and will not find women that act, dress, speak like men attractive. Femininity attracts masculinity and the other way around. One cannot survive without the other, society and we as humans hinge on the existence of both masculine and feminine traits. This is how our species is designed and our society built. This is also the best formula for the child since it gets to grow up in an environment with its biological parents and get the necessary masculine traits from its father and feminine traits from its mother thus ensuring the best possible future for the child.

If you think that there is no attack on manhood and positive male masculinity, and if you (for whatever reason) still think that feminism is the advocacy for the equality between men and women I suggest you think again. You might say "who cares if men are getting emasculated". Well, the feminization of men doesn't have a negative impact only on men, to quote Tomi Lahren *"is it just me or have men gotten really soft these days, I talk about the breakdown of the American family ruining our country and this is part of it, yeah I know that feminists are going to go crazy over this because there are women's studies classes dedicated to demonizing masculinity so there is one symptom of a larger disease, who would have thought that in 2016 we would be holding up frat boys as the last line of defence against an all-out pansy fest, this has nothing to do with sexuality by the way, more so it has to do with the helplessness of today's young men, it seems few can change a light bulb let alone change a flat tire or change oil, and that makes for pretty slim pickings for the females out there looking for a match. Chivalry is all but dead, and so is manliness...so who's fault is it? Is it our fault ladies? Are we getting too strong? Nah, I don't buy that, see a real man knows how to handle a strong woman so this isn't our problem. Maybe it's the way boys are raised these days, fatherless homes and no male role models. It's hard to learn how to be a man with no men around but even stable families are failing though...if you take your seven-year-old son to the ladies room that's your fault not his, please teach your sons how to be men because the women of the world are tired of the boys."*

ATTACK ON SEXUALITY:

In 2015 the results of a study on human sexuality came out. The study claimed that "that there is no such thing as an exclusively heterosexual woman." The study said that all women are either lesbian or bisexual.

"NBC News: 'Heterosexuality Is Just Not Working' - Women are increasingly opting out of heterosexuality because it is 'the bedrock of their global oppression,' NBC News asserted in a bizarre opinion piece this week. 'Men need heterosexuality to maintain their societal dominance over women,' writes Marcie Bianco for the NBC News website. 'Women, on the other hand, are increasingly realizing not only that they don't need heterosexuality, but that it also is often the bedrock of their global oppression.' 'As the status quo, heterosexuality is just not working,' she concludes, before explaining just how evil men are and how women are learning to live without them." (Source: breitbart.com) A few observations are necessary. This opinion piece was originally posted on NBC, a 'progressive' liberal news outlet. This literary masterpiece was written by Marcie Bianco, a feminist and a lesbian, what a shock. She is not the first, unfortunately, not the last feminist/lesbian that spews hatred towards men and advocated for women to become lesbians. Prior examples include Julie Bindel. In 2009, Julie Bindel wrote "*My sexual revolution - In the late 70s a group of lesbians in Leeds, known as revolutionary feminists (RFs), made a controversial move that resonated loudly for me and many other women. They began calling for all feminists to embrace lesbianism. Appealing to their heterosexual sisters to get rid of men 'from your beds and your heads', they started a debate, which reached its height in 1981 with the publication of an infamous booklet, Love Your Enemy? The Debate Between*

Heterosexual Feminism and Political Lesbianism (LYE). In this, the RFs wrote that, 'all feminists can and should be lesbians. Our definition of a political lesbian is a woman-identified woman who does not fuck men. It does not mean compulsory sexual activity with women.' To me, political lesbianism continues to make intrinsic sense because it reinforces the idea that sexuality is a choice, and we are not destined to a particular fate because of our chromosomes. I also suspect that it is very difficult to spend your daily life fighting against male violence, only to share a bed with a man come the evening. Then there's the fact that working with women towards a common goal means you develop a strong and passionate bond with them - why some feminists then block out the possibility of sexual relationships with their political sisters and instead turn to men for intimacy is beyond me." (Source: theguardian.com) As for the definition of the term 'a feminist' is concerned, Ann Coulter said it best: (a feminist) *"is an angry, man-hating lesbian."* They are constantly pushing the, yet to be proven, notion that homosexuality, bisexuality, pansexuality are innate preferences that can't be changed, while at the same time claiming that heterosexuality is either a social construct or a choice that people can and should change. Heterosexuality not working, you say? If this isn't heterophobia, I don't know what is. Is there a more pseudoscientific, oxymoronic, and postmodernist statement than this? As Kirk Lazarus said *"You went full retard...never go full retard."*

Empirically speaking, a growing number of women seem to change their sexual orientation more often than I change my socks.

Gloria Steinem (a feminist) said that women should separate their sexuality/sexual orientation from the need to procreate. Her books are being taught in every college in the U.S. Steinem and other feminists like her say that the only reason women marry men is because they are oppressed. I would like to give my counter-argument. If Steinem is correct, then why in the U.S. where women have been completely liberated, where homosexuality is not only tolerated but rather praised, women still choose to marry men even though they don't have to?

How dare I even assume that women are programmed to procreate and give birth? Well, there is a thing called the "Mommy brain". This is the evolution of a female brain that occurs during a woman's life. This change starts during pregnancy completing a new "mommy brain" about 6 months after giving birth. Due to this, a woman's stress circuit will become suppressed, her cortex will enlarge, and the rest of her brain will experience a shrinkage (she won't lose any brain cells) but her pathways will change and new networks will form until her brain is back to normal size. This rewires the woman's brain so that she is better equipped to dealing with the newborn (example: her hearing will become more sensitive, the scientific explanation for this is that this way she is better able to hear the cries of her infant). Supposedly, women aren't the only ones that experience changes due to them becoming a parent, recent studies indicate that men's brain changes once they become fathers.

Another example is related to hormone releases. Women attach to their male sex partners through the hormone oxytocin, which is the same exact hormone released in women while they are nursing their babies. Isn't this mother nature's way of saying procreation is a biological imperative?

These, amongst many other things, merely prove that men and women are made/programmed to procreate and last time I checked procreation cannot occur between members of the same sex.

First, they claimed that homosexuality is an exception to the rule, an alternative to heterosexuality. Now they are claiming that exclusively heterosexual women don't exist.

There is a reason as to why they are attacking women first, women are bearers of life, even though society and our civilization would not survive without one of the two sexes (men/women) it is my honest opinion that they are deliberately targeting women more because they know that it will have a greater negative effect of society if they "destroy" women first rather than men. Having said that, there is no doubt in my mind that they will eventually go after men, claiming that heterosexual men don't exist.

ATTACK ON THE KIDS:

Where will the line be drawn?
There is a deliberate attempt to sexualize and homosexualize children from the earliest age possible.

LGBT members and pro-gay activists argue that gay marriage should be legalized since it only affects the parties involved in that marriage. In other words, they claim that gay marriage and the gay movement will not adversely affect those who are not a part of this movement. This is a straight out lie. The gay agenda has nothing to do with equality. This chapter is dedicated to this aggressive movement that aims to destroy the family. The newest victims of their brain-washing experiment are kids, the most fragile and impressionable members of society. As you will see in the future more and more members of society will be attacked by this dogma-like movement, first they attacked the religious people, then they infiltrated science since they were unable to prove that homosexuality is something you are born with, then they went for the family and now they are even targeting kids.

Ontario, Canada, in February 2015 Kathleen Wynne, the then Premier of Ontario, (and a member of the LGBT) and her government introduced changes to the sex education curriculum in public schools. As these things usually go the reasoning for this was to stop discrimination and promote equality, at least on the surface.

This sex-educational curriculum "Health and physical education" consists of 244 pages. This curriculum was also developed by Benjamin Levin, former deputy minister of education, who pleaded guilty to three charges relating to making and distributing child pornography. He was sentenced to three years imprisonment. So a sex-ed curriculum made for kids was drafted by an LGBT member (Kathleen Wynne) and a pedophile (Benjamin Levin), how convenient.

There was an earlier attempt at a sex-ed curriculum in 2010, a curriculum so radical that when parents complained it was pulled and not implemented. Since then it has been under review outside of the public eye and not available for parents to see. The curriculum was supposed to be implemented in schools starting from September 2015. Kathleen Wynne did not keep her promise that she would consult parents before implementing the curriculum. She said that anyone opposing the sex-ed curriculum is a bad parent and a homophobe.

The Ontario Curriculum "Health and physical education" is meant for grades from 1-8 (from 6 to 13-year-old kids)
Here are a few examples:
- For grade 1 kids (6-year-old kids) on page 93 under the *"Human development and sexual health"* title, it says and I quote *"identify body parts including genitalia (penis, testicles, vagina, vulva), using correct terminology."* It is interesting to note that a few years ago the government abolished spelling in many of the elementary schools in Canada for grade 1 kids. I guess it's more important for these kids to know how to identify a vagina and a penis than it is to learn how to spell – priorities. They will know how to say penis and vagina but not how to spell them.

- Grade 5 (10-year-old kids) page 156 "*Female body parts that mature and develop as a part of puberty include the vagina.......Male body parts that mature and develop during puberty include the penis......During puberty, girls will develop breasts and get their periods for the first time.....Menstruation is the medical term for having a 'period'........It is how the female body gets ready for pregnancy.*" 10-year-old kids being taught about sex and pregnancy when then they haven't even entered puberty, why, is someone preparing them for something? Also, I thought gender is a social construct, that there are no differences between men and women.
- Grade 6 (11-year-old kids) page 174 and 175 I quote multiple passages "*new interest in relationships with boys or girls, confusion and questions about changes......Exploring one's body by touching or masturbating is something that many people do and find pleasurable.*" Kids at this age being taught about masturbation, again why? I'm not saying that masturbation is good or bad, moral or immoral I'm simply asking why are kids bombarded with it at this age.

Page 177 I quote "*assess the effects of stereotypes, including homophobia and assumptions regarding gender roles and expectations, sexual orientation, gender expression.......Can you give examples of some stereotypes that might have a negative effect on a person's self-concept and social inclusion? What can we do to change stereotypes and discrimination........Assumptions are often made about what is 'normal' or expected for males and females – for example, men take out the garbage; nursing is a woman's job; boys play soccer at recess and girls skip rope or stand around and talk; boys are good at weightlifting and girls are good at dancing. Assumptions like these are usually untrue, and they can be harmful.....Stereotypes are usually formed when we do not have enough information.*" No, stereotypes exist for a reason, because they are generally true, it doesn't mean that all stereotypes have a negative connotation. They talk about anti-discrimination while discriminating those who disagree with this curriculum. Gender roles are not made up-social constructs (I have already covered this earlier in this chapter).
- In grade 7 (12-year-old kids) on page 199 "*Thinking about your sexual health is complicated. It's important to have a good understanding of yourself before getting involved with someone else. It's not just about making a decision to have sex or waiting until you are older. It's also about things such as your physical readiness; safer sex and avoiding consequences such as pregnancy or STIs; your sexual orientation and gender identity.*" Why are 12-year-old kids being encouraged to have sex? Also at the age of

12, they are already bombarding them with LGBT ideology. As for "avoiding consequences such as pregnancy and STIs" how about you stop teaching them about sex at a young age if you want to avoid unwanted pregnancy and stop encouraging homosexual behavior if you don't want them to get STIs since it's far more likely to get STIs due to sexual interaction with a person of the same sex rather than with the opposite.

- Grade 8 (13-year-old kids) on page 216 children are expected to and I quote *"demonstrate an understanding of gender identity (e.g., male, female, two-spirited, transgender, transsexual, intersex), gender expression, and sexual orientation (e.g., heterosexual, gay, lesbian, bisexual), and identify factors that can help individuals of all identities and orientations."* How and why do they expect 13-year-old kids to know and understand the infinite number or gender identities when there is no scientific proof for any of them apart for the male-female binary?

This curriculum presents itself as anti-discriminatory, all-inclusive educational curriculum all about equality. In reality, it's here to sexualize children from the earliest age possible.

The parents of Ontario's elementary schools were so outraged that many of them pulled their kids from schools for days at a time and even whole weeks. They signed a petition to battle against the continuation of this curriculum. They have been demonized by the mainstream media as being homophobes and intolerant bigots.

Almost all psychologists, sociologists, psychiatrists agree that these topics should not be taught to kids as young as this, they claim it has a negative impact on their lives. So why is it then being pushed so heavily? Not that long ago they have tried to do the same thing in Serbia in the name of equality and tolerance.

Why is anyone (in the realm of science or not) who dares criticize the negative implications of this curriculum being labeled a homophobe or transphobe? Why are more and more kids being exposed to inappropriate material in the name of human rights? Where is the right of kids to be kids and not forced to learn about things most adults don't understand? Where is the right of parents to be the first educators of their own kids? Since when did the school take over this sacred parent-child bond? The answers to these questions will be addressed in a later chapter.

This is not education, this is called grooming, something pedophiles do to their victims.

INDIVIDUAL CASES OF LGBT AGGRESSION:

In France kids in kindergarten and pre-school are read books like "Jean a deux mamans" (translation: Jean has two moms) and "Tango a deux papas" (translation: a tango of two fathers, a book about a little penguin having two dads).

In Latvia, there are children's books called "The day Karlis was Karlina" and "The day Ruta was Richard", both of these books have a transsexual/transgender topic aimed at kids.

In the U.S.A. children are read books by the name "Heather has two mommies", "Daddies roommate", "Jacob's new dress", "My princess boy" all homosexualy/transsexualy themed. These books are meant for children as young as 2 years old.

In one school in Germany students and teachers "swapped sexes", in honor of gender equality day boys and girls cross-dressed.

The current stance of science (based on research and experiments) is that sex (male or female) in predetermined at conception, gender is a blueprint. Despite that you have situations like these:

- Kids as young as four are asked to choose their own gender with the option of being something other than male or female. Parents received a letter asking them whether their child preferred male or female (source: Dailymail)
- School told not to use terms like "boy", "girl", "ladies", " gentlemen" because it is not inclusive of transgenders. Instead of that, they were told to use a more inclusive term like "purple penguins." (source: Nationalreview). This happened in Nebraska, USA, no surprise there. It's being pushed in other places as well.

In Germany, 13-year-olds are given the following questionnaire which they must answer: *"Do you belong to the right gender?","When and why did you decide to be heterosexual?"* (didn't they tell us that you are born gay? Now you can choose your sexuality?) *"Is heterosexuality only a phase that you will overcome?", "Is it possible that your heterosexuality is a result of a neurotic fear of the people the same gender as you?"* So you are supposedly born gay, but heterosexuality is a social construct?

More and more TV shows, series and even cartoons are pushing this gay/trans movement. Here are just a few examples:

- Disney's hit show "Good luck Charlie" aimed for kids featured a lesbian couple raising a child.
- Disney's show "Star vs forces of evil" again for kids featured a gay kiss between its characters.
- Disney's admitted that their upcoming rework film "Beauty and the beast" in 2017 will feature first exclusively gay moment in a Disney movie.

If you think it's merely a coincidence that this is coming from Disney, think again. Check their previous "kid-friendly" movies.

In Australia I quote *"Teachers have been advised to no longer use the terms 'mum' or 'dad' and young boys are being encouraged to dress up as girls in new education guidelines. The instructions have been released by the NSW teachers' union on ways to address LGBTI issues within the school environment. The latest guidelines for 'non-gender-specific free play,' come in the wake of a string of drastic political correctness measures taken by Australian schools."* (source DavidIcke.com)

In Germany, I quote *"Anal sex practices, sadomasochism and adult sex toys should become known to German pupils through "theatrical performance," lectures or workshops, according to teaching materials promoted by a state-supported anti-homophobia project. Fourteen-year-olds in North Rhine-Westphalia (NRW), the most-populous state in Germany, may come across school classes making them aware of anal sex, sadomasochism and the use of sex toys, including dildos, as early as in the next school year, according to Die Welt newspaper. It all comes as part of an offbeat project called 'School of Diversity', jointly run by the regional education ministry and a number of LGBT advocacy groups to "reflect on tabooed, but very relevant themes [for teenagers]," as well as to promote diversity and tolerance in German society."* (source rt.com) Right....tolerance, demanding tolerance but denying the right of parents to raise their own children in accordance with their own set of values.

In the UK I quote *"Police and local government agencies in the United Kingdom are distributing a "pioneering" document for "empowering teachers to encourage and support" transgenderism in schools at the "earliest stages" after a four-year-old child identified as transgender. The*

"School Transgender Guidance" document has been distributed to all schools in the Cornwall area, and been named as "best practice" by the UK government's Department of Education. It says transgenderism can potentially be identified in those as young as two, and discusses powerful, irreversible and controversial treatments for prepubescent children. The document claims: "The purpose of this guidance is to deeper ember good practice in the field of school [primary and secondary] and colleges," and states that children as young as two years old can be identified as suffering from Gender Dysphoria." (source Breitbart.com) I wonder why they are suffering from Gender Dysphoria, it has nothing to do with all the constant LGBT brainwashing and propaganda they see everywhere they look, right?

In Australia: *"Australian school children are to be told that heterosexuality is not the norm, according to a new education department pilot program called "Proud Schools." "Heterosexism" is one of the evils that the Proud Schools program is intended to stamp out, along with "homophobia and transphobia," education officials have said. According to the minutes from the Proud Schools steering committee on March 22, 2011, the program focuses on reversing "the dominance of heterosexism rather than on homophobia." The program defines "heterosexism" as the practice of "positioning heterosexuality as the norm for human relationship," according to the Proud Schools Consultation Report. "It involves ignoring, making invisible or discriminating against non-heterosexual people, their relationships and their interests. Heterosexism feeds homophobia."* (source: lifesitenews.com) I guess Alex Jones (a journalist) wasn't too off when he said *"being straight is a crime"*

The headline reads: *"TEACHER FORCES TEENS TO QUESTION BEING 'STRAIGHT' 'Is it possible your heterosexuality is just a phase you may grow out of?" I quote the article "The mother of a Wisconsin teenager was stunned when her high school senior brought home a questionnaire assigned by his English teacher that asked, among several provocative questions. The questions included: "What do you think caused your heterosexuality?", "When and how did you decide you were a heterosexual?", "Is it possible that your heterosexuality is just a phase you may grow out of?", "Statistics show that lesbians have the lowest incidence of sexually transmitted diseases. Is it really safe for a woman to maintain a heterosexual lifestyle and run the risk of disease and pregnancy?", "Considering the menace of overpopulation, how could the human race survive if everyone were heterosexual?", "Is it possible that your heterosexuality stems from a neurotic fear of others of the same sex"? The mother, Marilyn Hanson, reviewed the questionnaire and thought it completely inappropriate for any class, but especially for a required English class, where, Hanson told WND, "They should be taught to read and write and prepare for college." "I really believe this was outright indoctrination to the homosexual viewpoint," Hanson said. "I could see this being discussed in a debate class, where both sides were presented. But the other side was not presented."Hanson told WND, "I think they're trying to shove [homosexuality] down our throats."* (source wnd.com) Again, people are born gay but conditioned to be straight according to them.

Report by the Dailymail under the headline *"Teach the pleasure of gay sex to children as young as five, say researchers" says: "Children as young as five should be taught to understand the pleasures of gay sex, according to leaders of a taxpayer-funded education project. Heads of the project have set themselves a goal of 'creating primary classrooms where queer sexualities are affirmed and celebrated'."* Equality apparently

In Denver, a 4-year-old girl was thrown out of pre-school because her parents did not want her to attend a sexual education class. The parents have found out that school was introducing provocative and homosexual images and stories in literature that was being read to the kids. I quote the article *"a 4-year-old girl was kicked out of a preschool last month when her parents raised questions about books read in her class, including ones that told stories about same-sex couples and worms unsure about their gender", the article continues "The girl returned home from school one day concerned that her daddy might not like girls anymore – and her mommy is a girl"* (source: Theresurgent)

In California, parents pulled their son out of school after they found out he was participating in a gay-pride ceremony without their knowledge. The boy was dressed as a girl and was explicitly instructed not to tell his parents that he was participating in such ceremonies. (source: Urianbrandon) Using kids as weapons and meat shields, oldest trick in the book.

"Swedish school bans 'him' and 'her' in bid to stop children falling into gender stereotypes. A pre-school in Sweden has decided to stop calling children 'him' or 'her' in a bid to avoid gender stereotypes. As well as the

decision to stop using the words, the taxpayer-funded school also carefully plans the color and placement of toys and the choice of books to assure they do not fall into stereotypes." (source: Dailymail.co.uk) Men and women are not equal, boys and girls are not equal.

Dolce and Gabbana – Elton John and his leftist minions spearheaded a campaign to boycott Dolce and Gabbana when they disagreed with children being born through artificial insemination especially to gay couples. Due to ongoing pressure from the media and the people, Dolce and Gabbana capitulated by blaming their views on the traditional Catholic values they were raised in. Bullying tactics 101.

Julie Bindel, prominent feminist and a gay woman (what a surprise), in an interview she said the following *"I hope heterosexuality doesn't survive actually."* The LGBT is about tolerance and equality (equal treatment) you say? Imagine the outrage if someone were to say "I hope homosexuality ceased to exist." That person would be sent to the guillotine in a blink of an eye. Did the same occur to Julie Bindel, NO, she got a standing ovation from the crowd – the leftist's definition of equality. This is the hypocrisy of the so-called progressive tolerant left (including the gay movement).

In the same interview, Julie Bindel said: *"I would actually put them in some sort of camp where they can all drive around in quad bikes, or bicycles, or white vans. I would give them a choice of vehicles to drive around with, give them no porn, they wouldn't be able to fight—we would have wardens, of course. Women who want to be able to see their sons or male loved ones would be able to visit or take them out like a library book and bring them back again."* Putting men in camps? And people say feminists don't hate men. Take them out like a library book? Knowing how often people read books nowadays (sarcasm intended) men might as well kiss their chances of ever exiting this misandristic camp goodbye.

"European feminists gang up on children's fairy tales - European kindergartens and schools may ban children's books and fairy tales that depict the traditional family. This is a request of the European Parliament Committee on Women's Rights. According to the committee, fairy tales should talk about sexual diversity. Norwegian experts believe that children benefit from watching porn. The European Parliament's Committee on Women's Rights and Gender Equality prepared a report that calls for a ban of all books that show the traditional family where the father is the

breadwinner and the mother takes care of the children in schools and day care centers of Europe. According to the authors, these books are bad for the future life of children, especially girls, and promote wrong behavioral patterns. In the future, it may prevent them from building a career. Feminists are concerned that children from an early age are constantly faced with "negative gender stereotypes" in television shows and commercials. The word "negative" in the report is synonymous with the word "traditional". Over time, the ban would be extended to television and advertising. So far it was decided to start with books. An example of alternative children's literature is a book "King and King" with kissing men on the cover. According to the report, this would help children to learn about the "true sexual diversity of society." In fact, such measures have already been taken in some countries, particularly in Scandinavian ones that consider themselves the vanguard of Western democracy. "Pravda.Ru" once reported about a Swedish toy manufacturer that issued a catalog before Christmas where girls were pictured shooting imaginary enemies with laser guns, and boys were depicted playing with dolls. Norwegian kindergartens in 2010 introduced a program of compulsory sex education focusing on sexual minorities. The report of the European Parliament also insisted that "homosexuality should be taught in kindergarten as a form of experience and knowledge." According to them, this will expand the concept of "gender identity" for children. "Sexual diversity should be obvious to children. Children need to know that this is normal when your parents are gay or lesbian." (source: pravdareport.com)

"Europe to destroy traditional family and sexual identity - Traditional words 'father' and 'mother' will be replaced with official terms Parent 1 and Parent 2 in Britain. The terms will be used in official documents. The authorities decided to make such a "politically correct" move to accommodate same-sex couples. The decision is another step towards the destruction of traditional families. The words 'father' and 'mother' will be removed from British passport applications before December 2011. This became an achievement of Stonewall group, which defends the rights of sex minorities. The US State Department tried to do the same before, but it was eventually decided not to remove the two words from US passport applications. Last year, the European Parliament published the brochure, which recommended not to use the words 'Missus' and 'Miss', 'Mademoiselle', 'Seniora' and 'Seniorita'. From the point of view of the European parliament, the use of such words was discriminating against

women because they directly indicated their sexual identity. They proceeded towards the protection of human rights. This is how they approach children's rights today. They think that children must be protected from the despotism of their parents - from any forms of traditional upbringing. In order to accomplish that, one has to destroy the traditional family first and to make the family become a form that enslaves and binds children. The movements for the protection of rights of sexual minorities are trying to undermine the traditional or natural family. They want to separate the process of procreation and childcare from marriage and family." (source: pravdareport.com)

California State Bill 48: a law that mandates that children as young as kindergarten (5-6-year-old kids in the U.S.A.) are now required to learn about famous homosexuals as part of their standard curriculum. Under this law, school materials can only promote positive topics regarding LGBT themes. The law states that parents will not be notified of such materials and can't exempt children from these classes. This bill forbids school from teaching kids the fact the homosexuality is statistically unhealthier than heterosexuality and has an exponentially higher rate of sexually transmitted disease. (for a long time I have been saying that California is America's Holland, a cesspool of liberal left-wing ideology)

Thanks to this bill: -textbooks and instructional materials must positively promote *"lesbian, gay, bisexual and transsexual Americans as role models"*

-children as young as 6 years old will be taught to admire homosexuality, same-sex marriages, bisexuality and transsexuality (cross-dressing and sex-change operations)

-children are to be taught to support the political activism of "lesbian, gay, bisexual, transgender, intersex and questioning (LGBTIQ) political groups"

-teachers are required to positively portray homosexuality, same-sex marriages, bisexuality, transsexuality

-school boards are required to select textbooks and other instructional materials that positively portray the LGBT lifestyle

-parents are not notified, nor are they able to exempt their children from this core curriculum

This bill is just one of many, not even including the ones that are yet to coming. They tried a similar thing in Serbia. Even though they did not succeed that doesn't mean they won't try again until they get what they want. There are many reasons why these kinds of laws are and will be pushed forward. These reasons are not as they claim equal rights and anti-discrimination. The real reasons are not on the surface and I will cover them at a later chapter.

Here I have listed only a small number of situations where there has been an obvious push by the gay agenda to attack the family and the kids. If I were to list all of the aggressive transgressions by the LGBT movement just in the time I have been studying this topic (last 6-7 years approximately) I would be forced to write 'War and Peace' version 2.0

If you look at modern entertainment (TV shows, media, series, movies and anything else) you will see a pattern. An ever-increasing number of characters on all of these platforms are either gay, lesbian, bisexual or transgender in both adult and kid shows. Just think about it. Look at your average TV show, there has to be a miserable married straight couple or a happily divorced and single straight ex-couple, if they are divorced it's always the men's fault, the man is always portrayed as an incompetent idiot who is a liar and a cheater, straight married couple are shown as being joyless because they have kids, gay couples are happily in love, gay couples are shown as excellent parents.

These are but a few of an ever-growing number of cases where the liberal-left wing (under the guise of the gay/LGBT movement) is attacking the nuclear family, kids and science/biology itself and all that and more in the name of equality and anti-discrimination. The irony – fighting "discrimination" by discriminating those who oppose their views and opinions.

GAY AGENDA 21

CHAPTER 6 "WHY IS THE GAY AGENDA BEING PUSHED?"

If there is an agenda what is its purpose? After all, there is no reason for an agenda to exist if it doesn't have an end goal. The gay agenda is no different. The two main goals of the gay/androgynous agenda are:

-to destroy the nuclear/traditional family

-to normalize and later down the line legalize pedophilia

THE DESTRUCTION OF THE FAMILY:

The traditional/nuclear (heterosexual monogamous) family unit always was and still is the bedrock of every civilization in the history of humankind. So by this definition, if someone wants to destroy the family and society as a whole they would need to eliminate one or both of these components (heterosexuality or monogamy).

History has shown that anytime a civilization, nation, people step away from this formula (heterosexual monogamy) their collapse follows. If society deviates from this formula the best case scenario, in very rare cases (Islam), they stagnate as a society. The Islam/Arab world used to be way more advanced than their European counterparts back in the Dark ages (from 7th to 11th century AD). One of the reasons it has stagnated for nearly a millennium is polygamy. As previously discussed, in a polygamous society rape, incest, homosexuality, and pedophilia tend to rise. The resurgence of the Islamic world occurred in the second half of the 20th century and continued in the 21st, at least for a while in some parts. The reason for this was the promotion of monogamy and family values. Thanks to this brief modernization and de-radicalization the Islamic world prospered (mainly Libya and Syria). To a lesser extent, this is true for Iran, Iraq, Afghanistan. Women had educational rights, a right to work, a right to wear heels and dresses, not hijabs and be covered from head to toe with a rag, a right to choose which man they want to marry and not be forced into marriage (Gaddafi's government used to give 50,000 dollars to newly-wed couples). I am not saying that they had it as good as western women, but they were, in certain regards, better off than they are now. This, of course, ended once the Western powers brought liberal democracy and human rights to North Africa and the Middle East and threw them back to the Stone age.

Polyandry is equally nonsensical since women haven't gained any evolutionary benefit from being promiscuous and having multiple husbands.

The point of this was to show that polygamy has yet to work in the course of humankind. There is a reason why every group of people that stood the testament of time practiced monogamy (including the period before any monotheistic religion introduced marriage). In an earlier chapter, I have elaborated why polygamy is bad for kids. Take this as an example, in the Muslim world a man can have 4 wives, from all of these wives he will probably have at least 4 kids in total. Do you honestly think he (or any man) can possibly devote enough time to every wife and every child? Of course, he can't. Some kids will basically be left without a dad in their life. The negative side of that I have already covered in the previous chapter. What kind of culture would not only tolerate but also encourage and celebrate a lifestyle that would leave children without one of their parents even though they are essential for the kid's development? Parents have a legal and, more importantly, a moral obligation to care and protect their children, to be involved in their lives not to "half-ass" that duty. Not only does that have a negative impact on the kids but it also isn't beneficial to society as a whole.

Despite all this, popular culture, media, movies, and TV-shows are promoting this. Monogamy is being looked down upon even though it has been proven time and time again that it is the best environment for raising children since they get a guaranteed mom and a dad. This was true way before Christianity formed marriage and is still true across the world in tribes where modern civilization and modern way of life haven't set foot.

When it comes to sexuality I have discussed this earlier. If homosexuality is innate and natural than the number of gay people should stay relatively the same throughout history. So why is there an increase of people who identify on some level with the LGBT spectrum? LGBT apologists say that that is due to the fact that society has become more open and tolerant towards homosexual and other LGBT behavior. Fair enough, on the surface, it seems like a valid argument. There is one problem though. If this hypothesis were true then in the countries that have openly accepted gay marriage and gay rights there should not be an increase of homosexuality, the numbers should not change drastically since there is no reason for gay people to hide there anymore. In some countries (US, Canada, Holland) gay marriage and gay adoption are legal. In many other western European countries, even though they don't recognize gay marriage, people who identify as gay can form an out-of-wedlock contractual relationship with all the benefits of marriage and are protected by the state. So why is it then, despite the fact that in contemporary western society homosexuality is not only tolerated and accepted but also celebrated, yet it is still rising. In many of these countries, gay people not only have the same right as heterosexuals but also have more rights when it comes to entering college and employment due to the "gay quota" schools and employers are required to have thanks to the new diversity programs and legislations. Not to mention all the anti-discriminatory laws that protect them, in other words, silence people who contradict the LGBT narrative. LGBT members are one of the, if not the best protected demographic group in Western Europe and America. Not only are they protected but also anyone who dares to, for whatever reason, disagree with them or challenge their views is deemed a homophobe, bigot, Nazi or any other kind of radical. So don't use the argument that gay people are at any kind of disadvantage in the west in the eyes of the law or society since anyone who merely has an opinion that rivals the LGBT narrative gets "quartered" medieval style. Despite the fact that in the west they are probably the most protected group and are welcomed with open arms (since homosexuality and the rest of the LGBT behavior is encouraged) their numbers are still rising.

So why is it that the LGBT members are growing in numbers then?

-(source New York Post): The headline says "*Millennials are the most bisexual generation of all time*" the article continues "*Bisexuality is booming, with the number of people who bed men and women more than doubling, a study says. Some 7.7 percent revealed they had bi romps in 2014, compared to 3.1 percent in 1990. In the same period the percentage of men who reported having had sex with at least one man rose from 4.5 percent to 8.2 percent. And the number of women who said they had bedded at least one female leapt from 3.6 percent to 8.7 percent. Lesbian sexual experiences are more likely to occur when women are young, the researchers found. In terms of attitudes towards same-sex relations, between 1973 and 1990, the percentage of adults who believed sexual relations between two adults of the same sex is not wrong at all rose only slightly, from 11 percent to 13 percent.*" Despite the opinion of the people on gay relationship not changing drastically, these same-sex relationships increased drastically in a small period of time. As I have said before the biggest number of LGBT members are bisexuals.

-(source CNN): the title of the report "*Bisexuality on the rise, says new U.S. survey*" the article says "*A growing number of women and men say they are bisexual, according to the latest national survey by the Centers for Disease Control and Prevention. As awareness about bisexuality has grown over the years, it could be getting easier for people to label themselves as bisexual, said Debby Herbenick, associate professor at Indiana University and author of the book "Sex Made Easy," who was not involved in the study. Researchers asked more than 9,000 people in the United States age 18 to 44 about the types of sexual experiences they have had, whether they are attracted to the same or opposite sex and whether they identify as being straight, gay/lesbian or bisexual. Interviews were conducted between 2011 and 2013 as part of the CDC's National Survey of Family Growth. Many of the findings about sexual behavior, attraction and orientation were similar between the current survey and the previous (2006-2010) family growth survey. Similar to previous surveys the group conducted, 1.3% of women and 1.9% of men said they were homosexual. However a few trends stood out. More women reported having had sexual contact with other women: 17.4% in the current survey compared with 14.2% in the 2006-2010 survey. And higher numbers of both women and men identified as bisexual, 5.5% of women and 2% of men, compared with 3.9% and 1.2% respectively in the last survey. The finding that women were more likely than men to say they were bisexual is consistent with what previous studies have found, said Casey E. Copen. Women were also more likely than men to report having same-sex sexual contact. Compared with 17.4% of women, only 6.2% of men said they had ever had this activity. Among women who reported being lesbian, the rate of 1.3% is consistent with other surveys. Over the last several decades, fewer women have been saying they are lesbian and more report being bisexual, similar to what the current study found. For example, among those who labeled themselves heterosexual, 12.6% of women and 2.8% of men had had sexual contact with the same sex.*" These and many more studies coincide with what I have been saying for years, that there is an increase of women/girls who identify as bisexual or have had or want to have a homosexual experience. According to Milo Yiannopoulos (who identifies as a gay man), he doesn't believe there are true lesbians, he says that homosexuality between women is a reactionary response. It is also worth noting that a majority of women who during their life say that they are lesbians or bisexual end up marrying a man and having a child with a man. Is it because of their natural need for procreation, thus proving humans are attracted to the opposite sex not by choice but due to biology? Procreation is a biological imperative. Take this for an example. In the early 2000s, there was a Russian electronic music group "t.A.T.u.", the singers were two women (who identified as gay and were a couple) who were one of the most prominent gay activists. Several years after their "love" as they called it ended, one of them ended up marrying a man and having a baby with that man.

People say homosexuality is normal because it has been around since the dawn of time. This is a retrospective assumption. A few problems exist with that statement. First of all, that is next to impossible to prove, unlike heterosexuality that has to have been present since the beginning of humankind or we would not be here. The other thing, while male homosexuality can be traced to around 2000 BC, female homosexuality has practically not been recorded by history. Those who defend homosexuality say that that is because women were, for the majority of history, in an unfavorable position compared to men. But the problem with this is that they neglect to look at those few cultures where women were considered equal to men and cultures where women were at the seat of power (India, Egypt that had many female pharaohs, England) and yet no accounts of female homosexuality.

Regardless of whether homosexuality is or is not a mental disorder the rise of homosexuality (and the entire LGBT pantheon) is a sign of what I call a social mental disorder.

Ben Shapiro says that precisely because homosexuality is increasing this means it is a social and not a genetic thing.

This is why many moralists and religious people have disagreed with the homosexual lifestyle on the basis that its rise is a result of rampant hedonism.

Why does the increase of homosexuality concern me and why do I care? First of all, I would like to clarify that I am not one of those who believes that all humans will become gay and that the human race will go extinct because of that. Not because that is not what some people want but because the family will be destroyed far before every single human identifies as a homosexual. Even though I don't agree with homosexuality because there is no proof that you are born gay, this chapter is amongst other things devoted not to the individual cases of homosexuality but rather to its rise in recent decades. It is a historical fact that every civilization, society is built and based on a heterosexual and monogamous family (could it be because it is proven to be the best?). Let's put it clear, no civilization in the history of known humankind managed to survive a different family structure and progress. No civilization to date survived the emasculation of men and/or masculinization of women. Just because homosexual behavior existed for whatever time, it is not an excuse to justify its increase in numbers, especially in such large numbers over a relatively small period of time. The truth is, from what we understand in history, there hasn't been one nation in the history of the world that has openly embraced the homosexual lifestyle and begun to practice the homosexual lifestyle that has endured. Every one of them has gone down. Every single one of them. Once rampant homosexuality takes place, then people don't take care of their children, they aren't concerned about the next generation. Every civilization has its foundation in the nuclear/ traditional family. If we look at history when a society starts embracing and promoting sexual deviancy (including homosexuality) past a certain number the collapse of that society is inevitable. In the last few decades (since at least the 1960s and 70s in North America, a bit later in Europe as well) there has been a push for exactly that.

Promiscuity, prostitution, abortion, and feminism: some other components of the destruction of the family I feel have to be addressed.

PROMISCUITY:

When it comes to polygamy (one man procreating with multiple women) you can only possibly defend it if we were living in a world where there is a shortage of humans (where mortality greatly exceeds natality), a world where humans are going extinct. So, the only solution is for men to impregnate as many women as possible, and since sperm is "cheap", men are only limited to the number of women they can impregnate in a set time. This is a fictional scenario where the existence of our species would depend on the birth of as many babies as possible to ensure that the human race has the best chance for survival. We do not live in this scenario, human numbers are going up every year, we live in a world where the number of men is roughly the same as the number of women on this planet (there are more women in the world but nothing to be worried about).

Polyandry (one woman sleeping with multiple men) makes no sense. Having one uterus to fill and one fetus at a time women gained no evolutionary advantage from being promiscuous. Let me put this in simple terms, sperm is cheap and eggs (women's eggs) are expensive. When it comes to procreation women are limited by the gestation period (9 months) while men are limited to the number of women they can sleep with. Imagine the number of women a single man can sleep with during 9 months if his only goal was to impregnate as many women and create as many offspring as possible. Women, on the other hand, are limited by time, no matter how many men they sleep with, they will only give birth to an X number of babies, all belonging to one man during a period of 9 months. The faults of polygamy I have already covered.

So regarding this we come to the conclusion that if you want to drastically increase the number of the population you implement polygamy (planet Earth doesn't have a problem of low population), or if you want to lower the population you implement polyandry since now multiple men are sleeping with only one woman but only one man becomes the father, due to pregnancy lasting 9 months, in that period there is no new procreation until the baby/babies are born.

One of the original talking points (with which I agree) of the first-wave feminist movement was the advocacy for men to stop acting like pigs/sluts. This all changed. The third-wave, the so-called radical feminism (modern-day feminism) and to an extent the second-wave have reversed this. Instead of advocating for men to start acting like men/gentlemen worthy of women, it tells women to praise promiscuity and encourages them to sleep around like sluts. Recent studies show that women in the west are more likely to cheat, commit adultery and sleep around than ever before. Instead of men becoming less like animals women are now as promiscuous as men according to new research.

A quote from Paul Joseph Watson (a journalist) for Infowars *"It's clear that rampant hedonism and promiscuity only make people more unhappy, all the studies show that. But we are being tempted into following lifestyles that leave us depressed, unfulfilled and lonely."*

So why am I against promiscuity? Why have modern women been brainwashed by feminism to become so promiscuous? Studies on men show that men prefer women who don't sleep around (i.e. women who have had less sexual partners). This is, contrary to popular feminist myths, not misogyny. There is an evolutionary and psychological reason etched in men's brains for this behavior. Take this as an example. Why would a man help raise a child with his woman/wife if he has doubts if that child is his at all, due to that woman being promiscuous? The whole point of sex is to procreate and pass on your genetic pool to the next generation. Why would a man marry a woman, go to work, financially support his wife and the child if that child is not his, but is of some other man that isn't investing time, emotion and resources in that child? Since people (men and women) marry and have sex to procreate if a man marries a woman that is promiscuous or has had a promiscuous past there is a chance that the child she gives birth is not going to be his. Why would he help raise a child that isn't his when he can go and find a woman with whom he can have kids of his own. It makes no sense for a man to be with a promiscuous woman since he can never be sure if she is faithful or if he is the father of the child she gives birth. This has become a bigger issue in recent decades since women have become so promiscuous. Listen ladies, I am not telling you how to act, I'm simply telling you what is the most likely response you will get from men due to your promiscuous behavior and that response is that men will not be willing to marry you and will only see you as sexual objects that will fade into obscurity.

Let's look at the vice versa situation. In a scenario where women wait before sex and don't open their legs as soon as they see a male reproductive organ, men are forced to become better men. Let me explain. Throughout history, men had two options of getting sex: marriage or prostitution. One of the reasons men used to marry is because they got guaranteed sex. Back in the days (in western society, North America and Europe) when marriage was not demonized as though it were blasphemy, men could get married only if they were worthy enough. This was possible in a number of ways: status, wealth, if the woman found the man attractive, funny, gentleman-like, from a good family, etcetera. So men needed to "earn" a woman's hand in marriage (in some cases they needed the approval of the woman's father). Out of many possible men (potential mates), women chose the best offer. It was a time where men competed with each other to win over a fair-maiden using whatever advantage they can get (all is fair in love and war). This competitive scene in the sexual market forced men to become better, either to improve or they would be left without a woman who would take them, thus leaving them alone. Ladies, imagine a world where men are trying to be the best possible version of themselves to impress you, I'm sure that in today's society you don't get to see that very often because chivalry is all but dead. Competition enhances performance, but the competitive scene in regards to men is all dried up. The competitive scene is no more. So why don't men do these things anymore, why don't they have an incentive to try and win over a girl and who is to blame for that? Sorry to say ladies but you are the ones to take the brunt of the blame or better yet the ones who are to be blamed are women who were brainwashed by the feminist doctrine and propaganda that told them that promiscuity will empower them.

Let me put this in perspective. If a man, in order to get sex has two options, first is marriage where he has to work, invest time and money and other resources and still has the possibility that the child his girlfriend/wife gives birth isn't his (due to her promiscuity), and the second option, is hiring a prostitute, or in modern terms picking a random drunk girl at a bar and having a one night stand in order to get sex. We have a situation of 'why buy the cow if you can get the milk for free' as the English would say. Why would a man go through all the hassle of marriage (if the marriage is bad for him) if he can get sex from some other woman with practically no effort or emotional attachment, zero strings attached? It makes no sense for him to work his ass off to get a woman to marry him if he can, with ten times the less effort, find a willing female to have sex with him and all this because women nowadays are more promiscuous than ever before. Men no longer have a need or drive to improve or impress women since more and more women literally have no standards with which man they sleep. As one woman, while criticizing female promiscuity, pointed out "I have heels bigger than your standards". Let me put this in the simplest possible terms, modern day women (in alarmingly increasing numbers) offer men nothing more than hookers do. I'm sorry to say it. So men are left with two options, go through marriage (work his ass off, invest time and money) with a woman that is a slut, or pay a slut and not have the added responsibility of marriage. Which one do you think a man would rather choose, both yield the same result (the result being the man ending up with a slut of a woman, unhappy since there are fewer and fewer women that are worth men's time and effort) the only difference is that for the first scenario he has to actually do something (a lot of things) and in the second he can get sex from a woman with next to no effort because women have become so promiscuous they have no standards.

Three things happened due to women in the west getting so promiscuous:
1) Men lose interest in marriage. Why marry to get sex if women are

practically opening their legs as soon as they see a penis?
2) Men stop trusting women. If a man knows that the growing number of women are sleeping around and are acting like sluts why would a man invest time, resources and emotion in that woman and her child if he can't be sure that the child is his? A man is more likely to work his ass off, to invest in his wife and the children if he knows the children are his. Married men with kids significantly outearn unmarried men.
3) Men stop being productive. Why better yourself if there is no need for that? There is no need for men to improve since it is easier to get sex with women without commitment than at any time in human history.

Why am I against the destruction of marriage and the family? First of all, there are those who would like nothing more than to destroy the family. The nuclear/traditional family is the foundation of any human civilization. Those who wish to destroy the family want to rebuild society in their image. In order for them to have the possibility to rebuild society they first need to destroy the bedrock of the "societal house"- the family.

There are those who say that that marriage is an oppressive failed institution and that because of that we should abolish this archaic institution and way of life. They usually point to the claim that that half of marriages end in divorces (previously I have shown that this notion is false). Science, on the other hand, does not agree with this. Study after study confirms the link between promiscuity and depression. When it comes to men and women the more promiscuous they are the more likely they are to be unhappy and emotionally unfulfilled in their lives. When it comes to women the more sexual partners they have had the higher chance is that their marriage (if they get married at all) will end in a divorce. Studies also show that married men earn significantly more than unmarried men. Other research concluded that married men and women are happier than unmarried ones. The demography (excluding transsexuals) which has the highest suicide rate in the west is single unmarried men. Also, both men and women with children are much more likely to be happy and fulfilled than those with no offspring. Studies show that men and women who have had fewer but more meaningful authentic relationships are far more likely to be happy than those who were promiscuous and have had more sexual relationships with no emotional involvement (a.k.a. one-night stands). Could it be, and forgive me for committing this outrageous thought crime, that women and men were biologically and psychologically programmed to procreate and co-exist since it ensures the continuation of our species and gives the children the best possible environment for being raised by their mother and father?

According to research the fewer sexual partners a woman had - it increases the chance of her having a successful marriage later on. If a woman had zero sexual partners before marriage she has around 90 percent chance of having a successful marriage, the more sexual partners she has this number drops. Once it gets to 21+ sexual partners in a lifetime she has under 20 percent of having a successful marriage. In the same study, 43 percent of married people reported being very happy while only 24 percent unmarried did. A different study says that people who have had fewer sexual partners have better sex. The study shows that the more sexual partners both men and women have had before marriage the higher negative impact it has on their sex life in marriage. The study indicates that the fewer sexual partners people have before marriage the better their sexual life in marriage will be. Its conclusion is that you have two options: you either decide to be promiscuous and end up having what they call mediocre sex with a lot of people or extremely great sex with one person and having a meaningful lasting relationship.

If you look up the rise of feminism in western culture what you will find is that the rise of feminism coincides with the explosion of divorce rates and the decline of women's happiness.

Like I said if you want to destroy a civilization you should destroy women. By that logic, if you want to save a civilization you should uplift women. Promiscuity in women brings the worst in men since they now have no drive to be productive or to improve themselves. If women would reverse the negative impact of feminist propaganda on society (i.e. stop being promiscuous) men would be forced to become a better version of themselves or they would be left without a chance of getting a woman. If more women had higher standards and would stop being promiscuous, men would not have any other viable option but to better themselves if they want to win over a woman. The only other kind of option for men who do not want to improve themselves would be to continue watching porn or hiring prostitutes, both of which are not adequate substitutes for the real thing (i.e. sex, marriage, family). Ladies if you want men to be more like gentlemen and worthy of your attention stop being promiscuous. I know, it's not okay for me to say that in order to save our society it's the women who need to become better so that men would be forced to follow and become better themselves but it is how it is. Men will not change if they have no reason/incentive to do so. You are the ones that can, by not being promiscuous and acting more ladylike, force men to become men that you want them to be.

This sexual/hedonistic movement got it all wrong, it claims to liberate and uplift people, yet this is nothing more than an oxymoron or better yet a paradox. The sexual/feminist liberation movement tells women that promiscuity is liberating and empowering. Studies done on both women and men prove that people who have had fewer but meaningful relationships in their lives are more likely to be happy compared to those that had more meaningless short-term sexual partners. The feminist movement says that for a woman marriage is oppressive and that kids are a burden even though countless studies indicate that men and women who are married (to the opposite sex) and have kids are far more likely to be satisfied in their lives compared to those who are single and/or have no offspring.

Note: I do not condone male promiscuity either. I don't approve of double standards. In no shape or form am I saying that it is okay for men to be promiscuous. Both sexes should stop acting like pigs. There are things that both men and women need to change about themselves if we truly want to make our society better.

PROSTITUTION:

From a historical perspective, men had two ways of getting sex, marriage or prostitution. Why am I against liberating and promoting prostitution in society?

Before I can criticize something we need to look at those defending it. The most common arguments in favor of legalizing prostitution revolve around women. The arguments boil down to either it's her body and she should be able to do whatever she wants with it or we should legalize prostitution so that women who are forced in illegal prostitution and sex trafficking would receive protection from the state.

First, we have to make a difference between women who are forced into prostitution because they have no other option and women who choose prostitution even though they don't have to.

The fact that in this day and age people (men, women, and children) are being forced into the sex slave industry is sad. I don't believe that legalizing prostitution will alleviate this individual and social problem for reasons I will come to a bit later. Those who are proponents of legalizing prostitution claim to have the best interest for women in their mind. I don't buy into this claim since it's mostly coming from men (who in my opinion only want to legalize prostitution to ensure they have guaranteed sex without commitment). Take into account that a large majority of women enter the prostitution industry because they had no other way of earning money to ensure their survival. So for many women, the reason for going into prostitution is financial dependency. Women are forced into prostitution due to the fact they have no other option of making a living. History has shown that the only viable way to guarantee that women don't have to enter the prostitution industry is to allow them to get educated and get a job which will make them financially independent thus they have no need for prostitution in order to buy essential and existential needs. If women have the opportunity to go to school and later on get a job, start a career they would not need to continue with prostitution. This is true across the world and history (post-Weimar Republic Germany, the Islamic world in the second part of the 20th century.) If you truly want to protect women from prostitution than give them an option to do something other than prostitution to ensure their existence. The decrease of female prostitutes in the late medieval period and post-medieval period coincides with the rights of education and rights of employment that women were granted.

That is the situation when women have no other option but to enter the prostitution industry if they want to stay alive. What about women who have the option to go to school/get educated and join the workforce/have careers but for some reason choose prostitution. They say women have the right to do whatever they want with their bodies. I would not agree with that if her choice has a negative impact on society. Another argument people use for legalizing prostitution is that women in prostitution have no protection from the state and by legalizing it they would get the needed protection. Let's examine that hypothesis. In the 1970s and 80s, America decided to resolve their prostitution problem by liberating the pornographic industry (note: it was the Rockefeller family that promoted prostitution and the pornographic industry at least since the 1920's). Why I am talking about the porn industry if the topic is prostitution? Simple, the porn industry is a derivative of the prostitution industry. The porn industry is modern day prostitution. It's a visual representation of the act of prostitution and a more "elite" kind of prostitution. The porn industry in America is one of the most powerful, in a financial sense, businesses. The porn industry is one of the fastest growing industries in the U.S.A. even though its power is vast as it is. So if the hypothesis that by legalizing prostitution women would receive help from the state is true then this should be evident in the porn industry as the most financially powerful form of prostitution. But this is not the case. Women/girls who have an option to go to school and get a job but decide to enter the porn/prostitution industry have no idea what awaits them. Despite what it seems to be on the surface the porn industry is not glitz and glamour. The porn industry presents itself as though everything is fine, everyone seems content, money, attention, and fame, but underneath all the superficial stuff lies the gritty truth that the porn industry doesn't want you to know and those who support it are blissfully ignorant and unaware.

The U.S.A. became tolerant towards the porn industry in hopes that prostitution will go down, but in fact, it had the reverse effect. In previous decades women/girls would finish school and get a job thus being financially secured. After porn liberation, the reverse occurred. America now has a problem that an ever-growing number of young women (early 20s in most cases) are choosing to join the porn industry despite having the opportunity to educate themselves and/or get the job. There are many reasons for this: popularization of pornography, feminism telling women that promiscuity will liberate them, and money. Many college-aged girls (some as soon as they turn 18) choose to enter the porn industry for the glamour and money. Like I said the porn industry is extremely financially strong so there is a lot of money around it. More and more girls in America are deciding to quit college (or never start it anyway) and enter the porn industry because the amount of money they would receive is tempting.

So what is wrong with this? Well, a lot of things. First of all these women/girls are not thinking about their future. Why would they, after all, they earn an obscene amount of money just for opening their legs. Well, it's only a matter of time before they are no longer able to make money this way. This is one of the things that the pro-prostitution and pro-porn industry brigade will never tell you. I will use the example from the porn industry but the same is applicable to classic prostitution. Why am I against women joining the porn industry? Because I hate them? Because I hate their "independence" as they call it? No, it's because unlike those who want you to join the porn industry I'm actually going to tell you the ugly truth. Most females that enter the porn industry are around the age of 20. If you ask a current young pornographic actress about the industry odds are she would say the most positive things: money, glamour, fame and all the attention she could possibly need. Not a bad deal it would seem, but don't get fooled by this facade. The popular culture only tells you the story of the current actresses, it does not tell the story of the older women who are no longer in the industry. The truth is that women in the porn/prostitution industry are limited by time. It's only a matter of time before the vast majority of them lose their jobs due to their age. The truth is that beauty, youthfulness, and attraction have an expiration date. The thing you will never hear from the pro-sexual-liberation crowd is what happens to women who reach a certain age. Simply put, once women reach a certain number of years they are, in almost all cases, not needed by the porn industry or the prostitution industry. They are expendable goods. The career of a pornographic actress or a prostitute relies on men finding them attractive. Since beauty has an expiration date once that date comes and men don't find them desirable they are no longer needed by the porn/prostitution industry. This is not because men hate older women. The reason is that men are biologically and psychologically programmed to seek out fertile women to procreate since that gives the best possible chance of the child being born healthy. The older the woman gets the higher chance of a miscarriage or the baby being born with a physical or mental deficiency. Men do this subconsciously, it's in their nature. So what happens to women who reach this point? Once women in the porn/prostitution industry reach a certain age (roughly not long after the age of 30) they are replaced by younger women/girls and the cycle continues. There is a big difference in the way current porn actresses view the porn industry as liberating on one side and older women who are no longer in the porn industry who plea for young women not to enter the porn industry. Many ex-porn actresses are advocating for girls not to get involved with this business.

All is good for them until they reach a point where, due to their age, they are no longer desired by men so they either lose their job because no man wants to hire them for their services in the prostitution industry or they get fired because they are no longer enough youthful-looking for the porn industry, due to there being a constant flow of new young girls joining the industry. What happens to these women? They end up being anything but financially secured. Their entire 20s they learnt only how to open their legs and after their services are no longer required what do they do now, nothing since they are not qualified for anything else. They end up being a burden to the government and society since they can no longer do the only job they ever knew how to do. They are not qualified for anything else but to spread their legs and now that they can't do that, they are left without an income and rely on the taxpayer-funded welfare state for existence. Wasn't the entire argument for legalizing pornography and prostitution for women to be secure and have financial support? How is that looking now when they become useless to society (they were useless before as well). They just become another social issue that needs to be taken care of. They end up not having any financial support whatsoever and are at the mercy of the system, not so glamorous now, is it?

Another argument people use is that if prostitution was legal you can tax them. Just because you can tax something doesn't mean you should, that's not an argument (in parts of rural China the government taxes the second child in the family, if the family wants to keep the child it has to give a portion of its annual food rations to the government, the alternative is they kill every child born after the first one, if twins are born than the mother can choose which one will stay alive, if she doesn't choose the authority decides instead of her). We could give them a pension you might argue. Most of the women in the prostitution/porn industry will end their career around the age of 30 (maybe a bit later if they are lucky). Would that pension be enough to ensure their existence? Another thing, on one hand, you have women who find a job by getting educated, be good at what they do, improving themselves and their skills and they continually do that until they reach the age of around 65 (depends where they live) and on the other hand you have women who from the age of 18 (or whenever they enter the porn industry or prostitution) till about they are at the age of 30 (if they are lucky a bit longer) do nothing more than spread their legs and you want to reward both of them with a pension when their careers have ended. So women would have two options, first spend at least 16 years of their lives getting educated and then spend another 40+ years working 8-hour shifts a day or, the alternative option, they spend around 15 or so years on their back with their legs spread after which they will receive a pension. Why would women ever go to school and find a job when they can just spread their legs and bingo, in a couple of years they will be getting paid by the government simply by doing nothing after their careers have ended. And somehow people think that both of these groups of women deserve the same reward, one that spends a quarter of her life in school and a further 2 quarters of her life in the workforce doing something useful for society, and the other that spends a fifth of her life laying on her back with her legs spread and the rest of her life laying on her back waiting for the government paycheck to arrive, the same paycheck those hard-working women and men are busting their ass off working 8 hours a day. Tell me what woman would choose work over prostitution/porn industry. It's the same principle with men and female promiscuity that I have already covered. Once her porn/prostitution career has ended one way or the other women are left with no way of earning money. Who will take care of them? The government, of course, thanks to the welfare programs, and by the government, I mean tax-paying citizens. Not like those citizens have kids and families to feed. I guess it's far more important for hard-working men and women, who actually do something useful in society, to have to pay for the existence of some ex-prostitute than to ensure the existence and well-being of their children. Parents with actual jobs have to feed their kids, but in this scenario, they would also have to give a part of their salary to the welfare programs so that ex-prostitutes and ex-porn actresses would have something to eat, NO thanks. Just because people were made mistakes and chose to be prostitutes doesn't mean that rest of the hard working society should have their salary lowered in order to help them. People need to start taking responsibility for their action and that includes stupid decisions. This is why I said I don't agree with the argument that a woman should be able to do whatever she wants with her body if that choice has a negative impact on society. You might say that after her porn/prostitution career inevitably ends she will have a husband to financially support her. First of all, what if that husband decides that he wants a divorce or dies, where does that leave her? It again leaves her at the mercy of society, not so financially independent now, is she? And second, believe it or not, there is a method to my madness. There is a reason why I have covered the topic of promiscuity before prostitution. I have stated before that men don't find promiscuous women desirable due to reasons I have previously covered. The more promiscuous a woman is or has been, the less chance there is she will find a husband, and if she indeed finds a husband there is a higher chance that that marriage will end in a divorced because of her promiscuity (or promiscuous past) leaving her again completely financially dependent when she is no longer needed in the porn/prostitution industry.

Another argument used by those who claim to have the best interest for women when they talk about legalizing prostitution is that by legalizing it women would receive social and medical security thus alleviating the potential of them contracting some disease due to their occupation. If people who participate in professions like that can ever be secure from sexually transmitted diseases than that should be visible in the elite echelons of this industry. Let's take a look at the porn industry again. The reason as to why I am using the porn industry as an example is because unlike the local brothel on your average street corner the porn industry is 1000 times wealthier and actually "cares" about its employees (until women reach the age of 30, then they get sacked). Imagine this, the porn industry has an actor or actress who brings them a lot of money, they have to options, first not care for their employees that earn them money and second care for them. The last thing the porn industry wants is to lose one of their best actresses that brings them a lot of money (at least until she gets old and is replaced by a younger one). To the porn industry, women are nothing more than expendable assets. By "care", I mean provide them with medical insurance and medical check-ups at the doctor's office due to their hazardous profession. Another thing the porn industry is reluctant to tell you (but which you can hear from ex-actors and ex-actresses) is that in the porn industry their employees have a regular doctors examination. This examination is very frequent, usually once a week. The examination is, as one might expect, to check for any sexually transmitted diseases they have contracted during work. Despite this weekly examination and millions of dollars invested by the most powerful prostitution-like industry (porn industry), a vast number of porn actors and actresses end up being diagnosed with some life-changing sexually transmitted disease. The numbers as to how many porn actors and actresses end up with some disease due to their work are unclear, one of the reasons being the porn industry with all its wealth and influence doesn't want this to get out in the public view. Most reports and research done on this subject indicate that most of these actors and actresses end up with HIV or some other disease at some point during work. The porn industry is wealthier than some countries and most legal businesses and it still can't save their employees from life-ruining diseases. A message to those who think that by legalizing prostitution we would help women gain adequate medical care. The porn industry has more financial power than most countries (and its wealth is still rising) and it still can't provide the medical security for its employees to protect them from sexually transmitted diseases. On what basis do you think that local brothels or any other prostitution facilities can, by legalization, possibly provide women with good enough health care if the titan of all prostitution (the porn industry) cannot do so? If the porn industry can't do it, no one can.

A message to pro-prostitution legalization members (mostly men who want to legalize prostitution because they are sexually frustrated and can't find a woman by conventional means) stop being hypocrites. If you were to ask these people would they approve of their own daughter joining the porn/prostitution industry or dropping out of school/college to join such industry odds are they would not approve of such a thing. If you would not endorse such choice and behavior from your daughter then you have no right to claim that you have the moral high ground for wanting to legalize such things.

A message to current and future parents. I have no right to tell you how to raise your children but if you truly want your children (especially daughters) to be financially independent and secure then the only way to ensure the best possible chance for that is to educate them and let them find a job. Any girl can open her legs, not all can do something useful with their lives. Unfortunately, our morally decrepit society, instead of praising women who are inventors, scientists, pilots, mothers (anything useful for the progression of society), it glorifies pornstars actresses and women who take off their clothes just to sell. These promiscuous women, the ones who have the option to be useful to society, to go to school, get a job and raise a family, but choose to enter the porn/prostitution industry are limited by time. They are limited by their youth and beauty. But what they don't tell you is that youth and beauty fade while intelligence and knowledge don't.

ABORTION:

Abortion is the "poster child" for the feminist movement. The feminist movement has always been about complete and unscrupulous liberalization of abortion. Before I criticize their point of view it's only fair I give you mine. There is no sugar coating it, abortion is a sad and sensitive topic. It is my honest opinion that there are certain extreme circumstances where a woman should have a right to choose an abortion (example: where there is a chance that a child will be born with a physical or psychological deficiency thus preventing it from having a normal life, if a pregnancy is a result of rape, or the birth of a child puts the mother at risk of losing her own life). As you can see I'm not for what has been proposed in Poland - that abortion should be illegal in absolutely all cases, but on the other hand, I'm definitely not for what is being pushed in the west (America, Canada, Western Europe). For decades they have pushed an agenda to allow women to have an abortion whenever they want regardless of the duration of pregnancy or whether she is in a relationship or married.

Is abortion murder? If murder is robbing someone of their right to live, what constitutes life?

When it comes to abortion people say that they are two prevailing theories that define life:
-religion: that says that life begins at conception
-science and law: that say that life begins with birth (exiting the womb)

This is not entirely true. Science is in neither one of these categories. Science is somewhere in the middle. Dare I say it, the current opinion of science is closer to the religious view of the beginning life than the one that law has.

Here lies the problem, how does one define live? When does one become a human being? If we knew the answer to this crucial question we would know if abortion is a murder or not.

It all depends on the variable you use to describe life and humanity:

1) Dependency: those that argue that abortion is morally sound say that there is nothing wrong with abortion since the unborn child is not human due to the fact it depends on the mother to survive and develop. So here the main thing is dependency. Even though it is true that an unborn child cannot survive outside the woman's womb, by this logic we should be able to take the lives of those whose lives are dependent in other ways (life support in a hospital). If a woman has a right to abort her unborn child on the premises of dependency then family members should be able to "cut the life supply" of their relatives who are in a coma or whose lives are completely dependent on a machine. People who are in a coma (or in a similar state) are dependent on a machine that keeps them alive, does this mean that their family members get to decide when their "air supply" is taken away from them just like the mother decides when she can carry out an abortion? If women can decide to have an abortion because she sees her unborn child as a burden then what stops people from deciding when their relatives will no longer get the care they need to keep them alive? (example: there are people who due to unforeseen circumstances need to constantly be hooked to a machine that monitors their health and situation, without that machine their life ends, they are equally dependant on that machine as an unborn child is on its mother).

2) Development: to counter the last point you might say that an unborn child is not yet human because it's not developed. Then development constitutes life, but what kind of development:

- consciousness: science says consciousness begins as early as 24 weeks of gestation but doesn't actualize until months after birth
- pain: If you define life when you can feel pain than life begins around 8 weeks after pregnancy
- heart: the heart begins pumping blood around at week 14 after conception
- brain activity: around 6 weeks of pregnancy
- heartbeat: 5 weeks
- at week 4 there are brain waves detectable
- at week 3 after conception the spinal column and nervous system are forming

The point I am trying to make is that there is no one stage of human/fetal development that can be taken as life-affirming, there are too many variables involved (these are only a few).

3) Non-human: those who encourage the liberalization of abortions say that the unborn child is not human therefore abortion is not murder since you can't kill someone that is not yet alive. There is a flaw in this logic since it puts more value on life the further it is in the stages of development hence why for people it's easier to empathize with a grown person rather with an unborn child. Problem with this is development itself, since it is completely dependable on what variable you use. In order to define life you must define development and since development itself it's dependant you end up defining life on an arbitrary scale. Another problem here is that this theory says that you are human if you are developed. If, as they say, a 9-year-old is more developed than a fetus shortly after conception than by this logic a 70-year-old man (with Alzheimer's) is more developed than a 10-year-old boy. Development doesn't end after birth, again depending on what development point we are talking, people develop different things at different times in their life. People continue developing long after they are born. Does this mean that a born child is not human because it is not and will not be fully developed for a while? What about people with a disease that have lost their sanity, are they less valuable than a sane person just because they are no longer fully developed (by this logic we should implement eugenics).

The last thing I want to touch upon in connection with development is the development of unborn babies within the womb. The abortion rights pushed forward by feminists and LGBT groups, would allow women to carry out an abortion up until the moment of birth. Lest take into consideration the following example. In certain cases, babies are born prematurely. In these scenarios women give birth to a child a few weeks, sometimes a month or even two months before schedule. Even though these babies were born before the end of the 9-month gestation period, they end up growing into completely healthy, normal, developed people who live normal lives and contribute to society. Now, in case of abortion, this baby, while still in the womb, weeks before the end of the gestation period, would not be considered a living being. In the first case, where a woman gives birth to a healthy child after 8 months of pregnancy, the child is considered a living human being. In the second case, where we allow women to abort their babies up until the moment of birth, women can commit an abortion of that same exact 8-month old baby without any remorse or repercussions. The only difference between these two scenarios is the will of the mother.

The whole argument of abortion depends on do you think is the unborn child alive or not. If it's alive than it's a murder and if it's not alive abortion is not a murder, therefore not immoral.

All these theories about when life begins are dependent on numerous variables and interpretation. The zygote contains all the necessary material for a human being. The final theory, life begins at conception - this is the only definition of when life begins that is independent. All those other theories that rely on the development stages are arbitrary since there is not one single date during the pregnancy stages when all these and other signs of development occur at once since they all occur in different stages.

There are three countries in the world that allow abortion up until the moment of birth (China, North Korea, and Canada). In these countries, life is constituted when you leave the birth canal. By this logic, if a woman has carried her child in the womb for nine months and then suddenly commits an abortion she has done nothing wrong. Canada in 1991 - two midwives caused the death of an unborn child due to negligence and because the child died while still in the birth canal nobody was charged because the child wasn't considered a human being. Also in Canada - in 1996 a woman shot her child in the head as it was exiting her birth canal and was not charged with anything because it was not fully outside her body thus not considered a human being by law.

All this stems from the popular feminist theory "my body my choice". Another tactic used by feminists is the belittling of the unborn child. A happy expected mother uses words like baby, joy, and miracle, but if the pregnancy is unwanted they use terms like a cluster of cells, blob, ball of tissue, parasite, and other words to diminish the meaning of pregnancy and life. Abortion is presented as a women's right but truthfully it's a purely ethical question. In regards to the law, it's not the law that influences human behavior, it's the human societal consensus which allowed the law to exist in the first place. In other words, the law doesn't dictate human behavior since humans created law, without humans there would be no law but without law, humans would still exist. There are more abortions because we think it's not a big deal, abortion is about not valuing human life. The thing about abortion that I personally find sickening is the lack of mourning. Regardless of your opinion on abortion, I cannot be the only one who thinks how abhorrent it is that women who carry out an abortion (regardless of reason) don't have a mourning period. They act as though nothing had happened, as though abortion is just another thing to do. They are emotionally excluded from any responsibilities. The worst thing is some of them, instead of being sad and going through grief like a normal human being, are celebrating abortions as though it is something to be proud of. Even though I think there are extreme instances where abortion is something a woman should have a right to (in extreme circumstances), I don't think that abortion should be the first thing a woman does but rather the last resort if other less invasive options fail. What world do we live in where women are actively celebrating and praising abortions?

Lena Dunham, a prominent feminist said *"I can say I still haven't had an abortion, but I wish I had"*

Leaving the pro-life vs pro-choice debate on the side I would like to address the reason why abortion has been popularized in recent decades and why it's being pushed as a woman's right to cover its true nature and agenda. Regardless of your stance on abortion, there are things about its promotion and popularization that people should know.

The key thing I would like to address is Planned Parenthood, one of the most sinister, taxpayer-funded organizations in the world.

They are responsible for the genocide of unborn children and organ harvesting. Planned Parenthood and abortion itself is highly supported by leftists. Planned Parenthood crimes include open genocide. How do they do this? By various methods, their favorite being abortion. During the first 3 months of pregnancy doctors plunge a tube with an edged tip into a womb, then they use the suction power of the tube to tear up the child while it's still alive and then suck the pieces outside of the mother's womb. This is called suction aspiration. An even more disturbing way of abortion is called dilation and curettage, in this version of an abortion, doctors use a curette with which they chop up the baby inside a womb and them scrape what is left right out. As the abortion takes place later down the development stages the methods of abortion become more gruesome. There is the dilation and evacuation method in which doctors use a forceps to crush the baby including the brain and spine, the pieces are then removed. As the last result doctors use partial-birth abortion, in this method doctors use an ultrasound to find the babies legs, pull the baby in the birth canal, they deliver the entire baby except the head and then they stab the baby with a pair of scissors, insert the suction tube in the skull and suck the brain out. The eeriest part about this is that the last way of abortion is the most preferred one since it ensures that the internal organs are best preserved, which are intended for harvesting later on.

Around 1 million babies are being aborted each year in America alone (that is worse than Communist China), out of those 1 million around 700.000 are African American babies, if you divide that by the number of days in a year you get a number that is close to 3000 babies being aborted every day only in the U.S.A. Abortion is one of the most lucrative businesses in the world.

Planned Parenthood supporters claim abortion accounts for only around 3 percent of what the organization actually does. Planned Parenthood, the leading organization in the abortion business admits to committing approximately 300.000 abortions per year, though this number has been rising each year in the past few decades. 300.000 abortions per year equals to 822 abortions per day just by Planned Parenthood alone, that numbers equals to 34 abortions per hour. Every hour, on average, 34 abortions are being performed in the U.S., and that is just based on the numbers they are willing to admit in the U.S.A., not including Europe where Planned Parenthood has bodies of operation. Planned Parenthood doesn't only deal with abortions, the other stuff they deal with is contraceptives, promotion of correct use of condoms, sexual health, and sexual education. All of these are secondary to their main goal which is the killing of the innocent. The number of the supposed 3 percent is insane. They get around 2.5 million patients annually for all of their services (just the ones they admit). Divide those 2.5 million patients, on their own accounts, with the annual 300.000 abortions that they claim and you get that more than 8 percent of their patients get an abortion. As you can see that number is more than double the 3 percent they claim. According to analysis Planned Parenthood commits around 33 percent of the total abortions in the U.S.A.

In an earlier chapter, I mentioned Planned Parenthood and Margaret Sanger. It is not a secret that Margaret Sanger was a eugenicist. Nowadays she is rightfully blamed for the "black genocide" since the majority of aborted victims are African American unborn children. Most U.S. Planned Parenthood clinics today are located in black neighborhoods. Margaret Sanger was one of the leading eugenicists pre World War One. It has been well documented in recent years with video evidence to back up this claim that Planned Parenthood is harvesting and selling organs and other body parts of aborted babies. This was admitted by high ranking members within the Planned Parenthood's hierarchy.

Margaret Sanger not surprisingly, being one of the original feminists, didn't oppose homosexuality. In 1947, Sanger, then the president of America's Planned Parenthood Federation, said in an interview that European women should stop having babies for the next 10 years. She said: *"From my view, I believe that there should be no more babies"*. She defended her remarks by saying that that is more practical, intelligent, humane and not antisocial.

Gloria Steinem, another pro-gay feminist, is one of if not the most notable proponents of liberating abortion. She gained prominence during the second wave feminism and is best known for having a clothing line that proudly says *"I had an abortion"*. No surprise the T-shirts with this inscription is sponsored by Planned Parenthood. In recent years the long-lasting speculation that she has been financed by the C.I.A. has been proven.

FEMINISM:

I don't think anyone described feminism better than Mark Passio when he said *"Neo-feminism is an act of war. Neo-feminism, modern day feminism which has nothing to do with classical feminism, is a program of social engineering, mind control which is specifically targeted at women in order to incite a war between the sexes in a divide and conquer strategy. The long-term goal of this manipulated gender war is to weaken both genders to such an extent that it becomes much easier for the entrenched ruling class to subjugate both women and men under their world-wide system of totalitarian control. There is no bigger divide than men vs. women. The social engineers have specifically focused their efforts on cultivating this gender war because, through it, they can create maximum social tension, instability, and chaos because the fabric of a society is the familial bond between man and woman, make no mistake about that."*

The gay movement and the feminist movement are intrinsically linked since they have the same goal. The amalgamation of these two movements aims to destroy the family. Feminism, similar to the gay movement differs in its presentation on one hand and its true purpose on the other. Supposedly feminism is a movement for equal rights between women and men, so why does it still exist in countries where men and women do have equal rights then? In truth, feminism has become a movement of misandry that aims to break up the family and separate men and women. Modern day feminism, as a movement for equality between the sexes, has been debunked more times than I can list in a lifetime. But since I am a misogynistic, chauvinistic male pig that wants women to stay in the kitchen don't take my word for it, listen to women (Lauren Southern, Tomi Lahren, Christina Hoff Sommers, Karen Straughan, Julia Tourianski, Brittany Pettibone etc.) that are against feminism and have debunked popular feminist myths like: rape culture in the west, gender pay-gap, patriarchy is inherently evil, women are oppressed in the west, sex being a social construct that is redefined as gender, all men are evil, feminism is for equality between men and women. If you doubt my claim check it for yourself, I dare you to listen to modern day feminists and tell me if they truly want equality or supremacy.

In truth, this is what feminism teaches women/girls :

-all men are sexual predators and are by nature evil

-don't have kids and if you do kill them (abortion)

-it tells women to become lesbians (is there any surprise that, statistically speaking, there are more women who identify as homosexual in the feminist movement than in the general population, since feminism promotes hatred towards all men)

-tells women that promiscuity will liberate them

Let's take a look at the real world.

The National Survey of Family Growth (in the U.S.) compiled a report. The survey was done on women in regards to first sexual experience, non-marital sexual partners, overall happiness, and the results are in. For all of these individual results the age bracket for women varied from the age of 12 till the age of 26+ (I will only show the 2 sides of the spectrum since they all have a downward or upward spiral) :

-Number of lifetime sexual partners: if a girl had her first sexual experience at the age of 12 or younger she will have over 20 lifetime sexual partners, if a girl had her first sexual experience after the age of 20 she will have around 3 lifetime sexual partners, this shows that the earlier a woman has her first sexual experience the number of her lifetime sexual partners is going to be higher.

-sexually transmitted diseases: if a girl had her first sexual experience at the age of 12 or younger she has a 20 percent chance of having an STD, if a girl had her first sexual experience after the age of 20 that percentage drops to about 5 percent

-women in stable, successful marriages in correlation with the number of sexual partners. The study has shown that the more sexual partners a woman has in a lifetime the less chance she will define her marriage as stable or successful. The less sexual partners she had in a lifetime the higher chance that she would define her marriage as successful and stable

-out-of-wedlock pregnancy: if a girl had her first sexual experience at the age between 15 and 18 she has a 50 percent chance of out-of-wedlock pregnancy, if a girl had her first sexual experience after the age of 20 this percentage is less than half of that

-the more non-marital sexual partners a woman had during her life the higher chance of out-of-wedlock pregnancy. If she has 16-20 sexual partners in a lifetime she has around 50 percent chance of out-of-wedlock pregnancy.

-if a girl had her first sexual experience at the age of 12 or younger she has over 40 percent chance of a out-of-wedlock pregnancy, that percentage drops to less than 10 percent if the girl had her first sexual experience after the age of 20

-out-of-wedlock birth, in 1950 only 4 percent of children were born out-of-wedlock, in 2012 a bit over 40 percent, 1/3 out of every 100 children conceived each year are aborted

-if a woman had 21+ sexual partners in her lifetime the chances of abortion is 50 percent, that number diminishes as the number of sexual partners lowers

-if a girl had her first sexual experience at the age of 12 or younger the chances of her having an abortion are around 33 percent if a girl had her first sexual experience after the age of 20 the percentage drops to about 10

-chance of single motherhood (despite the constant rhetoric of feminists, single motherhood is not better than a child being raised by a biological mother and a father): if a girl had her first sexual experience at the age of 12 or younger she has around 65 percent chance of being a single mother, if a girl had her first sexual experience after the age of 20 that number drops to around 15 percent. The perils of single motherhood and the unwillingness of men to be with promiscuous women I covered earlier

-single motherhood percentage: the more sexual partners a woman has in her lifetime, the higher chance she has of being a single mother. Single mother households have been rising since the 1970s.

-family structure and child abuse: the least chance of a child being abused is if it is living with its biological parents who are married, that significantly rises if parents are unmarried and in single-parent households, the highest chance of a child being abused is if it is living with a single parent and the single parents partner who is not the child's biological parent

-problems behaviors of children (in which they included: lied about something important, stole from a store, damaged school property, gotten drunk, hurt someone enough to need a doctor, had to bring parents to school, skipped school without permission) are more likely to occur with children of divorced parents compared to those who are living with parents who are married

-mothers living in poverty: if a girl had her first sexual experience at the age of 12 or younger she has a 33 percent chance of living in poverty, if a girl had her first sexual experience after the age of 20 the chance of poverty drops to around 11 percent

-happiness percentage: if a girl had her first sexual experience at the age of 12 or younger she has only a 20 percent chance of being happy in life (by their own statements), that number goes to 50 percent if she has her first sexual experience after the age of 20

The results of this study have been confirmed in newer studies in recent years.

All of this feminist, promiscuity, sexual liberation propaganda is being pushed, even though all the studies show that if a woman wants happiness in her life the best path is marrying a man in a stable, secure, loving marriage and having kids. Note: I am not saying women ought to be prude while men can act like pigs, studies on men indicate the same thing, promiscuity equals depression and loneliness. The best chance of a man being happy is by marrying a woman (a non-feminist woman that is) and having offspring. Married men are more likely to be happy, they live longer (contradicting popular belief), they earn more. Single unmarried men are the most likely demographic in western society to commit suicide (not including transsexuals).

Believe it or not I don't hate women, on the contrary, the reason as to why I am criticizing women is because I don't want them to end up like women in the west who were brainwashed into embracing feminism. I've seen what happens to western women who go down the road of feminist ideology and it isn't pretty. If you don't believe me just ask western men. In the west, men are giving up on marriage altogether and avoiding women completely – this is called "the sexodus". In the last 15-20 years, American men have, in increasing numbers, moved to Europe (especially Eastern Europe) in search for feminine women who value family, traditional life, and marriage. Now men are moving towards Asia since women in Europe are making the same mistake (embracing feminism) as those in the U.S. And what I would call "normal women", the ones that have evaded the feminist dogma, who are looking for high-value men and are looking to settle down and start a family, are left wondering where have all the good men gone. Short answer you and your promiscuous lifestyle drove them in search of greener pastures. Be strong, independent women, no one is saying that you shouldn't, just don't go down the extremist road of "I don't need a man". It's that precise ideology that will leave you lonely with two dozen cats in your empty apartment trying to compensate for not having a family/kids.

There is a direct correlation between the rise of feminism on one hand and the rise of divorce rates and women's unhappiness on the other hand. Thanks to feminism, believe it or not, women are now unhappier than ever before. The testament to that is evident once one takes into consideration that the pharmaceutical-drug industry is being kept afloat by unhappy and unfulfilled career women who dope themselves with anti-depressant drugs in a desperate and in vain attempt to numb the pain which resulted from their life choices, mainly caused by pro-feminist mantra (abortion, promiscuous lifestyle, anti-male, anti-kids, and anti-family rhetoric). Nowadays, women care more about their careers than starting a family and having kids. They spend their productive years trying to reach "the corporate dream" instead of finding a man with whom they would be happy. The inevitable happens, once they reach a certain age (usually mid-30s or after) when they realize their reproductive clock is winding down, it's too late since they are no longer desired by men due to their age. There is a phenomenon in the U.S, Canada, U.K, where women spend their best (fertile) years climbing the corporate ladder and once they reach the stage in their lives where men won't impregnate them (because men are programmed to seek fertile women) they turn to their own sex. Women are now compensating for not having children by having pet animals. Again, believe it or not, I am not against women getting educated, getting a job, having a career, progressing in a certain field, but what I am against is women and men putting their jobs and careers in front of their families and children, since this will ultimately leave them unhappy and unfulfilled, not to mention the harmful effect the lack of parental involvement has on kids, which can manifest years or even decades later. Women have fallen for the same trap men did 5 thousand years ago, men and women are now slaves to the government. Men and women were made to procreate (have children), they were not made to have a job and serve the state.

The main reason why I am criticizing the feminist movement is because it is so prevalent with women yet its ideology has proven to leave women unhappy. It is only right that if I criticize feminism that I have the same attitude towards the male version of feminism – MGTOW (an acronym for Men Going Their Own Way). Members of this group include frustrated men who spew hatred towards all women as though all women are sluts and gold-diggers. This movement started rather innocently (just like the first wave feminism), it focused on real-life issues that plague men in western civilization (marriage courts favouring women when it comes to divorce and getting custody of children, men accounting for over 90 percent of all workplace injuries and deaths, men account for over 90 percent of all deaths in war, men have a measly 15 percent chance of winning custody of their children in case of the divorce, men are 3 times more likely to be homeless than women, men are 5 times more likely than women to commit suicide), but just like feminism it morphed into straight out hatred towards the opposite sex, further spreading the abyss between men and women. While feminism tells women that they don't need men, marriage, children, MGTOW tells men that marriage is a prison sentence. It also advocates for the abolition of marriage as an institution, it tells men that they don't need women and that they should continue watching porn for the rest of their lives because all women are the same. Two movements same result. Both of them aim to divide men and women and destroy the family.

The sexual market value of women. Not many women want to hear this but I believe it's something that needs to be said. To quote Lauren Southern *"men are born poor and grow rich while women are born rich and die poor"*. What does this mean? Before answering, we first must take a look at what women find attractive and desirable in men and vice versa. Women seek masculinity, strength, power, status, resources, financial security (this does not change even if the woman is completely financially independent), while men seek chastity, youth, fertility, childbearing years (women between the age of 20-30). Women in their 20s have the traits that men are biologically programmed to seek out, long hair, hip-to-waist ratio, youth, all these are indicators of health and fertility. Why do men seek out these kinds of women? Because a woman in her 20s (her best childbearing years) gives the best chance of a baby being born without physical or mental deficiency. Why would a man choose to have kids with a woman if her age increases the chance of the child not being born healthy? Men are programmed to seek women who are fertile – for reproductive purposes. This means a woman's sexual market value starts diminishing not to long after the age of 30 (I covered this when I talked about prostitution), on the other hand man's market value increases after the age of 30 because most of the things women find desirable in men (status, stability, ability to financially invest in the woman and their child) they tend to achieve after the age of 30. Women, instead of using their prime fertile years to get a high value man, a man who is willing to marry then and with whom they will be happy and start a family, they spend their 20s (and ever increasingly their 30s) sleeping around with as many sexual partners as they possibly can while being drunk, drugged and so on. Once the shit hits the fan and they realize their chance of finding a man are decreasing by the passing day (due to their lifestyle, age, and the fact that men don't find promiscuous women desirable) it's too late, men have moved on to younger women who actually want to settle down and have kids. Like it or hate it it's a fact, after the age of 30 (thirty-ish) the chance of a woman finding a man declines and for men after the age of 30 their sexual market value goes up. This is my advice for women, get educated, find a job, be independent, but don't neglect family and kids. We live in a society that openly praises women who are climbing the corporate ladder while demonizing women who want to become mothers (nowadays the first thing a woman gets asked after giving birth is "when are you coming back to work"). Parenthood – is the toughest and most important job a man and/or women can possibly do.

Geriatric mothers: in western society (America and Europe) there is a problem with regards to women waiting to have kids. No matter how much feminist dogma and gender studies rhetoric you have been brainwashed with, medicine and science can't negate the negative impact a woman's age has on childbirth. The Royal College of Obstetricians strongly advises women to have children between the age of 20 and 35 to minimise any chance of damaging the child during childbirth (I would like to argue that this should be moved up to 25, reasons are plenty, by this time the mother will most likely be finished with school and might even have a job, another argument I will use is one that scientists recently started using and that's that women should wait after the age of 24-25 to have children since before this age the woman's brain is not fully developed thus according to research the babies brain will be underdeveloped as well). In Europe, depending on which country, 20-25 percent of pregnancies are with women over 35. Age in women affects fertility, it is estimated that around 20 percent of women at the age of 35-39 are infertile. Older mothers are at risk of developing medical conditions such as gestational diabetes, high blood pressure, and other chronic diseases, they are also at risk of pregnancy complications like premature birth and low lying placenta. If a woman has children at a later age she is not the only one that will experience negative effects. Figures in England and Wales show that chances of having a baby with a genetic abnormality are 1 in 500 from the ages of 35 to 39 (age of the mother when she gave birth), 1 in 250 from the ages 40 and 44, and 1 in 70 after 45. Mothers over 40 are particularly vulnerable to stillbirths, interventions during labor, cesareans. Even though medical professionals strongly advise against it, women are now more likely to delay pregnancy until they are in their late 30s or even early 40s. At 20 years old a woman has a 1 in 1500 chance of a baby having a Down syndrome, at 25 it's 1 in 1300, by 30 years it's 1 in 900, by 35 years old it's 1 in almost 400 at the age of 40 it's 1 in 112 and at the age of 45 the chance of a baby being born with Down syndrome is 1 in 28. Most experts in these fields say that after the age of 32 (age of the mother at childbirth) there is an increase of a chance that the baby is not going to be born healthy (physically and/or mentally). Another problem is the lack of responsibility of women. Since women are now waiting later in life to have children and since abortion has become something to be proud of, many of these geriatric mothers choose to have an abortion when they find out that their child is suffering some kind of disease or has hormonal deficiency (because of the mothers age) while still in the womb. The one thing they are blatantly ignoring is lack of their responsibility since it's their bad decision to have children at an older age that resulted in those kids having deficiencies in the first place. So the state comes into play to relieve women of their responsibility for their decisions and actions. Its women's selfish actions (waiting until they get old, old for childbearing years) that end up costing children they give birth normal lives and the state is here to alleviate women of any responsibility and guilt, thorough the liberalization of abortion. Lets now draw parallels between this and feminism. During the campaign to legalize gay marriage and allow abortion up until the moment of birth in Ireland, one could have heard the pro-abortion feminist chanting '*Hoes need abortion*' over and over again on repeat. And what did the state of Ireland do? It came to the rescue. It came to help promiscuous women, 'hoes' as they call themselves, to nullify the natural result of sexual intercourse. So now women, with to morals, can practice a promiscuous lifestyle to the fullest, and if heavens forbid, they end up pregnant, the state shows up as a friend and grants them the right to kill their own babies. This lack of female responsibility and maturity for their actions is a sign that we, as a society, are heading towards a downward spiral, with, quite frankly, practically no signs of improvement. Let me show you another thing, let's take Africa and Europe for example. On one hand, we have Africa, a cesspool of diseases and decay, not a forgiving environment for raising kids but yet Africa, the continent with the highest mortality on planet Earth is booming with population rise. On the other hand Europe, the supposed staple of cutting-edge science and medicine, but yet it has the highest rate of children born with a physical or mental deficiency of any continent. To put it bluntly, Europe has a problem with an ever-increasing number of children being born retarded. I'm not saying that the only reason for this is the choice of women to have children at an older age but it certainly helps in that regard. I am sure that women, in the name of self-defense, will say that they have the right to first focus on their career (no one is saying that you don't have a right to have a career) and then decide when to have a family. But what about the rights of a child, the right to be born physically and mentally healthy? The older a woman gets in regards to childbearing (most experts say after the age of 32) the chances of that child acquiring those rights diminishes. Focus on other things all you want, no one is stopping you, just don't complain to the world when you give birth to a mentally challenged child. It's women's selfish decisions that end up costing children normal lives.

Aaron Russo: I highly suggest listening to the interview the late Aaron Russo gave, amongst other things he mentioned feminism. He got this information from Nick Rockefeller, no surprise since it was the Rockefeller dynasty that funded the feminist-abortion movement, amongst other things.

According to him, there are two reasons feminism is being pushed, contrary to popular belief it has nothing to do with equal rights between men and women, although it is presented as such. The first reason is tax-income. Let's factor in that the ratio of men and women is roughly 50:50 percent on this planet, in 1950's men were the ones who went to work while women stayed at home. Since the state can't tax the stay at home mother, they promoted and pushed women in the workforce so that they can tax them just like men. The state doesn't care about women's independence, the state only believes in the creed of greed. The second reason is much more important but is dependent on the first one. Once they got both men and women in the workforce (a.k.a. slaves of the government, the so-called "corporate slaves", Charles Bukowski said "*slavery was never abolished, it was only extended to include all the colors*"), someone needed to take care of the children – introduce daycare facilities, also known as state organized brainwashing. The reason as to why the Rockefeller family promoted feminism is not female independency but rather child dependency. Since now both men and women (both equal idiots) are more concern with work and their careers the kids are left at the mercy of the state – all planned. Now, neither the mother nor the father can tend to their kids, thus the kids are raised by the state (TV, internet, smartphones, the "educational system"). The state wants to control the future, and they will control the future by controlling the present youth (kids/children). Since parents are too busy at work, thus depriving children of the necessary love and affection they need, the government comes as a "savior" to indoctrinate the children, to zombify them, to make them into clones to serve their future agenda. While both men and women are now nothing more than ant-workers, the state has become the new parent and let me be clear IT WILL NOT DO A BETTER JOB AT RAISING CHILDREN THAN A BIOLOGICAL MOTHER AND FATHER. You want to know why, because it's not meant to do so, it's meant to program children (through formal education a.k.a educational indoctrination) into following the paths of their true parents – a path of mindless automatons, like lambs to the slaughter. If you have any doubts as to whether it is deliberate, let's take a look. Let's take into perspective two families, one in the 1950's America and the other in modern day America and Europe. In 1950's the father went to work while the mother stayed home with the kids (motherhood - the most important job a woman can do in her life, same as fatherhood), married couples had more children, and the salary of one working parent was enough to support the whole family. Nowadays both parents are working (sometimes more than one job), they have fewer children (one or two if they are lucky) and yet they are not economically strong as their 1950's counterpart. So let me get this straight, a family with multiple kids and one parent working lived better than the family with fewer children and both parents working. In terms of financial gain, financial security and economic prosperity we get this equation "one working parent with more kids is better than both working parents with fewer or no kids at all." It doesn't take a genius to figure out that it should be the exact opposite.

Mark Passio said: *"The neo-feminist agenda continually reinforces the notion that women are the same as men, not just having equal rights as men, but the same in characteristics and abilities as well. This was one of the main techniques to influence women to join the corporate workforce, which removed them from their traditional role as nurtures of the young. Children were then largely turned over to the State-run indoctrination system of public schooling in order to shape their beliefs and destroy their health and morals. The State ends up being the nanny, or the mother figure or the father figure because of this. It's a side effect of the whole agenda to bring women into the corporate workplace. I am not saying that women should not have careers, I am just saying that there was an alternative agenda, an alternative motive at work when this was done."*

For the record I would like to state that, even though I don't think the traditional system (working husband and a stay at home mom) was all bad as feminists claim, I do believe it needed change (mostly because too much dependant on the husband, if the man was normal then it was okay, but if the man started abusing his position problems would arise) but it changed into another system that is riddled with problems and dare I say it is worse than the traditional one. Now kids are, at an increasing rate, left without both a father and a mother and I am sorry but that is something I can't agree with. It is the role of fathers and mothers (from both a law and a moral perspective) to be parents first and foremost. I don't agree with people who try and justify that their career is more important than their own children who need parental investment for their full development. You don't really know what you got until it's gone, don't wait until the state supersedes you as parents because it will if you let it. I would like to propose the system that is somewhere in between these two, a system where women have the right to get educated, find a job and have professional careers, and choose a man that suits their needs, but also where both parents (fathers and mother) are firstly parents and spouses, and secondly bakers, engineers, astronauts or whatever career. This would be possible if the state would go out of its way and allow mothers and fathers to be parents. Of course, the all-knowing state in its present form would never allow this since it conflicts with their plan to raise the kids in the way it sees fit. To quote Paul Joseph Watson of Infowars "*the last thing the government wants is for happy, independent, secure families to raise their own children*."

Feminists say that they are now finally independent from men (those evil oppressive men). Though I have nothing against people, including women, being independent (including financially) today's women aren't independent. In the 1950s and 60s women used to be "dependent" on men who were their husbands and with whom they had children, now women are dependent on the government, the same government that seeks to destroy the relationships between women and men so it could take control of parental rights over children. Why do feminists want big government? Governments in the west have become masked Socialists states. Historically speaking, women are the majority of the population that votes for Socialism (they brought Hitler democratically into power as well, let's not forget – National Socialism is Socialism with a national element, another version of Socialism). The government alleviates any responsibility for women. For example: in the west, due to female promiscuity it is inevitable some will end up pregnant. If she decides to have an abortion (the man/husband doesn't have a say in the matter) who will pay it? She can, through the government, force the man to pay for her abortion which leaves us in this paradigm "her body, her choice, his wallet." This is done through the welfare state, which Socialism is famous for (maybe famous isn't the right word). Women's bad decisions in life (like promiscuity) are negated by the willingness of the government to help them evade repercussions of those decisions. Today's western women, instead of being married to a man, they are married to the state. The state has become their new god. The state has become some sort of surrogate-husband. Despite what you may think this all-knowing benevolent being called the state could not care less about women, the only reason it is doing this is to achieve its own goal of destroying the family thus becoming the de facto parent of the children.

Mark Passio said: *"The conditioned woman is being engineered to love the State for the small perks they are given by it. This is what I call the unholy matrimony between women and the government. On a subconscious level, they have bought into the State as the protective father figure and this itself is an expression of parental abandonment issues, or perhaps not having a strong father figure during their formative years. Emotional, spiritual and sexual connections between men and women are being eroded and eventually eradicated by the State. The State continually positions itself to be psychologically accepted as the 'provider', 'protector' and 'husband'. The vast majority of women in our society will not, unfortunately, speak out against the State for these reasons."*

As I have said, women aren't the only ones that are under the attack from the feminist movement. Mark Passio said: *"The war on authentic men takes the form of the emasculation of the human male, a process which breeds out the sacred masculine dynamic, the willingness to stand up to tyrants and bullies with physical self-defensive force. The long-term agenda is to create a feminized man that will not ever challenge the State, and to simultaneously condition women to view the State as an all-powerful husband/father figure."*

Here is an example from history. In World War One Germany lost millions of people (almost all men, military men to be more precise). After the Great War ended, millions of women and kids were left without a husband and a father in their lives. The German government appeared as a friend. The women started looking at the government/the state as a husband figure and the provider while the kids saw the state as a father since their real fathers died on the battlefields. Both mothers and children saw the state as the male figure because they needed to compensate for not having a real male figure in their lives. This gave the German government unprecedented power which like all governments it abused. Since mothers and their fatherless children saw the state as the male parent the state indoctrinated them (especially the kids) with ideology it saw fit. This is true in both the Weimar (Soviet) Republic and in Hitler's Germany.

Supposedly (though I cannot guarantee the validity of this claim) Adolf Hitler once said: "*First you get the women, then you've got the children, so follow the men*". Whether this quote actually comes from Hitler is less important, what is important is that it perfectly describes the elite's intentions. What I do know for a fact, is that throughout history Socialists aimed their plans more towards women than men (this includes both classical Socialism/Communism/Marxism and Nazism a.k.a. National Socialism which is Socialism with a national element). The reason being that the elite know that if they brainwash women, men will follow (remember women were the ones who democratically voted Hitler into power and nowadays women are more likely to vote for Socialist policies than men). Men are programmed to chase after women, so if the elite can indoctrinate and brainwash women and make them jump into the well, men would follow.

While the feminist movement aimed to exclude the man/father from the family this is only the beginning. The state now wants to supplant both men and women as parents and become the only "parent" so that it can, through indoctrination, create new generations of obedient slaves who are just smart enough to listen to orders but dumb enough to never ask question.

Feminists say that being a mother is unfulfilling. Let me put this in the simplest terms possible, he who controls women controls the future because through the control of women he controls future generation. Since when did being a parent (mother or father) become such a disgusting thing? Feminists say that being a mother is unfulfilling because throughout history it's mostly men who were at the seat of power and influence. To that I have to say this, while men went hunting, or went to war to ensure the existence and survival of their wives and children, women spent upbringing, shaping and molding those future rulers at the seat of power and influence. The hand that rocks the cradle rules the world. Feminists also say that being a mother is not a real job, on the contrary, there is no greater and more important job for society than child rearing. While an average workday is 8 hours long, being a parent is a 24/7 job.

Mark Passio: "*Why specifically target women? Since women possess the capability of influencing men, most men will adjust their attitudes and behaviors to conform to women's likes and preferences. Therefore if the ruling class can influence the minds of most women, the men and children of a society will ultimately follow. Additionally, women ultimately control at a biological level the human reproduction process by way of their control over the selection of males with whom they choose to reproduce. Taking both of these factors into consideration, it is women who ultimately decide which traits and characteristics are passed down to future generations of humanity.*", he also said: "*The inauthentic woman, the non-authentic woman, or the socially-engineered woman is being, above all else, culturally conditioned to no longer be attracted to any of the qualities of an authentic man. Such qualities include: high holistic intelligence, true confidence, and high self-esteem, being very vocally opinionated, having very masculine features and an overall masculine look, independence, a rebellious attitude towards 'authority', and placing very high value on individual freedom. Such traits are, of course, seen as highly dangerous to the goals of the ruling class, who wish especially to see society produce weakened men since weakened, emasculated men are very unlikely to resist the State, while strong, independent thinking men are more likely to resist the control of the State. That's why they want to breed out these qualities out of the human male. And that's why they don't want women to find those qualities attractive in a potential partner.*" This correlates perfectly with what I said: "if you want to destroy society destroy the women".

It's next to impossible to talk about brainwashing and manipulating women without at least mentioning Edward Bernays. Edward Bernays – manipulator extraordinaire and public propagandist. He's targeted audience were mostly women. It's his propaganda pieces that hooked women onto cigarettes (it also didn't help the fact that in previous decades doctors encouraged the usage of these cancer-sticks claiming they are healthy). How? He concluded that you can sell virtually anything (whether it be a product or an ideology) to women if you convince them it will make them independent. Sound familiar? – feminism.

In 1990 Anthony Ralph Epperson wrote "The New World Order", here I will only cover chapter 29 called The Attack On The Family:

-page 130: "*The desire to destroy the family unit is, as has been briefly alluded to in previous sections of this study, one of the goals of the New Age-Humanist-Communist movement.*"

-page 131: "*the concept of marriage is that of a male husband and a female wife. Homosexual or lesbian marriages are not legal. But that can change anytime those who make the laws decide to change it*"

-page 131: "*there are some who want the family unit to be destroyed altogether. The destruction of the family unit has been the goal of the communists and socialist for over 140 years. Karl Marx the so-called father of communism wrote that that was the goal of the party-abolition of the family*" You can find proof of this in Karl Marx's Communist Manifesto (examples: page 24 "*abolition of the family*", page 24 "*The bourgeois family will vanish as a matter of course*", page 29 "*the dissolution of old moral bonds, of the old family relations, of the old nationalities*", page 33 "*But these Socialist and Communist publications contain also a critical element. They attack every principle of existing society. The practical measures proposed in them – such as the abolition of the family.*", page 52 "*What will be the influence of communist society on the family? It will transform the relations between the sexes into a purely private matter which concerns only the persons involved and into which society has no occasion to intervene. It can do this since it does away with private property and educates children on a communal basis, and in this way removes the bases of traditional marriage - the dependence of the children on the parents.*"). The only thing that the Marxists did correctly is identify that the monogamous reproductive union between a woman and a man is the foundation of modern civilization, but everything else is pure propaganda and demagoguery. Contrary to Marx's and Engels's brainwashing the family isn't an oppressive institution.

-page 131: "*Robert Owen the so-called father of socialism wrote: in the new moral world, the irrational names of husband and wife, parent and child, will be heard no more. All connection will result of affection, the child will undoubtedly be the property of the whole community*" Remember all those laws banning the words like "mother", "father", "wife", "husband", "boy", "girl" that they are implementing across Western Europe and North America which I covered in one of the previous chapters? Melissa Victoria Harris-Perry is an American writer, professor, television host, and political commentator who used to work for MSNBC. She was featured in an ad campaign in which she said "*we always had a private notion of children, your kid is yours and totally your responsibility, we haven't had a very collective notion that these are our children. Part of it is we have to break thru the private idea that the kids belong to their parents or kids belong to their families, and recognize that kids belong to whole communities.*" More collectivism, what could possibly go wrong?

-page 134: "*So the problem in China is not too much population. It is too much communism. It is too much New world order. So the family unit in*

China, the cornerstone of their civilization for centuries, has essentially been destroyed by the communist party. And it was not destroyed by mistake. It was planned that way. And the Bolshevik communists in the Soviet Union HAVE NEARLY DUPLICATED the "success" of the Chinese communists"

-page 135: *"talking about the U.S. "in 1988 the supreme court decided that the husband has no right to stop his wife from having an abortion. The appeals court which passed that decision onto the supreme court, had stated that the husband has no right to veto his wife's decision to have an abortion as such a decision only concerns her"* It only concerns her they say? Unless it's the man that is forced to pay for the murder of his own child through abortion, but then again wives and husbands are supposedly equal.

-page 135: *"in 1979 Sweden passed a law that punishes parents who spank their children"* This, or so they claim, is done to protect the kids from those evil parents. Protecting kids by taking them away from biological parents and letting them be adopted by strangers. Though presented as such, these child-protection laws have nothing to do with actually protecting children. They are only there to present biological parents as unfit to be parents, the result of this is that the state decides who is "worthy" of being a parent when it comes to adoption and in the end, the state itself will become the parent.

-page 135: *"and the traditional family as known for centuries will cease to exist. And some will be pleased. American Home Economics Association redefined the family in 1979 as two persons who share resources, share responsibilities to one another over time"* Gradually changing the definition until they reach the desired result.

-page 137: *"The attack on the family in America has taken several clever and unique twists. The family destroyers have resorted to cleverness to disguise their original intent: they do not want the parents to know that the destruction of the family is their goal. So they conceal their purposes by quietly causing problems that create intense pressures on the family. One of the methods utilized is that of inflation. Inflation is simply defined by a dictionary as an increase in the money supply, causing prices to go up. That means that whoever controls the money supply controls the price level. Increase the money supply, and prices rise. Decrease the money supply and prices go down (called Deflation.) Once Inflation or Deflation has been documented, the government economists point with pride at the supposed perpetrators: the public. They never direct their attention at the real culprit in America: the privately owned Federal Reserve System. This private banking establishment has complete control over the quantity of money in circulation. Therefore, they have the ability to create Inflation or Deflation whenever they choose to do so. The rising price level without a corresponding increase in a family's income causes the wife in a family unit who has chosen to care for her own child at home to leave the nurturing of the children to others in order to seek gainful employment so that she can increase the family's earnings"* Feminism never had in mind making women financially independent. It was promoted so that women would join the workforce and be taxed by the government, while the state would slowly become the children's only parent due to the absence of biological parents who were slaves of the system.

-page 138: *"The planners have been extremely successful, as the number of working mothers has been steadily increasing. According to a report issued in 1987, more than 44 percent of women work outside the home, compared to only 32 percent in 1960. Of women with children under one year of age, close to 50 percent are currently employed, a figure that has doubled since 1970. But, what happens to the child when they are placed into daycare centers? Are they better off? One group of individuals who feel that they are not are the doctors inside the American Academy of Pediatrics who have reported that the children placed in these centers are subject to all sorts of diseases caused by bacteria, viruses and parasites. They are more than 12 times as likely to catch flu viruses and 15 to 20 times more likely to catch other diseases than children under maternal care. So the daycare center has a negative impact on the health of a child placed there by a working mother. When the child gets sick, the mother must take time off from her job to care for the child, or to place the child in the hands of the medical fraternity. If the mother gets paid by the hour, and only gets paid when she is on the job, this frequent sickness costs the family additional revenue. And the only time that the mother sees her child, other than evenings or weekends, is when the child is sick and not feeling well. This does not tend to support warm mother-child feelings. But there is another lesser known problem when the mother is not directly involved in the care of the child. Until fairly recently, the assumption that care by the mother was the best kind of childcare went unchallenged. John Bowlby's widely acclaimed book entitled MATERNAL CARE AND MENTAL HEALTH, published in 1951, concluded that the "warm, intimate, and continuous" care of the mother or permanent mother substitute was essential to the "development of character and mental health." He called the absence of this mother-child relationship "maternal deprivation" and said that it was likely to result in "maladjustment of the child." This was the consensus view of the vast majority of psychologists, psychiatrists, pediatricians, and the general public until the medical and professional organizations capitulated to the demands of the feminist movement in the 1970s. The continuing debate over Dr. Jay Belsky's recent "heresy" is testimony to the power of the feminist/daycare lobby in academic and professional circles. Belsky, a professor of child psychology at Pennsylvania State University, was, a decade ago, one of the influential voices that saw no harm in institutional childcare. Now, he says, convincing research shows that non-maternal care for more than 20 hours per week for children under a year old is a "risk factor." Daycare at that young age can impede secure parent/child relationships and lead to rebellious and aggressive behavior, or shy and withdrawn behavior in the preschool and early years. His views have caused him much grief, as colleagues and feminists have come down hard on him for his views. They have impugned his research, his credentials, and his motives. Even Dr. Benjamin Spock, certainly no "conservative" in other matters, has also resisted the push for group child care, especially before the age of three. He has taken a position that appears to be out of character for him. He has written: "It is stressful for children to have to cope with groups, with strangers, with people outside the family." And another certified Harvard liberal, Professor Burton White, warns parents: "Unless you have a very good reason, I urge you not to delegate the primary child-rearing task to anyone else during your child's first three years of life." But the debate is certain to continue. Those who want to destroy the family will continue to urge mothers to leave the home and "become fulfilled in the workplace." When the mother goes into the workplace to "become fulfilled," or to increase the family's income, she leaves the care of the children to others. Those who warn against such practices will continue to be scorned by the feminists and others who have a hidden agenda: they want to destroy the family."* A 2001 National Institute of Child Health and Development study revealed the link between the long hours of non-maternal care for young children and aggressive behavior. Who would have thought, children are better off being raised by their parents than by strangers, mind-blowing conclusion.

-page 139: *"And in some cases, the destruction of the family has not gone unnoticed. Newsweek magazine of January 12, 1981, carried an article by Dr. Jonathan Kellerman, a psychologist, and author. He wrote this: "However, when one examines the role government has played in its relationship to the family, it is clear that not only has there been no support, on the contrary there has been a systematic erosion of the family, perpetuated by executive, legislative and judicial branches of government. The trend of the last two decades toward more government intervention and control has carried with it a clear message to families: you are not competent to decide how to live your life — we know better."And some in America have discovered that the psychologist was correct. An article in the Arizona Republic reported that "Family life [was! harmed by government, poll says." The article quoted pollster George Gallup, who said that: nearly half of those who responded to his organization's 1980 survey on the American family believe the federal government has an unfavorable influence on family life. And the government is once again using the tax laws to discriminate against families with full-time mothers. The present tax code favors families whose mothers enter the workforce over families with full-time mothers. Those parents who do not send the mother out into the workforce must subsidize those who do."*

-page 141: *"The planners have experienced their desired result: marriage has become the least desired relationship in Russia."* He is referring to the former Communist USSR.

-page 141 and 142: *"Perhaps the entire scenario was placed into perspective on the side of the government "experts" by B. F. Skinner, the chairman of the Harvard Department of Psychology, who wrote this about in his book entitled BEYOND FREEDOM AND DIGNITY: "My book is an effort to demonstrate how things go bad when you make a fetish out of individual freedom and dignity. If you insist that individual rights are the 'summum bonum,' [meaning the highest good,] then the whole structure of society falls down." So, those who want to destroy the family want the world to turn the society over to them. And those running the society continue to destroy it. The strategy is not new. In fact, it has been the strategy of this conspiracy for centuries. They cause the problem. Then they solve the problem with more government. And the people are convinced that their solution is desirable, generally because that is the only solution offered. And the end result is less freedom for the people. And it works nearly every time."* Ordo ab Chao (order out of chaos) is a 33 degree Freemason motto, David Icke calls it Problem-Reaction-Solution. The principle goes something like this: first you create a problem (the WEST creating and financing the Third Reich, or killing millions of innocent people in the Middle East based on falls premises thus creating the Migrant Crisis), then after the reaction of the general public you present the solution to the people who have suffered, the result is centralization of power in fewer and fewer hands (that's how the few control the many)... League of Nations (today's UN), EU...create war and then present yourself as the "savior" to the starving masses, this always leads to loss of individual freedom - especially freedom of speech/thought and freedom of privacy (Big Brother). More often than not it is precisely those people who present the solution that have caused the problem in the first place. For example - marriage is falling apart, says the state, therefore it needs to be firstly redefined and secondly abolished. Marriage is not a failed institution, it's not marriage that is failing, its people that are failing thanks to the manipulative brainwashing that they have been force-fed. Apply this exact method on the family, the government defines biological parents as unfit to raise their own children, the government takes away the children (for adoption, and later down the line to raise the children itself). But I'm sure that the state will do a better job at raising the children than the biological parents by giving the children needed attention and care for their full development (by replacing the father and mother) since the government has proven to be good at other things, right? OH yeah, never mind, I take that back.

Margaret Sanger, a founder of Planned Parenthood, eugenicists and an icon of the contemporary feminist movement, in 1934 wrote an 8 piece article for the enactment of a marriage license in the American weekly magazine. This would not allow couples to have children without further application for a parenting license which would only permit the birth of one child per license. Here are some excerpts from those articles:

- Article 3. *"A marriage license shall in itself give husband and wife only the right to a common household and not the right to parenthood."*

- Article 4. *"No woman shall have the legal right to bear a child, and no man shall have the right to become a father, without a permit for parenthood."*

- Article 5. *"Permits for parenthood shall be issued upon application by city, county, or state authorities to married couples, providing they have the qualifications needed for proper rearing of the child"* Again, it's the state/government that decides who is "fit" to raise a child, of course, the state would like nothing more than to classify all women and men willing to be parents as unfit so that it can be the only "parent".

- Article 6. *"No permit for parenthood shall be valid for more than one birth."* One of Sanger's public admirers is none-other that the wicked witch of the west a.k.a. Killary Hilton, another feminist icon who received the

Margaret Sanger Award (the highest award the genocidal Planned Parenthood gives away) in 2009.

In Scotland, there are steps to transfer guardianship of every child to the state through the "Named Person Act." This involves assigning every child under the age of 18 a state guardian such as a social worker or a teacher. They would then act as the final word in any decisions involving the rearing of the child. In such a society the parents would not be able to question the states approach to raising children, from decisions about sex education to shaping a child's political views and even children spying on their parents (*cough* "1984" *cough*). According to this legislation, the new social worker or teacher will have the power to make the decision about children that their parents do not consent and to interact with the child without their parent's knowledge or approval. Of cause, in the classic totalitarian way, the parents don't have a way to opt out of this 'Named persons act'.

"Shocking law for Scottish state to oversee entire childhood through a 'named person' - another major step to Huxley's no-parents Brave New World – the most blatant and disgusting example of the state deleting the rights of parents to bring up their own child (and they want the same everywhere). Scottish children to be given a "named person" from the state from before birth to 18 to oversee their upbringing, and you are taking this Scotland?" (source: Scotsman.com and davidicke.com)

A society where the state defines parenthood is about as authoritarian as it gets. If there is one thing that all totalitarian ideologies have in common it's an obsession with the destruction of the family. By destroying the family the state gets to raise impressionable kids and mold them in whatever shape it desires, and what all totalitarian, collectivist dystopias want is an obedient, subservient, mindless society comprised of sub-humans (üntermenschen). They don't want nuclear families where the children are raised by their biological parents and where the family is independent (including financially) from the state. What they want is for the future generations to be zombies, clones, and automatons who have no free will but who only do the bidding of the government. To them we represent nothing more than a ball of clay which they mold in accordance to their own distorted vision of the world.

What they want is a uniformed society that is obedient, to quote Huxley's Brave New World - Revisited in Chapter 3 Over-Organization *"Their conformity is developing into something like uniformity. But uniformity and freedom are incompatible. Uniformity and mental health are incompatible too. . . . Man is not made to be an automaton, and if he becomes one, the basis for mental health is destroyed."*

One problem though, there is one thing standing in their way – the family, which for their plan (the plan to destroy society and create a new one) to come into fruition must be destroyed. The family is the enemy of totalitarianism.

At this point, you are probably thinking what do these four topics have to do with homosexuality and the gay movement. You probably think there are no connections and that these are all completely unrelated topics. At the very beginning of this book, I have said that the issue regarding the gay movement/lifestyle is far broader and complex than most people think. Most people think it's only about legalizing gay marriage. This is false, this topic is so much more. How you may ask. For starters, the gay movement and the feminist movement (from the second wave feminism onwards at least) have had the same goal and that is to destroy the family. They are basically one and the same, equal goals posing as two separate equal rights movements. Secondly, when it comes to promiscuity and abortion they are intrinsically linked to the feminist movement (they derived from it), thus they are automatically linked to the gay movement. Feminism teaches women that promiscuity empowers them. Promiscuity and abortion did exist earlier but never to this extent, their liberation and popularization come from the sexual liberation/revolution movement and the original one of these movements was the gay liberation movement from which all others derived from.

Sexual liberation is a form of control in the false name of freedom. There is a big difference between what we are told is going on and reality, in the words of George Orwell 'Freedom is slavery', the complete inversion of stated goals as opposed to the truth. Through this new age bread and circuses, we are conditioned to be content in our own slavery, as Aldous Huxley would phrase it.

PEDOPHILIA:

The second reason as to why gay/LGBT movement is being pushed is to, later on, normalize and legalize pedophilia. It was never about gay rights to begin with. Pedophilia is the final stage of the sexual liberation agenda. Even Milo Yiannopoulos (a gay man) said that after the gay and transsexual movement the next one is the push for pedophile rights.

Homosexuality and pedophilia are linked in more ways than one, both as a movement and as a behavioral pattern. In Ancient Greece, homosexuality was present there, but it occurred between a grown man and a boy - pedophilia (usually when the boy was left without biological parents due to war or other causes).

If we take that the entire LGBT population represents around 3-5 percent of the entire population in the U.S.A, and out of that the gay population is anywhere between 1-2 percent. According to one study in the U.S, around 33 percent of child molestations are committed by homosexuals. So 1 to 2 percent of the population commits a third of crimes involving sex with kids, and no one sees the problem with that?

Gay marriage and gay rights were never the end goal, they were only a forefront or a mask for the main movement. After gay marriage was proclaimed legal in the U.S. in 2015 it took mere weeks for psychiatrists and psychologists to start advocating for the redefinition of the word pedophilia. The plan is to redefine pedophilia as a legitimate sexual orientation.

"'Gay' laws set stage for pedophilia 'rights' In 1973, the American Psychiatric Association declassified homosexuality from its list of mental disorders after intense lobbying by homosexual-rights groups. The organization calls pedophiles "minor attracted people," and the website states its purpose is to "help mental health professionals learn more about attraction to minors and to consider the effects of stereotyping, stigma, and fear. True pedophiles have an exclusive preference for children, which is the same as having a sexual orientation. You cannot change this person's sexual orientation. If the APA would declare pedophilia a sexual orientation on a par with homosexuality, it would have huge ramifications for existing anti-discrimination laws." (source: wnd.com and FoxNews) Go back to chapter 3 and read what Nicholas Andrew Cummings had to say about the APA. Apparently now it's bad to stigmatize against pedophilia.

"PEDOPHILIA THE NEXT 'SEXUAL-RIGHTS' REVOLUTION?" the article says "The underlying assumption that has led to the increasing legitimization of same-sex marriage is now fueling a growing effort in academic circles to mainstream pedophilia. Once considered taboo, psychologists are beginning to walk down the same path LGBT activists established more

than 50 years ago, insisting that pedophilia is an inborn "sexual orientation," not a learned sexual behavior. If people are born with a sexual attraction to minors, the argument goes, their "orientation" should be accepted as normative and not stigmatized. Last fall, the American Psychological Association caused an uproar when the latest edition of its vaunted Diagnostic and Statistical Manual of Mental Disorders called pedophilia a "sexual orientation." (source wnd.com)

Similar to how homosexuality was first normalized and then legalized (based on the false premises of the born this way myth) the same methods are merely applied to pedophilia, years ago they started reclassifying pedophilia as a sexual orientation. In order to legalize it, they first have to normalize it. Who is trying to normalize pedophilia? If you look at the history of the second part of the 20th century and modern day politics it is easy to see that the normalization of pedophilia is coming from the Left side of the political spectrum.

Harriet Harman (member of the Uk's Labour party), in 2014 was exposed to having links with the Pedophile Information Exchange (PIE), in the 1970s she was a legal officer for the national council for civil liberties when she suggested that child porn should not be considered indecent if the child consented or was not harmed and that banning child pornography would lead to an increase of censorship. These claims were verified by her own documents and she never apologized for them.

In may 2013 the American Psychiatric Association tried to reclassify pedophilia as a sexual orientation. They did, however, withdraw this claim thanks to the people's outrage. The APA (American Psychological Association), the one that in the 70s decided that homosexuality was no longer a mental disorder, also backtracked on the decision. The two APA's (American Psychiatric Association and the American Psychological Association) are nefarious for pushing sexual liberation, including the normalization of pedophilia.

Edite Estrela, a member of the European Parliament for the Socialist party (what a surprise). In 2013 she was an author of the controversial report named "Sexual and reproductive health and rights". The European Parliament rejected the draft report by a narrow margin of votes. What does this report say? The report called for compulsory sex education, masturbation and gender identity for newborn babies onwards, as well as theories about sexuality and same-sex relationships to children as young as four.

Here are parts of the report:

-Page 6: *"whereas sexual and reproductive health and rights touch every human being at every stage of life"* Where does every stage of life begin, 18 years old? 15? 10? From birth? Since when did our society accept that children have sexual and reproductive rights and why is the government concerned with the sexual rights of children?

-Page 7: *"whereas an estimated five million young people aged between 15 and 24, and two million adolescents aged between 10 and 19 are living with HIV1"* Not saying these are the only reason but 78 percent of homosexuals are infected with STDs and they account for over 50 percent of all AIDs cases. Also, it doesn't help that more and more people are promiscuous and homosexual.

-Page 9: *"whereas young people are widely exposed, from an early age, to pornographic content, especially through access to the internet, whether at home or at school"* I wonder how did that happen. Not like the Rockefeller's pushed the porn industry.

-Page 14: *"Calls on the Member States to make sex education classes compulsory for all primary and secondary school children and to ensure that space is made available for this subject in school curricula; stresses the importance of regularly reviewing and updating the teaching of sex education and of placing special emphasis on respect for women and on gender equality"* What other gender identity? The only other gender identity apart from women is a man as far as science and objective reality is concerned, there are no genders besides male and female.

-Page 14: *"Calls on Member States to ensure compulsory, age-appropriate and gender-sensitive sexuality and relationship education, provided in a mixed-sex setting, for all children and adolescents (both in and out of school)"* Again we see the push to get rid of the parents as schools become first and main educators while neglecting the natural rights of parents.

-Page 15: *"Underlines that sexual education must include non-discriminatory information and convey a positive view of LGBTI persons"* Only positive views? What about all the diseases that homosexual behavior brings, not to mention the much higher chance of a homosexual ending up with an STD in comparison to a heterosexual, so much for objectivity but I guess feelings are more important than facts.

-Page 15: *"Asks Member States, in the context of sexuality education, to focus on the prevention of sexually transmitted infections (STIs), including HIV, by encouraging safe sexual behavior and facilitating access to means of protection"* Or you can just discourage behavior which promotes and celebrates promiscuity and homosexuality, just a thought. The list goes on. Before you say that this report isn't in force just you wait, this is but the beginning, they won't stop here.

Nick Clegg – British Liberal Democrat (big shock) – called for sex education for 7-year-olds in the summer of 2014. This is not the first time something like this was proposed. In 2011 a government-backed drive advocated teaching about homosexuality to 4-year-olds by integrating it into the curriculum. Mock my word this is not the last time you hear stuff like this.

One of the ways they are pushing this on children is trying to lower the age of consent arguing that it is arbitrary and obsolete. Most of the people who are pushing for the lowering of the age of consent are gay activists, no surprise there if you look at previous decades. Peter Tatchell, a notorious LGBT advocate, with links to the Labour party has strongly advocated abolishing the age of consent.

A news article reads *"I'm a pedophile, but not a monster"*. The pedophile in question is a grown man named Todd Nickerson. In the article, this self-proclaimed pedophile calls for readers to be understanding and supportive of pedophiles. He talks about drooling over pictures of underaged girls. On the other post, he contemplates if a 6-MONTH-old baby can consent to sex. He describes his desires as a different form of "sexual orientation". Todd described how he has to relieve himself (masturbate) in the bathroom after fantasizing about a 5-year-old girl. SALON, a left-wing news outlet that posted the story in the first place deleted the post but you can still find other media sites talking about this deleted post. This isn't the first time SALON did something like this. Back in 2012, they posted an article titled *"Meet pedophiles that mean well"*. Why are pedophiles being given platforms?

When are children old enough to be taught about sex? According to the Left - no age is too young.

Jimmy Savile – more than 50 years of allegations, at least 34 rapes, over 100 indecent acts, the youngest known victim was a boy of 8 years old. This psychopath was never brought to justice even though he was doing this for decades. One of the reasons for that is the fact that the BBC (left wing) played an integral role in covering his pedophile scandals for decades. This is why his victims are now suing the BBC. Why was TV presenter Jill Dando murdered right before she was about to expose *"big name stars at the BBC who were involved in the abuse of children."*

Sarah Nyberg – a transgender who in 2015 confessed to being a pedophile. What did the people do? Progressives (leftists) flew to her defense categorizing her as a victim. Sympathy for pedophiles, yes because they are the true victims and not the children.

Allen Ginsberg - (a leftist poet) was a homosexual, supporter of and a member of NAMBLA (North American Man/Boy Love Association – a pedophile organization), again the link between the gay and the pedophile movement.

The Guardian (left-wing news outlet) also published an article titled *"Pedophilia, bringing dark desires to light"* in which it pushed for pedophilia to be reclassified as a sexual orientation.

At a Cambridge University in July 2013 at a conference presentation, it was claimed that pedophilia is normal for males. This conference was attended by Ken Plummer, an Essex University sociology professor. At one of his lectures he said *"pedophiles are told that they are the seducers and rapists of children, they know their experiences are often loving and tender ones, they are told that children are pure and innocent devoid of sexuality, they know both form their own experiences of childhood and from the children they meet that this is not the case"*

"FOX COMEDY FEATURES 6YO 'TRANS' BOY WEARING BONDAGE BDSM GAG, the scenes show the boy dressing like a girl and commenting how the dress he's wearing "kind of breezes on my vagina." A sickening new "comedy" show on FOX features a 6-year-old boy wearing a bondage gag. The FOX show is named "The Mick" and it aired on January 1st, 2017. It was created by Dave Chernin and John Chernin, both sons of top Hollywood executive Peter Chernin (Who is a mega-donor to the democratic party, what a surprise, a leftist involved in pedophilia), Another forced scene shows one of the characters awkwardly praising Planned Parenthood" (source: Dailymail.com / infowars.com)

"'I'm a normal guy. I just fancy six-year-olds: 'Virtuous' pedophile who is aroused by girls aged under 13, Gary Gibson, 65, of Oregon says is aroused by girls aged six to 13, A self-described 'virtuous pedophile' who admits to being sexually attracted to girls as young as six. Gary Gibson, 65, of Oregon, has set up a non-profit organization - the Association for Sexual Abuse Prevention, The Christian ex-teacher, whose family has a history of incestual child abuse. 'My grandfather sexually abused my mother and I think at least one of his sisters, and my father's woman was known on the streets to be

one that invited the little boys into her house and did things with them,' he said in a video published last month. 'So, I think, she is a pedophile. I know for a fact my father sexually abused several of my sisters – nearly all of them. 'When I was six, my two older sisters taught me to play "go to sleep". My understanding was I was to get them to take their panties off and get them ready to sleep. I don't think it was abuse, but it left me with the impression that little girls want to be touched. During a recent interview, Gibson explained why he is attracted to young girls - but not young boys or teenagers. The 'comfortably out' pedophile, whose wife is a nurse, said he is normally not aroused by teenage girls and does not have any desire for young boys. 'When they pass 12 they tend to get into themselves, start to make themselves look older, and I like things natural - so there we are,' he told The Sun in the UK. 'When they start wearing lipstick and stuff like that I don't find it very appealing.' Despite his attractions, Gibson added he is 'a normal everyday person'." (source: Dailymail.com) A few things I would like to point out. Putting the word 'virtuous' in the same sentence as the word 'pedophile' is as sick as it gets. Here you can see a prime example of early sexual experiences and child sexual abuses playing a key role in the development of sexual deviancy.

"Pedophiles want same rights as homosexuals - Using the same tactics used by "gay" rights activists, pedophiles have begun to seek similar status arguing their desire for children is a sexual orientation no different than heterosexual or homosexuals. Critics of the homosexual lifestyle have long claimed that once it became acceptable to identify homosexuality as simply an "alternative lifestyle" or sexual orientation, logically nothing would be off limits. "Gay" advocates have taken offense at such a position insisting this would never happen. However, psychiatrists are now beginning to advocate redefining pedophilia in the same way homosexuality was redefined several years ago. B4U-Act calls pedophiles "minor-attracted people." In July 2010 Harvard health Publications said, "Pedophilia is a sexual orientation"." (source: greeleygazette.com)

To the people who claim that pedophilia has nothing to do with the gay movement. While the Pedophile information exchange (PIE) was active it had links with the National Council for civil liberties, Scottish minorities group, Gay liberation front from south London. Pedophile information exchange was also involved in gay rights conferences (example: in 1975 campaign for homosexual equality). NAMBLA (North American Man/Boy Love Association) – it was the first U.S.A. member of the International lesbian and gay association, the group was a regular part of the gay and lesbian events. They gradually became too controversial to be associated with them publicly, similar to PIE in the U.K. But unlike PIE, NAMBLA never disbanded.

Harry Hay - the founder of the gay rights revolution, homosexual himself, Communist, labor activist (what a coincidence) constantly advocated the inclusion of NAMBLA (North American Man/Boy Love Association) in gay-pride parades. His biggest influence was Alfred Kinsey, a psychopath I will cover later on. Remember the name, Alfred Kinsey.

"Pedophilia Being Taught As 'Sexual Orientation' in California Schools - Government school officials in California think it is "really important" to teach children about pedophilia and pederasty in the classroom because it is a 'sexual orientation.' That is according to a top official for California's Brea Olinda School District, who admitted to parents that it was being done — and that it would continue, despite the outrage. The stunning admission came after a parent-information meeting last month for the Brea Olinda Unified School District (BOUSD). Stephanie Yates, founder of Informed Parents of California, asked school officials why they were 'teaching pedophilia in school to 9th graders.' But instead of a denial that such an atrocity was taking place, a top school official confirmed it was happening and acted like there was nothing wrong with it. Horrified, the mother turned activist expressed shock at Torres' admission. 'So sex between a man and a boy is a sexual orientation?' she asked. Torres did not deny it. 'It's something that occurred in history, and so this is really important for us to include,' the assistant superintendent said, implying that yes, sexual relations between a man and a boy — properly considered rape under the laws of every state — is a 'sexual orientation.' Establishment propaganda outlets disguised as news organizations such as Salon and Slate have also been working to normalize and redefine pedophilia and pederasty as a 'sexual orientation.' LGBT movement hero Harvey Milk, who is celebrated in California's fake "history" textbooks as a great figure, was known for raping minor boys, at least one of whom later committed suicide. There seems to be a trend here in California. There was a time when exposing children to far more mild obscenities was a crime. Now it is considered 'education.'" (Source: freedomproject.com)

"VICE Pushes Pedophile Acceptance - Vice becomes the latest outlet to push for destigmatizing pedophilia." (Source: blazetv.com)

"Shocking TEDx Videos Try to Normalize Pedophilia - A number of TEDx videos have been shocking people around the world. It seems that the current conversation in the culture wars is trying to redefine pedophilia. The

message is clear: 'Accept pedophilia.' Mirjam Heine, a medical student, presented a Tedx Talk at the University of Wurzburg in Germany on May 5, 2018. She said, 'Pedophilia is an unchangeable sexual orientation.' Continuing she was saying, 'Just like, for example, heterosexuality, no one chooses to be a pedophile. No one can cease being one.' Heine continued, saying, 'We must accept that pedophilia is a sexual preference.'" (Source: charismanews.com)

There are other connections between homosexuality and pedophilia, including those that most dare not talk about fearing repercussion. There is a link between same-sex attraction and sexual abuse in childhood. Plenty of research indicates that a strong link exists.

Before things became too politically correct and before it became impossible to conduct objective unbiased research (due to the influence of the LGBT lobby) there were studies that showed a link between homosexual behavior and sexual abuse in childhood. All of this stopped not too long after the turn of the new millennium. Nowadays it is next to impossible to do such research because anyone who dares question the narrative (the born this way myth) is scrutinized and quartered by the most anti-scientific group on the planet - the pseudo/quasi-intellectual LGBT and pro-LGBT ideologues.

A 2001 study found that while straight men outnumber gay men by 44 to 1 in the U.S. the incidents of gay men molesting children is around 44 times higher than among straight men.

Another U.S. study, also in 2001 found that among 942 adult men and women the incidents of childhood sexual abuse for those attracted to the same sex was far higher. While straight men reported childhood abuse 7 percent of the time, this was 47 percent for gay men. 1 percent of straight women and 22 percent of gay women reported sexual abuse in childhood.

Other research indicates that homosexuals are disproportionately more likely to be pedophiles in comparison to heterosexual people.

There is also empirical evidence that came to a similar conclusion. An undercover video demonstrated the following. When a man asked men in a gay bar on a Friday night whether being gay was strictly genetic, not only did numerous gay men admit they did not believe it was genetic but they openly admitted to very early sexual experiences affecting their attraction to the same sex as well as being perpetrators of sexual abuse among boys and males under age of consent (which this being in the U.S. is 16 years old). An even worst thing is what clinical psychology concluded - that sexual abuse is a cycle that often leads to victims becoming perpetrators. The people truly behind this agenda are well aware that unless children are exposed to sexual experiences and abuse at an early age the odds of them following a sexually deviant lifestyle are minimal.

How will all this normalization for pedophilia play out in the field? It will certainly be no different than their earlier sexual liberations. The ones that are pushing this (leftists) will use a mixture of tactics revolving around sympathy and empathy directed at the general public, aimed to make them feel sorry for pedophiles. They will present pedophiles as victims of societal oppression while ignoring the true victims – the children. Similar to other movements of its kind they will present pedophiles as ordinary men (much like you and I) they will emphasize their humanity while blatantly ignoring and concealing their sick, twisted and perverted mind. There is no doubt they will (and already have) show pedophiles as the oppressed ones in society putting them in a state of perpetual victimhood while waiting for human empathy of the normal population to kick in.

One of the arguments used by pro-gay activists used to be that gay marriage should be legal because homosexuality is different from pedophilia. They said that homosexuality, unlike pedophilia is consensual between two adults. Though that argument is solid the tables have turned. In 2015 as soon as gay marriage was legalized in the U.S.A. (some 2 weeks later approximately) there were psychologists and psychiatrists that proposed to redefine the word pedophilia as a normal sexual orientation. So they used the difference between homosexuality and pedophilia to legalize gay marriage then almost immediately started using the foundation of gay marriage to reclassify pedophilia as a legitimate sexual orientation on par with homosexuality.

It is clear that, for one reason or another, people and organizations on the left side of the political spectrum have been (and continue) to be sympathetic towards pedophiles (or victims of societal oppression as they call them). This is not a surprise seeing how the left was the one that pushed the whole sexual liberation agenda in the first place, so why would pedophilia be exempt? The fact that the left is acting as pedophile enablers and apologists is significant for something I will cover later down the line.

To quote a modern day philosopher, whom I shall mention again at the very end, *"If pedophilia is normalized, I will consider it a sign that civilization is all but dead, and all that remains is a hedonistic culture, I will not partake in such a culture and I would rather riot in the streets than be complicit in such a degeneracy."*

CHAPTER 7 "WHO IS PUSHING THE GAY AGENDA?"

Answering this question is not as hard as one might think. Knowing the reason for the existence of such an agenda, we can narrow it down to those who are pushing for its fruition. The goal of such an agenda being what it is, it is no surprise that it is being pushed by those who want to destroy the family and/or are pedophiles. It is irrespective whether they are homosexuals themselves or not. Could I name you the people who have directly orchestrated this agenda? Of course not, to quote Eric Kaiser *"the real power is always the entity you don't see"*. Despite me not being able to tell you the exact names of the people on the very top I can tell you the people and organizations through which this agenda is being forced on us. Talking about people on the top, to whom am I referring to?

This world is run by pedophiles:

In almost every pedophile case in every country in the world top politicians, judges, celebrities, billionaires and other members of the establishment are always connected.

In 2008 American financier Jeffrey Epstein, whose friends include some of the most powerful people on the planet, was convicted for soliciting an underage girl for prostitution, he is a registered sex offender. One of Jeffrey Epstein's friends was Bill Clinton. According to the Alliance to Rescue Victims of Human Trafficking regarding Epstein, *"everyone in his inner circles knew he was a pedophile"*. Jeffrey Epstein provided underage sex to elites via his private island and plane. Bill Clinton, a known serial rapist to anyone who bothered to do research into the Clinton family crimes, has flown at least 26 times on this plane in three years.

In 2010 Laura Silsby, a former director of the New Life Children's Refuge, was arrested for attempting to traffic 33 children out of Haiti. Laura and her lawyer were later arrested for involvement in an international trafficking ring. Bill Clinton intervened to secure the release of all the Silsby's co-conspirators, he also helped Silby's sentence get reduced from conspiracy and child abduction to just *"arranging irregular travel"*.

In 2014 the London police publically said they believed allegations that *"a ring of prominent politicians and members of the establishment abused and terrorized children as young as 7 more than 30 years ago and went on to kill three young boys."* In 2016 for reasons yet to be explained they closed the investigation.

Former Child protection manager Peter Mckelvie said the following *"there has been an extremely powerful elite amongst the highest levels of the political classes for as long as I have been alive, and I'm 65 now, and there has been sufficient reason to investigate over and over again, certainly for the last 30 years and there has always been a block and the cover-up and the collusion to prevent that from happening".*

Cyril Smith was a British Liberal (what a surprise) Member of Parliament, abused boys for 4 decades and was protected by the British establishment.

In the 1970's Roman Polanski, actor, producer, writer and a convicted statutory rapist (sexual activity in which one of the individuals is below the age required to legally consent). Polanski was arrested for having sex with a 13-year-old girl before fleeing America. In 2003 Meryl Streep, actress, gave a standing ovation for Polanski, an admitted and convicted pedophile. Her support did not end there. In 2017, regarding Polanski, she said *"I'm very sorry that he's in jail"*

Corey Feldman, an actor, said that in the 1980's *"the number one problem with Hollywood was and is and always will be pedophilia", "I was surrounded by them (pedophiles) when I was 14 years old", "there was a circle of older men that surrounded themselves around this group of kids and they all either had great power or had connections to great power in the entertainment industry", "there is a lot of sick corrupt people in this industry"*

Jim Cusack, an actor, said *"Hollywood is a whorehouse filled with crazy people"*

In 2016 Elijah Wood, an American actor, gave an interview where he made several claims *"young actors are being abused in Hollywood", "Hollywood is in the grip of child abuse scandals similar to Jimmy Savile", "pedophile ring is being protected in Hollywood", "Hollywood is full of organized child sex abuse"*

In 2010 in Portugal numerous prominent individuals were convicted for their involvement in the sexual abuse of more than 100 orphan children. They included a TV presenter, members of Parliament, a governor and a UNESCO ambassador.

These are only a handful of documented and proven cases where the elite have been exposed to having a role in organizing and/or participating in sex scandals with children. I'm not even going to go deeper in the rabbit hole regarding newer scandals like Pizzagate and Milogate.

Your counter argument, I am sure, will be that we live in a world where the state/government and its agencies will protect us and our children. You could not be more wrong.

"Pentagon workers found to have downloaded child pornography - Dozens of Pentagon staff and contractors with high-level security clearance have been found by US federal investigators to have downloaded child pornography." (source: theguardian.com)

"The Child Porn-Pentagon-NSA-CIA Link 'They' Don't Want You to Know - Even though there is evidence, the Pentagon, the NSA, and the CIA do not want to investigate and prosecute their highly-disciplined, high-profile, and high-ranking child pornographers. Some of the top ranking defense personnel, intelligence analysts, and federal law enforcement officers in the United States are pedophiles who access and download child pornography on their work and home computers. In 2006, an undercover Internet child pornography investigation, called Operation Flicker, was conducted by the Immigration and Customs Enforcement (ICE), a federal investigative agency. ICE revealed a list of 5,200 Pentagon employees (with high-level security clearances) suspected of subscribing to child pornography websites, and asked the Pentagon to investigate its employees." (source:anonhq.com)

"Flashback: Pentagon caught in massive child porn cover up." (source: newstargate.com)

"More Than 200 Pentagon Employees Were Caught With Child Pornography." (source: livingresistance.com)

Daniel Cohn-Bendit, a French-German politician, in 1994 he was elected in the European Parliament, his entourage included members of the Communist libertarian leftists (who would have thought). In his earlier days, he used to run a kindergarten. In 1982 on a French TV-talk show he gave an interview in which he said the following statements *"I work with children, very small children, WOW, the things they do to me"*, *"I wipe their arse and tickle them, they tickle me, we cuddle"*, *"Did you know that the sexuality of a child is something fantastic?"*, *"you know, when a little girl of 5 years starts to undress you it's fantastic, it's fantastic because it's a game and absolutely erotic-maniac"*

Alex Jones, journalist, founder of Infowars and one few men ever to be invited to the Bohemian Grove as a reporter. The Bohemian Grove is one of the most secretive organizations in the world. This organization is an all-male club in California where the most powerful elite (politicians, economists, business leaders, globalists, sports figures, actors, entertainment industry stars) gather once a year. It usually takes place after the Bilderberg Group meeting. Before Alex Jones was invited, for decades there were rumors speculating the sexuality of members of this all-male club. You could say that the only useful thing the hippie movement ever did was that they were the first ones to keep an eye on this group, usually during their protests. According to numerous reports during the 1980s and 1990s both outside the Bohemian Grove (mostly thanks to the hippie protesters) and people on the inside (mostly employees working inside) this club, filled with the most powerful men on the planet, was overflowing with homosexuals. In 2000 Alex Jones was invited in the club to make a report. According to him, people who attend the Bohemian Grove are also members of the Bilderberg Group and the Trilateral Commission (founded by David Rockefeller and Zbigniew Brzezinski). Alex said that during his visit there, male prostitutes were shipped to service the elite members. He states that there were men following him around trying to get his *"attention"* by whistling while he was there. Spy-magazine and Vanity-fair have also reported about homosexuality in the Bohemian Grove.

Richard Nixon, ex-member of the Bohemian Grove, said *"The Bohemian Grove, which I attend from time to time is the most faggy goddamned thing you could ever imagine"*

Sigmund Freud: for some odd reason considered one of the greatest minds of the 20th century. In reality, his mind was nothing short of sick. This psycho-psychologist proposed a theory that aimed to normalize pedophilic-incestual relationships. Freud said that from birth children develop a sexual attraction towards their parents. According to him, as soon as a mother breastfeeds her son for the first time he expresses sexual desires towards her (Oedipus complex), the same behavior, according to Freud, is normal between a father and his daughter (Electra complex). This was Freud's theory on infantile sexuality, a theory that says that humans are sexual at birth. The same theory is being used by modern Leftists/Liberals/ Progressives who advocate that the age of consent should be abolished and that children should be taught about sexual intercourse as early as possible. This should not come as a surprise to many since Freud was "sexually attracted" to his own mother and despised his father out of jealousy because he could not have her. Freud believed that this is why men become socially awkward – because they have to suppress their sexual desires towards their mothers due to social stigma. Once Freud's father passed away Freud was reportedly happier hoping he can finally "be with his mother." A sick and deranged mind, yet celebrated and revered in the scientific community. Freud's so-called scientific research inspired the work of Alfred Kinsey, another pseudo-scientists who shall be mentioned in greater detail.

Hollywood: it should come as no surprise that every movie and TV series that comes out of Hollywood must have AT LEAST one of the following requirements:
- "the protagonist and/or antagonist is divorced" they are promoting the notion that married people are miserable and that divorced people are happy even though all the studies show the complete opposite (unless it's homosexual couples – they are presented as being happily married and great parents)
- "the female is dominant, controlling, violent and better than a man" I'm guessing she is better in every aspect imaginable for no other explainable reason than the fact she is a woman
- "the male is aloof, feminine, overly-sensitive, and/or cheating" masculinization of women and the emasculation (feminization) of men
- "in the family at least one character must be a gay, lesbian, bisexual" They used to claim that homosexuality was equal to heterosexuality, now, again and again, we see a pattern where homosexuality is being put on a pedestal and above heterosexuality.

Michael Swift, a gay activist. In 1987 he was asked to contribute to an editorial essay to the "Gay Community News". The following is the full text titled the "Gay Manifesto":
"We shall sodomize your sons, emblems of your feeble masculinity, of your shallow dreams and vulgar lies. We shall seduce them in your schools, in your dormitories, in your gymnasiums, in your locker rooms, in your sports arenas, in your seminaries, in your youth groups, in your movie theater bathrooms, in your army bunkhouses, in your truck stops, in your all male clubs, in your houses of Congress, wherever men are with men together. Your sons shall become our minions and do our bidding. They will be recast in our image. They will come to crave and adore us.

Women, you cry for freedom. You say you are no longer satisfied with men; they make you unhappy. We, connoisseurs of the masculine face, the masculine physique, shall take your men from you then. We will amuse them; we will instruct them; we will embrace them when they weep. Women, you say you wish to live with each other instead of with men. Then go and be with each other. We shall give your men pleasures they have never known because we are foremost men too, and only one man knows how to truly please another man; only one man can understand the depth and feeling, the mind and body of another man.

All laws banning homosexual activity will be revoked. Instead, legislation shall be passed which engenders love between men.

All homosexuals must stand together as brothers; we must be united artistically, philosophically, socially, politically and financially. We will triumph only when we present a common face to the vicious heterosexual enemy.

If you dare to cry faggot, fairy, queer, at us, we will stab you in your cowardly hearts and defile your dead, puny bodies.

We shall write poems of the love between men; we shall stage plays in which man openly caresses man; we shall make films about the love between heroic men which will replace the cheap, superficial, sentimental, insipid, juvenile, heterosexual infatuations presently dominating your cinema screens. We shall sculpt statues of beautiful young men, of bold athletes which will be placed in your parks, your squares, your plazas. The museums of the world will be filled only with paintings of graceful, naked lads.

Our writers and artists will make love between men fashionable and de rigueur, and we will succeed because we are adept at setting styles. We will eliminate heterosexual liaisons through usage of the devices of wit and ridicule, devices which we are skilled in employing.

We will unmask the powerful homosexuals who masquerade as heterosexuals. You will be shocked and frightened when you find that your presidents and their sons, your industrialists, your senators, your mayors, your generals, your athletes, your film stars, your television personalities, your civic leaders, your priests are not the safe, familiar, bourgeois, heterosexual figures you assumed them to be. We are everywhere; we have infiltrated your ranks. Be careful when you speak of homosexuals because we are always among you; we may be sitting across the desk from you; we may be sleeping in the same bed with you.

There will be no compromises. We are not middle-class weaklings. Highly intelligent, we are the natural aristocrats of the human race, and steely-minded aristocrats never settle for less. Those who oppose us will be exiled.
We shall raise vast private armies, as Mishima did, to defeat you. We shall conquer the world because warriors inspired by and banded together by homosexual love and honor are invincible as were the ancient Greek soldiers.
The family unit-spawning ground of lies, betrayals, mediocrity, hypocrisy and violence--will be abolished. The family unit, which only dampens imagination and curbs free will, must be eliminated. Perfect boys will be conceived and grown in the genetic laboratory. They will be bonded together in communal setting, under the control and instruction of homosexual savants.
All churches who condemn us will be closed. Our only gods are handsome young men. We adhere to a cult of beauty, moral and esthetic. All that is ugly and vulgar and banal will be annihilated. Since we are alienated from middle-class heterosexual conventions, we are free to live our lives according to the dictates of the pure imagination. For us too much is not enough.
The exquisite society to emerge will be governed by an elite comprised of gay poets. One of the major requirements for a position of power in the new society of homoeroticism will be indulgence in the Greek passion. Any man contaminated with heterosexual lust will be automatically barred from a position of influence. All males who insist on remaining stupidly heterosexual will be tried in homosexual courts of justice and will become invisible men.
We shall rewrite history, history filled and debased with your heterosexual lies and distortions. We shall portray the homosexuality of the great leaders and thinkers who have shaped the world. We will demonstrate that homosexuality and intelligence and imagination are inextricably linked, and that homosexuality is a requirement for true nobility, true beauty in a man.
We shall be victorious because we are fueled with the ferocious bitterness of the oppressed who have been forced to play seemingly bit parts in your dumb, heterosexual shows throughout the ages. We too are capable of firing guns and manning the barricades of the ultimate revolution.
Tremble, hetero swine, when we appear before you without our masks."
Just one question, why will you never hear about this in the media?

THE DUNEGAN TAPES / THE NEW ORDER OF BARBARIANS:

The New Order Of The Barbarians: On March 20th, 1969, Dr. Lawrence Dunegan attended an astonishing lecture at a meeting of the Pittsburgh Pediatric Society. The lecturer was Dr. Richard Day who at the time was Professor of Pediatrics at Mount Sinai Medical School in New York. Day had previously served as Medical Director of Planned Parenthood Federation of America. Dr. Dunegan had been a student of Dr. Day's at the University of Pittsburgh and was thus well acquainted with him. Dr. Day had asked the attendees not to take notes or record what he was about to tell them during that lecture. The reason, Dr. Day implied, was that there would be negative repercussions – possibly personal danger – against him if it became widely known that he had talked about the information. Dr. Richard Day gave a lecture about the future plan for humanity. This plan wasn't meant only for the 20th century but rather it was meant to continue in the 21st century as well. When he got home that night, Dr. Dunegan wrote down much of what he had heard from Dr. Day during that lecture, notes which he kept to himself for almost 20 years. In 1988, Dr. Dunegan recorded on tape his memories of that astonishing lecture back in 1969 – these tapes have come to be known as "The Dunegan Tapes". "The Dunegan Tapes" in fact consists of 2 different tapes made in 1988.

I will be quoting directly from the tapes Dr. Lawrence Dunegan made himself in 1988 with my own commentary after a certain quote if needed (some of the things he said in the recording are either his own recollections of the lecture or quotes from Dr. Richard Day that he made during the lecture, if a text is in double quotation this means that that text is a direct quote coming out of Dr. Richard Day's mouth):

Just keep in mind that Dr. Richard Day was a Rockefeller family insider.

- Tape 1:

"He said – as we listened to what he was about to present – he said. "Some of you will think I'm talking about Communism. Well what I'm talking about is much bigger than Communism""

""everything is in place and nobody can stop us now.""

""Everything has two purposes. One is the ostensible purpose which will make it acceptable to people; and second, is the real purpose which would further the goals of establishing the new system and having it.""

"He was very active with population control groups, the population control movement, He said the population is growing too fast. Numbers of people living at any one time on the planet must be limited or we will run out of space to live. We will outgrow our food supply and we will over-pollute the world with our waste." Something fans of Aldous Huxley's – Brave New World Revisited should be familiar with

"People won't be allowed to have babies just because they want to. Most families would be limited to two. Some people would be allowed only one."

"Well, from population control, the natural next step then was sex. He said sex must be separated from reproduction. Sex is too pleasurable, and the urges are too strong, to expect people to give it up. Chemicals in food and in the water supply to reduce the sex drive is not practical. The strategy then would be not to diminish sex activity, but to increase sex activity, but in such a way that people won't be having babies." Again, something Huxley alluded to in 1932 in his original book – Brave New World

"Contraception would be very strongly encouraged, and it would be connected so closely in people's minds with sex, that they would automatically think contraception when they were thinking or preparing for sex. And contraception would be made universally available." Huxley also predicted this in his dystopian society. It's worth noting that Margaret Sanger (who I mentioned earlier) is the one who is credited with inventing the contraceptive pill while she worked for Planned Parenthood.

"marriage itself would be diminished in importance. He indicated some recognition that most people probably would want to be married... but that this certainly would not be any longer considered to be necessary for sexual activity."

"No surprise then, that the next item was abortion. "Abortion will no longer be a crime. Abortion will be accepted as normal", and would be paid for by taxes for people who could not pay for their own abortions. If school sex programs would lead to more pregnancies in children, that was really seen as no problem. Parents who think they are opposed to abortion on moral or religious grounds will change their minds when it is their own child who is pregnant. So this will help overcome opposition to abortion. Before long, only a few die-hards will still refuse to see abortion as acceptable, and they won't matter anymore."

"Homosexuality also was to be encouraged." People will be given permission to be homosexual." Everyone will be given permission to have sex, to enjoy however they want. Anything goes. In this regard, clothing was mentioned. Clothing styles would be made more stimulating and

provocative. Recall back in 1969 was the time of the mini skirt when those mini-skirts were very, very high and revealing. He said, "It is not just the amount of skin that is exposed that makes clothing sexually seductive, but other, more subtle things."

"Technology. Earlier he said. Sex and reproduction would be separated. You would have sex without reproduction and then technology was reproduction without sex. This would be done in the laboratory. He indicated that already, much, much research was underway about making babies in the laboratory." Huxley again

"Divorce would be made easier and more prevalent. Most people who marry will marry more than once. More people will not marry. This would tend to make the marriage relationship less stable and, therefore, tend to make people less willing to have babies. But one of the effects of easier divorce laws was to create instability in the families."

"Euthanasia, everybody has a right to live only so long. The old are no longer useful. They become a burden. You should be ready to accept death. And after you have had enough of them and you're no longer productive, working, and contributing, then you should be ready to step aside for the next generation." Huxley said in Brave New World that all people (he envisioned a world that is constantly populated by no less and no more than 2 billion people) would have the same life expectancy of 60 years, and then die of natural causes because they were designed biologically to do so.

"A big item – [that] was elaborated at some length – was the cost of medical care would be burdensomely high. Medical care would be connected very closely with one's work, but also would be made very, very high in cost so that it would simply be unavailable to people beyond a certain time. And unless they had a remarkably rich, supporting family, they would just have to do without care." Obamacare anyone?

"He said there would be new diseases to appear which had not ever been seen before. Would be very difficult to diagnose and be untreatable — at least for a long time. Some years later, as AIDS ultimately developed, I think AIDS was at least one example of what he was talking about. I now think that AIDS probably was a manufactured disease." In the book "Behold a Pale Horse" the author William Cooper said that AIDS is intended to decrease the population.

"Cancer - he said, "We can cure almost every cancer right now. Information is on file in the Rockefeller Institute, if it's ever decided that it should be released. But consider - if people stop dying of cancer, how

rapidly we would become overpopulated. You may as well die of cancer as something else. But at least for the time being, letting people die of cancer was a good thing to do because it would slow down the problem of overpopulation."" How convenient that he mentioned the Rockefeller family. This sinister family full of psychopaths funded the eugenics program in the U.S. at least since the nineteen hundreds onwards.

"Somewhere along in here there was also something about accelerating the onset of puberty." Why? Pedophilia?

"But the major religions of today have to be changed because they are not compatible with the changes to come. The old religions will have to go. Especially Christianity. Once the Roman Catholic Church is brought down, the rest of Christianity will follow easily." Whether you agree with religious views or not, destroying religion was always one of the Marxist plans.

"In order to do this, the Bible will be changed. It will be rewritten to fit the new religion. Gradually, keywords will be replaced with new words having various shades of meaning." Ever heard of the Gay Bible?

"Another area of discussion was Education. And one of the things in connection with education that I remember connecting with what he said about religion, was – in addition to changing the Bible – he said that the classics in Literature would be changed. But he said, the casual reader reading a revised version of a classic would never even suspect that there was any change. And, somebody would have to go through word by word to even recognize that any change was made in these classics; the changes would be so subtle. But the changes would be such as to promote the acceptability of the new system." Something George Orwell predicted in "1984"

"As regards to education, he indicated that kids would spend more time in schools, but in many schools they wouldn't learn anything. Overall, schooling would be prolonged. For most people, it would take longer to complete their education. So that a lot of school time would be just wasted time. Students would have to decide at a younger age what they would want to study and get onto their track early. Studies would be concentrated in much greater depth, but narrowed. You wouldn't have access to material in other fields, outside your own area of study, without approval. People would be very specialized in their own area of expertise. But they won't be able to get a broad education and won't be able to understand what is going on overall." In translation, people will not be able to see past their education a.k.a. indoctrination.

"Education would be lifelong. Adults would be going to school. There'll always be new information that adults must have to keep up. When you can't keep up anymore, you're too old. This was another way of letting older people know that the time had come for them to move on and take the "demise pill". If you get too tired to keep up with your education, or you got too old to learn new information, then this was a signal – you begin to prepare to get ready to step aside."

"Some books would just disappear from the libraries. Some books contain information or contain ideas that should not be kept around. And therefore, those books would disappear. Further down the line, not everybody will be allowed to own books. And some books NOBODY will be allowed to own." By this point, Orwell is probably rolling in his grave.

"Another area of discussion was laws that would be changed. Gambling laws would be repealed or relaxed, so that gambling would be increased. He indicated then that governments would get into gambling. And, at the time, we were already being told that would be the case. "Why should all that gambling money be kept in private hands when the State would benefit from it?" was the rationale behind it."

"Drug use would be increased. Alcohol use would be increased. Law enforcement efforts against drugs would be increased. On first hearing that it sounded like a contradiction. Why increase drug abuse and simultaneously increase law enforcement against drug abuse? But the idea is that, in part, the increased availability of drugs would provide a sort of law of the jungle whereby the weak and the unfit would be selected out. There was a statement made at the time: "Before the earth was overpopulated, there was a law of the jungle where only the fittest survived. You had to be able to protect yourself against the elements and wild animals and disease. And if you were fit you survived. But now we've become so civilized - we're over civilized - and the unfit are enabled to survive only at the expense of those who are more fit." And the abusive drugs then, would restore, in a certain sense, the law of the jungle, and selection of the fittest for survival. News about drug abuse and law enforcement efforts would tend to keep drugs in the public consciousness. And would also tend to reduce this unwarranted American complacency that the world is a safe place, and a nice place. The same thing would happen with alcohol. The vulnerable and the weak would respond to the promotions and therefore use and abuse more alcohol. Again, much more in the way of psychological services would be made available to help those who got hooked on drugs and alcohol. The idea being, that in order to

promote this - drug and alcohol abuse to screen out some of the unfit - people who are otherwise are pretty good also would also be subject to getting hooked. And if they were really worth their salt they would have enough sense to seek psychological counseling and to benefit from it. So this was presented as sort of a redeeming value on the part of the planners. It was as if he were saying, "you think we're bad in promoting these evil things - but look how nice we are - we're also providing a way out!"

- Tape 2 :

“"we" – we take control first of the port cities... New York, San Francisco, Seattle... the idea being that this is a piece of strategy. The idea being that if you control the port cities with your philosophy and your way of life, the HEARTLAND in between has to yield. I can't elaborate more on that but it is interesting, if you look around the most liberal areas of the country – and progressively so – are the seacoast cities; the heartland, the Midwest, does seem to have maintained its conservatism. But as you take away industry and jobs and relocate people then this is a strategy to break down conservatism. When you take away industry, and people are unemployed and poor they will accept whatever change seems to offer them survival; and their morals and their commitment to things will all give way to survival. That's not my philosophy. That's the speaker's philosophy.” Take a look at the last U.S. presidential election. The majority of coastal areas (California, New York etc.) voted for Killary Hilton (she had liberal policies especially regarding abortion) while most of Trump supporters were Midwest central more conservative Americans.

“Patriotism would go down the drain then.”“One of the upshots of all of this is that with this global interdependence then national identities would tend to be de-emphasized” One of the goals of Marxism was to destroy nation states.

“gun control is a big element in these plans......and everybody should be restricted in gun ownership.” Once again no surprise here. The liberal “progressive” leftists want to legalize everything (especially if they can put it on the human rights bandwagon) except the right to defend yourself and your family. It’s been a lifelong dream of all Leftists throughout history to ban guns.

“Very important in sports was sports for girls. Athletics would be pushed for girls. This was intended to replace dolls. Baby dolls would still be around, a few of them, but you would not see the number and variety of dolls. Dolls would not be pushed because girls should not be thinking about

babies and reproduction. Girls should be out on the athletic field just as the boys are. Girls and boys really need not to be all that different. Tea sets were to go the way of dolls, and all these things that traditionally were thought of as feminine would be de-emphasized as girls got into more masculine pursuits. Just one other thing I recall was that the sports pages would be full of the scores of girls teams just right along there with the boys' teams. And that's recently begun to appear after 20 years in our local papers. The girls' sports scores are right along with the boys' sports scores. So all of this to change the role model of what young girls should look to be. While she's growing up she should look to be an athlete rather to look forward to being a mother." I have elaborated on this enough in past chapters. Here you see more of the feminist-trendy propaganda that seeks to blend men and women as though they are the same. Like I said replace men's masculinity with femininity and replace women's femininity with masculine traits. This is the goal of the "gender equality" push – create a society of one gender, one gender that is unable to reproduce.

"Movies would gradually be made more explicit as regards sex and language. There would be pornographic movies in the theaters, on television. He said something like, "You'll see people in the movies doing everything you can think of." He went on to say that... and all of this is intended to bring sex out in the open." Just the thing we need to bombard young impressionable kids with.

"As regards music, he made a rather straightforward statement like, "Music will get worse." Lyrics would become more openly sexual. He went on to say that the music would carry a message to the young and nobody would even know the message was there. Entertainment would be a tool to influence young people......but the changes would be all aimed at the young, who are in their formative years" Just take a look at modern-day commercial rap (or better yet crap) – the worst genre of music that ever was. It promotes drugs, alcohol abuse, degrading women, unadulterated sexual liberation.

"Then, was the statement admitting that some scientific research data could be – and indeed HAS been – falsified in order to bring about desired results. And here was said, "People don't ask the right questions."

"People would be more and more used to the idea of relinquishing some national sovereignty." Marxism

"Privately owned housing would become a thing of the past. The cost of housing and financing housing would gradually be made so high that most people couldn't afford it. People who already owned their houses would be

allowed to keep them but as years go by it would be more and more difficult for young people to buy a house. Young people would more and more become renters, particularly in apartments or condominiums. More and more unsold houses would stand vacant. People just couldn't buy them. But the cost of housing would not come down. People would not be able to buy these and gradually more and more of the population would be forced into small apartments... small apartments which would not accommodate very many children." Marxism aimed to destroy private property. Just look at ex-Communist Russia. Anthony Ralph Epperson in his "The New World Order" writes page 134: *"So the problem in China is not too much population. It is too much Communism. It is too much 'New World Order' So the family unit in China, the cornerstone of their civilization for centuries, has essentially been destroyed by the Communist Party. And it was not destroyed by mistake. It was planned that way. And the Bolshevik Communists in the Soviet Union have nearly duplicated the 'success' of the Chinese Communists. The September, 1988 Reader's Digest magazine carried an article called Should We Bail Out Gorbachev? In which they discussed life in the Soviet Union. This is one of the comments made in that article: 'At least 13 million urban families still must live in communal apartments or dormitories, sharing bath, kitchen and even bedrooms with other families. In Moscow, newly constructed apartment complexes are crumbling.' So a great percentage of the Russian families do not have a place to live separate from other people. Married life does not seem exceptionally attractive to a young couple contemplating marriage. So, if the Communists are trying to destroy the family in Russia, one of the ways to do it would be to not construct enough government owned apartments or houses. And that is exactly what they have done."* Both Dunegan and Epperson are referring to so-called "small or mini apartments" (some even refer to them as "caskets" or "coffins"). These "homes" can accommodate 2 people at most (usually a couple) and no kids (which is the aim of the elite anyway). These apartments have in recent years gained massive popularity in the U.S. where more and more couples are opting for these so-called homes without the intention of having children (all planned in advance by the elite).

- Tape 3: Though not original, the third tape was made in 1991. The interviewer was Randy Engel, Director of the U.S. Coalition for Life. She interviewed Dr. Lawrence Dunegan regarding his original tapes from 1988. The following are excerpts from that interview.

Randy Engel: *"Speaking of children, I gather that this speaker... he kept on making the point about, well, old people, they're going to go by the wayside, so I presume that the emphasis for these controllers for this New World Order is really an emphasis on youth."*

Dr. Lawrence Dunegan: *"Absolutely. Yes. Emphasis on youth. This was stated explicitly. People beyond a certain age... they're set in their ways and you're not going to change them. They have values and they're going to stick to them. But you get to the youth when they're young, they're pliable. You mold them in the direction you want them to go. This is correct. They're targeting the young. They figure, "you old fogies that don't see it our way, you're going to be dying off or when the time comes we're going to get rid of you. But it's the youngsters we have to mold in the impression we want."" Now Something on homosexuality I want to expand on, I don't think this came out on the original tape, but there was, first of all, "We're going to promote homosexuality." And secondly "We recognize that it's bizarre abnormal behavior. But, this is another element in the law of the jungle, because people who are stupid enough to go along with this are not fit to inhabit the planet and they'll go by the wayside"." "And when I remember the one statement and remember the other statement, I believe AIDS is a disease which has been created in the laboratory and I think that one purpose it serves is to get rid of people who are so stupid as to go along with our homosexual program. Let them wipe themselves out. This is I think what happens... "If you're dumb enough to be convinced by our promotion of homosexuality you don't deserve a place and you're going to fall by the wayside sooner or later. We'll be rid of you. We'll select out... the people who will survive are those who are also smart enough not to be deluded by our propaganda."* Many, including the late William Cooper in his book "Behold the Pale Horse", have stated their opinion that AIDS will be used to wipe out the homosexuals. If this is true do you still think it's a good idea that homosexuality is increasing and is being promoted?

Randy Engel: *"But of the sexualization of the population... when he said on the tape, basically, "Anything goes", I think that is what we're seeing. It's not so much that, let's say, someone may not adopt the homosexual style for himself, but as a result of the propaganda he certainly will be a lot more tolerant of that type of behavior too."*

Dr. Lawrence Dunegan: *"With the power of propaganda you dare not be against homosexuals, otherwise you get labeled homophobe. You dare not be against any of our programs for women, otherwise you're a male chauvinist pig. It's like anti-Semitism." "What this boils down to me is these people say, "No, we take the place of God; we establish what will change and what will not change, so if we say that homosexuality or anything is moral today... wasn't yesterday, but it is today. We have said so, and therefore it's moral. We can change tomorrow. We can make it immoral again tomorrow". And this is the usurpation of the role of God." "I am god. WE are gods, because we decide what is moral what is moral tomorrow, what is going to be moral next year. WE determine change."*

Randy Engel: *"But with regard to change, he seemed to acknowledge that there were a couple of entities which traditionally blocked this change and therefore made people resistant to constant manipulation. And of course one of those is the family, and that would include grandmothers, grandfathers, our ethnic background and so forth and I guess I was impressed by everything he seemed to mention whether it was economics, music... had the overall effect of diminishing the family and enhancing the power of the state."*

Dr. Lawrence Dunegan: *"It has an ostensible purpose, and then it has a REAL purpose."*

Randy Engel: *"But that little statement about words, that "words will be changed. And people say, "That's not important". Of course, you know that's VERY important, otherwise, why would they bother to change it? Otherwise, why go through all this rigmarole if it isn't important? It's obviously important for them because they know WITH THE CHANGING OF WORDS YOU CHANGE IDEAS. I suppose they're going to come up with a pedophobia for those who have difficulties with pedophilia."* Changing the definition of words - Orwell would be proud.

Dr. Lawrence Dunegan: *"They're exerting a lot of effort and time to change it and they're not exerting effort on things that are NOT important, so yes, you're absolutely right. And to dictate the truth WE use. Sex education is NOT education. It's conditioning, and we should never use the term "sex education". It's a misnomer. If they control the vocabulary, then they can control the way we can think and the way we can express ideas among ourselves and to anybody. But "sex conditioning", "sex initiation" is much more accurate."*

Randy Engel: *"This Dr. Day was very much into the whole population control establishment, and he was of course in favor of abortion. So, inevitably, if you are going to go about killing the young, especially at the pace we seem to have adapted ourselves to in this country, then invariably you're going to have to do something about all those aging populations.*

Because, the few children who are born, after all, they cannot be expected to carry this tremendous burden of all these people."

Randy Engel: *"We've already discussed "sex without reproduction", then you also said the technology would be there for "reproduction without sex" and this is a whole other area because it's contradictory. If a land is so overpopulated, then you would want to diminish sexual activity, get rid of pornography, get rid of everything that was sexually stimulating. But, no. It's a contrary. You want to Increase sexual activity but only insofar as it doesn't lead to reproduction. That was the message, right?"* Huxley

Dr. Lawrence Dunegan: *"Yes. Now, reproduction without sex... what you would get then would have all the desirable attributes of a human being without any claim to human rights. The way we do it now, we say, you're human because you have a father and mother... you have a family and so you're a human being with human rights. But if your father was a petrie dish and you mother was a test tube, how can you lay claim to human rights? You owe your existence to the laboratory which conveys to you no human rights."* Huxley again

Randy Engel: *"In "Brave New World". I can remember reading Brave New World in high school, and thought, "Boy, is this fantasy land". Thirty years later and I said, "This is scary". There seems to be kind of a similarity between his writings and the talk given by Dr. Day, because you get kind of a mixed message in Brave New World, that these things are not really good. It would be better if man still had a sense of humor, a sense of privacy, if the family still existed.. but, it's inevitable. They're going to go. Too bad. I feel a little sorry about that. A little sentiment, but the New Order has to come in and we have to make room for it."* ...need I say more...

Dr. Lawrence Dunegan: *"I can't remember on the original tapes, did I mention the phrase where he said, "This time we're going to do it right!" ?"*

Randy Engel: *"No. You didn't."*

Dr. Lawrence Dunegan: *"There were so many details to remember. But when he mentioned bringing in the New World Order, he said, "This time we're going to do it right"."*

- Tape 4: The fourth tape was recorded during the second interview in 1997. He emphasized the notion of "sex without reproduction and reproduction without sex" (this, of course, has Huxley written all over it). During this interview Dr. Lawrence Dunegan said:

"because sexual instincts are so strong you might think that at first we might try to deemphasize sex but that's nearly impossible to do because

feelings are so strong, so the plan is to go the other way to encourage sexual activity, promote sexual desire, but do it in such a way that's directed away from reproduction. Contraceptive devices would be promoted in such a way that it would just be instinctive, natural when you were thinking about sex you would automatically connect it with contraception." Huxley said the same exact thing back in 1932

"When he was asked whether homosexuality was mentioned during the original lecture, Dr. Lawrence Dunegan replied: "That would be promoted, not just merely tolerated or permitted but actually to be promoted, the idea being that no child can ever result from a homosexual union."

"In regards to abortion he said "Even though that in 1969 abortion was a crime in every state, the lecturer told us that it won't be for long and that soon abortion will be seen as a right and be tax supported. The idea was to promote early sexual activity among the kids, connecting it strongly with the use of contraceptives, they would be taught that these two naturally go together, and with the realization that with more sexual activity there would be more pregnancies, but no need to worry about cluttering the planet with unwanted babies because then abortion would be available as a backup."

I strongly encourage you to either read the transcript of the tapes (only the first three tapes have transcripts) or to listen to the audio-tapes (especially the first two originals since they were recorded based on notes made right after the lecture). The tapes talk about a thousand different things, which I have not mentioned since they are not directly linked to the topic at hand.

JAFFE MEMORANDUM:

On the 11th of March 1969, Frederick S. Jaffe wrote a memo to Bernard Berelson called "Center for Family Planning Program Development." Frederick S. Jaffe was a vice president of Planned Parenthood (what a surprise). One of the organizations he consulted was the Rockefeller Foundation (even bigger surprise). In 1978 he was awarded the "Margaret Sanger award", Planned Parenthood's highest award (named after the psycho-witch herself). This memo advocates measures of population control that are rather disturbing. It consists of 9 pages. The first 8 pages talk about why and how the population should be decreased or kept at a maintainable level. Interestingly enough, the same exact reasons and methods mentioned in Jaffe's memorandum that are used as a justification for the policy of population control (examples: overpopulation, scarcity of resources, the control of birth rates, limiting population) are also mentioned in Aldous Huxley's 1958 work "Brave New World – Revisited." The 9th page of the memorandum is the most interesting, it summarizes the plan to alter society.

- Page 1:
"To: Bernard Berelson
From: Frederick S. Jaffe

This memorandum is responsive to your letter of January 24th, seeking ideas on necessary and useful activities relevant to formation of population policy, defined as "legislative measures, administrative programs, and other governmental actions that are designed to alter population trends or that actually do alter them." My observation will be limited to the United States" For at least a decade I have been saying that the U.S. is one big experiment. Once the elite figure out that something works in the U.S. (by works I mean "has disastrous consequences that the elite wants") then those methods are implemented into Western Europe, after that the rest of Europe and in the end the rest of the world.

"Apart from the abstraction that in the long run, a zero rate of population growth is inevitable, the arguments to justify an explicit U.S. policy now of encouraging a specific universal limit on family size. That an explicit U.S. policy to encourage or compel smaller family size in the U.S. in necessary" These nut-jobs are the same as "Church of Euthanasia" members, "The Greens or the Environmentalists" and "Global Warming Alarmists" (don't worry Global Warming does not exist). These people say things like "the world is overpopulated", "in order to save mother Earth humans must die" or "kill yourselves to save Earth". That is the unfortunate necessary bad side of freedom of speech, every nut-job has the right to say something stupid. These are the same people who advocate mass uncontrolled immigration from non-developed countries into the West. Let me get this straight, they promote "population control", "limitation of birth rates" or "reduction of the population" in Europe and North America to "save mother Earth as they say", but still support uncontrolled immigration of non-Europeans into Europe. So according to them, Europe and North America are overpopulated so they want to limit or reduce the population while at the same time promoting the increase of population of Europe and

North America through uncontrollable immigration of non-native Europeans into those same continents. Please, someone, explain to me the logic these "geniuses" use.

"The debate thus far (in government, within Planned Parenthood) has only with a few notable exceptions virtually ignored current actual U.S. fertility behaviour and its implications for public policies and programming. It has not seriously grabbled with public policies in other areas with the predictable political consequences of a major effort to adopt and enforce an anti-natalist U.S. population policy."

- Page 6:

"Fiscal and Monetary Policy which appears to regard inflation as a concomitant of full employment and thus, to accept relatively high (or at least preventable) unemployment levels as necessary. Yet, more women enter the labor market under condition of full employment and the relationship between employment of women and lower fertility seems well established. An example is needed if, in effect, the question: How much inflation could or should we risk to achieve lower fertility? (X% risk of inflation = Y% increase in women's employment = Z% reduction in fertility.)" In America The Federal Reserve System (a private centralized bank) prints money like crazy (a.k.a creates that money from thin air. Since unlike the Russian Ruble or ex-Gaddafi's Libyan dinar, the U.S. dollar is no longer backed by gold it is slowly being devalued) causing inflation, devaluing the dollar and destroying the U.S. economy. The worse the economy got (deliberately by the elite) the more women were pushed into the workforce which resulted in the decrease of fertility and birth rates since now women choose careers over having kids even though practically all studies show that both men and women are more likely to be happy if they have kids. But I dwelled on feminism long enough. Like I said feminism has nothing to do with empowering women or making them more independent, it's simply a tool that the elite use to achieve their goal.

"Welfare Policy" Ah, welfare – the "great" invention of the Socialist Utopia, the utopia that never was.

- Page 8:

"Is it feasible to expect that society will accept policies which curb fertility universally – is it more likely that those who are powerful will favor and adopt policies which affect primarily those who have less power or are powerless?" The same way Planned Parenthood used to and still targets

primarily black neighborhoods. Planned Parenthood – they planned for there to be no parents in the hood so that the government can "become" the de facto "parent".

This is the 9th page:

Table 1. Examples of Proposed Measures to Reduce U.S. Fertility, by Universality or Selectivity of Impact

Universal Impact	Selective Impact Depending on Socio-Economic Status		Measures Predicated on Existing Motivation to Prevent Unwanted Pregnancy
Social Constraints	**Economic Deterrents/Incentives**	**Social Controls**	
Restructure family: a) Postpone or avoid marriage b) Alter image of ideal family size	Modify tax policies: a) Substantial marriage tax b) Child tax c) Tax married more than single d) Remove parents' tax exemption e) Additional taxes on parents with more than 1 or 2 children in school	Compulsory abortion of out-of-wedlock pregnancies	Payments to encourage sterilization
Compulsory education of children	Reduce/eliminate paid maternity leave or benefits	Compulsory sterilization of all who have two children except for a few who would be allowed three	Payments to encourage contraception
Encourage increased homosexuality	Reduce/eliminate children's or family allowances	Confine childbearing to only a limited number of adults	Payments to encourage abortion
Educate for family limitation	Bonuses for delayed marriage and greater child-spacing	Stock certificate-type permits for children	Abortion and sterilization on demand
Fertility control agents in water supply	Pensions for women of 45 with less than N children	*Housing Policies:* a) Discouragement of private home ownership b) Stop awarding public housing based on family size	Allow certain contraceptives to be distributed non-medically
Encourage women to work	Eliminate Welfare payments after first 2 children		Improve contraceptive technology
	Chronic Depression		Make contraception truly available and accessible to all
	Require women to work and provide few child care facilities		Improve maternal health care, with family planning as a core element
	Limit/eliminate public-financed medical care, scholarships, housing, loans and subsidies to families with more than N children		

Source: Frederick S. Jaffe, "Activities Relevant to the Study of Population Policy for the U.S.," Memorandum to Bernard Berelson, March 11, 1969.

Let's go over these one by one:

- At the very top, it says "Proposed measures to Reduce Fertility" (if you look up recent and older studies one thing becomes apparent very quickly and that is that fertility levels in both men and women have been on a decline for decades)
- Social constraints: restructure family: "postpone or avoid marriage" (marriage is less frequent as it is, more young people are avoiding marriage all together even though all the studies show that unmarried people are more likely to be unhappy compared to married ones)
- "alter the image of the ideal family size, educate for family limitation" (Chinese – Communist style?)
- "Compulsory education of children" (does this include sexual education I covered earlier?)
- "Fertility control agents in water supply" (Fluoride? Fluoride is known to reduce the fertility levels in women. Read The Dunegan Tape 1 again)
- "Encourage increased homosexuality" (I think this needs no explanation, this is the main reason I am covering this memo)
- "Encourage women to work, require women to work and provide few child care facilities" (The feminist movement is no exception to the "It has an ostensible purpose, and then it has a REAL purpose" rule)
- "Tax married more than single, remove parent's tax exemption, additional taxes on parents with more than 1 or 2 children in school"
- "Compulsory abortion, compulsory sterilization of all who have two children except for a few who would be allowed three" (go back to the transcript of the Dunegan tapes and read them again)
- "Confine childbearing to only a limited number of adults" (isn't reproduction a right of every human being that can conceive naturally?)
- "Permits for children" (Margaret Sanger said it back in 1934)
- "Discourage of private home ownership, stop awarding public housing on family size" (Communism? Read the Dunegan tapes again)
- "Encourage sterilization, contraception, abortion" (so that only a select few elites can procreate?)

This memorandum is a dream come true for the gay/feminist coalition. Just look at all the things that have been accomplished that were stated in this memorandum or are being pushed and promoted now.

THIS CHAPTER IS DEDICATED TO ALL THE SCEPTICS THAT AS SOON AS THEY HEAR THE WORD AGENDA REFLEXLY SCREAM "CONSPIRACY THEORY" OR "CONSPIRACY THEORIST" WITHOUT DOING ABSOLUTELY ANY RESEARCH.

GAY AGENDA 21

CHAPTER 8 "HOW IS THE GAY AGENDA BEING PUSHED?"

There will be 3 stages of human enslavement. I call them "1984", "Brave New World" and "Transhumanism"

1984 and Brave New World: Over the decades many have argued which one of these novels is better and which one more accurately represents the future of mankind. I think neither is better since they both show the same future intended for humanity only at different timelines. For some reason, people think these are two completely unconnected books. I have an alternative proposition, that they complement each other. There is a reason I call "Brave New World" the unofficial sequel to "1984" even though "Brave New World" was written earlier than its counterpart. How dare I make such a claim?

It is my honest opinion that the "Brave New World" is a continuation of "1984." On first glance, it makes no sense since "Brave New World" was published in 1932 while "1984" was published in 1948 but bear with me. Here are the reasons for this claim.

In "1984", George Orwell only alludes to the goals that are accomplished in "Brave New World."

In "1984" Orwell imagined a dystopian society in which he said some interesting stuff. Even though the traditional/nuclear family still exists in "1984", in the book it says that that will soon change. In this world, people are allowed to marry and have a family only in the interest of procreation, even though he writes that this is only a temporary right. They will have this ability only until the government finds a way to control the reproductive system, procreation and birth control. According to the book, their scientists are confident that in the near future they will be able to separate sex and reproduction seeing that sex is too powerful of an emotion. The scientists also mentioned that soon they will be able to abolish the orgasm. It's also mentioned that the educational system will be used to indoctrinate kids against their parents - further dissolution of the family. The goal of the state/government is to "become" the new parent by taking the reproductive rights away from men and women, and this will take place when technology becomes more sophisticated and when there is no need for conventional means of conception. O'Brien, a character that is a part of the establishment in "1984", said the following *"We have cut the links between child and parent, between man and woman. No one dares to trust a wife or a child any longer. But in the future, there will be no wives. Children will be taken from their mothers at birth, as one takes eggs from a hen. The sex instinct will be eradicated. Procreation will be an annual formality like the renewal of a ration card. We shall abolish the orgasm. Our neurologists are at work upon it now. There will be no loyalty, except loyalty towards the Party. There will be no love, except the love of Big Brother."* – "Children will be taken from their mothers at birth, as one takes eggs from a hen." how reminiscent of Karl Marx's and Frederick Engels's 'Manifest of the Communist Party' in which they write on Page 40: *"All children will be educated in state establishments from the time when they can do without the first maternal care."* and on Page 49: *"Education of all children, from the moment they can leave their mother's care, in national establishments at national cost."* Just remember that Melissa Victoria Harris-Perry (whom I mentioned in chapter 6) said that children should not be raised by their parents but by entire communities. If this isn't Communist talk I don't know what is.

It is worth mentioning that "1984" has a lot in common with Ray Bradbury's masterpiece "Fahrenheit 451" published in 1953. In "Fahrenheit 451", another dystopian society, the protagonist's wife is disgusted with the thought of having children. Her female friends are proud of having multiple abortions and more than one divorce. In this world more and more couples are unwilling to have children since motherhood and fatherhood are deemed as something unwanted. Similar to "1984" where documents (historical documents) are either rewritten or burned, in "Fahrenheit 451" books are forbidden and if found burned, while those in possession of books are killed or jailed. Decades after his book Ray Bradbury wrote a letter regarding his novel, at the end of the letter he wrote: *"There is no one way you can burn a book. But the world is full of people running with lit matches in their hands. Every minority: Baptists, Irish, Italians, Zionists, homosexuals has a will to spill kerosene and ignite the fuse."* This was his response to the offended people after being criticized for not implementing more female main characters in his novels. The LGBT community is not burning books they disagree with (even though they have written a Gay Bible in which Jesus was a homosexual) but they and their supporters are committing censorship in other ways. I have already covered how the liberal-left pro-gay members infiltrated the scientific community and pulled homosexuality off the list of mental disorders without any research but rather because it fit the popular narrative at that time. Another propaganda piece that they are propagating is the born this way myth for which they have yet to find any proof but are happily teaching kids about it in elementary schools around the U.S.A and Europe.

In "Brave New World" Aldous Huxley takes this to a whole new level. If "1984" is a dystopian nightmare then "Brave New World" is a living Tartarus on Earth. Orwell only alluded to the things that are completely in fruition in "Brave New World." In this world there is no marriage, family of any kind, kids are made in test tubes and raised by the state. Kids are made, not born, in laboratories. The words "mother" and "father" are considered curse words (go back to chapter 5 and look again at the laws I have stated that are banning the words like "mother", "father", "husband", "wife", "boy" and "girl" then come back and tell me if it's all just a conspiracy theory). The "bad old days" of a mother and father raising their own kids are gone. Sex does exist but it doesn't lead to reproduction (sex without reproduction – something Dr. Lawrence Dunegan talks about) because men and women are programmed from birth to associate sex with contraception (again, something Dr. Lawrence Dunegan talks about in his tapes). The book describes this to be subconscious, as soon as they think about sex they immediately think about contraception because they are programmed from birth to do so. Sex is, alongside the imaginary drug called "soma" used as a form of new age "bread and circuses" to keep the populace fed and under control. Huxley said that the primary goal of "soma" is to keep the population content in their own slavery since they know of nothing better than that with which they are presented. Since sex does not lead to reproduction the population is maintained through births in laboratories (the population in this world does not change, it always stays at 2 billion). Here you can see the true meaning of "sex without reproduction and reproduction without sex". If you still think it's a conspiracy theory go and listen to the Dunegan tapes again. When it comes to relationships (if you could call them that) in "Brave New World" they are eerily similar to our own world, or the world we are slowly but surely entering. The relationships as we know don't exist, in "Brave New World" people have multiple sexual partners and adultery is rampant. Relationships are not monogamous and last for 3 months at best, long-term relationships and marriage don't exist. If by any chance anyone has a long-ish term relationship or emotionally invests in their sexual partner they are sent to rehabilitation by the state, because the state doesn't want people showing genuine affection to one another. In one of the chapters, a female character named "Lenina" is talking to her female friend. Lenina is proud that she is cheating on her boyfriend (even though boyfriend isn't something akin to our definition of the word) but is mad at him for having another girlfriend while he is in a "relationship" with her. Long-term relationships don't exist, sex is only used to keep the population satisfied in their hedonistic ways. The whole reproductive system and the system of raising kids are controlled by the government. From birth (birth in this book means hatching from test tubes) kids are bombarded with rhetoric that "soma" is good, family and marriage are old-fashioned (an archaic institution of a bygone era), kids laugh at the thought that a female once gave birth to children. All of the characters in this novel are unhappy with their lives but they don't know anything outside the narrative they were fed their entire lives, they are conditioned to use the drug "soma" anytime they feel sad, depressed or lonely thus they spend a large portion of their week in a vegetative state not changing their way of life since it is the only way of life they know of. They, as Huxley said enjoy their servitude. A quote from Huxley's Brave New World – Revisited Chapter 4 Propaganda in a Democratic Society *"In Brave New World non-stop distractions of the most fascinating nature (the feelies, orgy-porgy, centrifugal bumble-puppy) are deliberately used as instruments of policy, for the purpose of preventing people from paying too much attention to the realities of the social and political situation."*

"Brave New World" represents a feminist utopia, a true depiction of the "sex without reproduction and reproduction without sex" statement. Nowadays, feminists say that they don't need men for reproduction since scientists have designed synthetic sperm, while men (members of MGTOW) say that they don't need women or marriage since they have porn, prostitutes, promiscuous women and in the future they will have sex-robots.

"The Sexodus: The Men Giving Up On Women And Checking Out Of Society" (source: Breitbart.com)

"This Is Why Men Are Giving Up On Women And Why Women Are Giving Up On Men - Statistics are suggesting that there will be more people who will stay single now than at any other point in history. Men and women are both checking out of the dating scene in droves, and it leaves many people wondering why this is happening in such large quantities. And why right now?" (source: rebelcircus.com)

"Why Young Men Are Giving Up On Marriage - Fewer young men in the US want to get married than ever" (source: worshipgh.com)

"Young men giving up on marriage: 'Women aren't women anymore" (source: lifesitenews.com) Why you may ask yourselves, it's because marriage no longer benefits men like it used to.

"Modern Men Prefer Porn Over Marriage, Study Reports - Young men are choosing pornography over marriage, a new study is reporting." (source: newseveryday.com) Remember when I said that men are choosing porn, prostitutes and easy women over marriage?

"The real goal of sexbots and artificial reproduction is making women obsolete" (thefederalist.com)

"Sexbots: Why Women Should Panic - Sex with robots will be 'the norm' in 50 years, say experts." (source: Breitbart.com) The first stage of transhumanism.

"SEX ROBOTS ARE BECOMING A BETTER OPTION THAN WESTERN WOMEN" (source: returnofkingsw.com)

"Scientists Have Made The Best Artificial Sperm Yet, And They're Breeding Mice With It" (source: sciencealert.com)

"Scientists claim they can create babies without men by injecting eggs with artificial sperm" (source: mirror.co.uk.)

"Scientists use skin cells to create artificial sperm and eggs" (source: theguardian.com)

"Scientists Have Made Artificial Sperm, and They Used It to Fertilize Eggs" (source: futurism.com)

"No men OR women needed: Scientists create sperm and eggs from stem cells" (source: dailymail.co.uk) Many years ago people laughed when I said that it's only a matter of time before science finds a method by which procreation can occur without a woman or man or both.

"Scientists Have Created the First Artificial Embryo Without Using an Egg or Sperm" (source: gizmodo.com)

"Sperm Made From Female Bone Marrow, Men Obsolete?" (source: science.slashdot.org) Are men obsolete? I guess feminists can finally be happy, their goal is achieved.

"Death of the father: British scientists discover how to turn women's bone marrow into sperm - British scientists are ready to turn female bone marrow into sperm, cutting men out of the process of creating life. The breakthrough paves the way for lesbian couples to have children that are biologically their own. Gay men could follow suit by using the technique to make eggs from male bone marrow." (source: dailymail.co.uk) One of

the ways artificial insemination is going to be pushed is as a right for homosexuals to have kids of their own, not even adoption rights are enough for them apparently. What about those kids born with genes from 2 women or 2 men, what about them, did they have a say in the matter, did they choose this – to not have a father or a mother? No, of course not, their rights are not important. Who cares about the kids, it's more important that homosexuals have rights at the expense of the rights of a kid to have a mother and a father.

"Chinese scientists may have made males obsolete by successfully engineering artificial sperm." (source: someecards.com)

"Men could have babies WITHOUT women by creating artificial eggs from skin cells - Scientists are working on an experimental technique which could one day remove women from the baby-making process." (source: thesun.co.uk)

All of these, and many more, examples of perversion of the natural process of reproduction are only possible in our time – a time where morals are considered a social construct, a complete inversion, where up is down and down is up, moral is immoral and immoral is moral. Not only does this raise many moral and ethical questions but also the repercussions are unknown. Will kids that are "born" (better term is made) this way be normal without deficiencies, not to mention those in the scientific community that are against combining genes of 2 women or 2 men and creating these chimera babies claiming that there are negative consequences for the child born that way. The elite are trying to make women and men obsolete one step at a time. Our species will not survive the separation of the sexes. But that is just it, those who are pushing this agenda would like nothing more than the annihilation of our species as we know it. I said it once I'll say it again the elite have stated their goal, they want to make the population bisexual and later on asexual. Why? In order for the state to achieve its goal of taking over the reproduction process they have certain steps. First, they will make men and women unwilling to procreate (this is more clear now than ever before) and in the end, men, and women will not be able to procreate which is when the state takes over the reproduction process away from those that can conceive naturally. Thus parental rights are transferred from mothers and fathers to the state.

In 1958 Huxley wrote "Brave New World - Revisited" in which he admitted that the family is going to be destroyed by sexual liberation. Here is a quote in which he reflects on his original "Brave New World." From Chapter 3 – Over organization: *"The society described in Brave New World is a world-state, in which war has been eliminated and where the first aim of the rulers is at all costs to keep their subjects from making trouble. This they achieve by (among other methods) legalizing a degree of sexual freedom (made possible by the abolition of the family) that practically guarantees the Brave New Worlders against any form of destructive (or creative) emotional tension."*

There is, after all, a significant difference between "1984" and "Fahrenheit 451" on one side and "Brave New World" on the other side. In "1984" and "Fahrenheit 451" books are banned and whoever is in possession of one is punished (the people are controlled by fear), while in "Brave New World" books are not banned, they don't need to be banned because people don't want to read (people haven't got any interest in books thus the ruling elite have no need for banning books). This is done, as Huxley described, through genetic standardization, post-natal conditioning, electroshock therapy, the use of a drug called "soma" and hypnopedia from cradle to grave. In "Brave New World" people love their servitude. I don't think I need to tell you which prediction is more accurate.

These novels (1984 and Brave New World) are not works of madmen but rather are a prediction and a warning for the future. Both Orwell and Huxley got their information from the same place. Both were members of the Fabian Society in London. The Fabian Society (a Socialist school) is a precursor of the Frankfurt School in Germany (another Socialist school) which I will cover later on. There is a reason why Orwell only alluded to the stuff Huxley developed in such great detail in his book. Orwell only had partial knowledge because he left the Fabian Society after he disagreed with their view for the future plans for humanity. Meaning Huxley knew more because he stayed a member for a longer time thus getting more information. The majority of people think that Orwell named his novel "1984" just by flipping the last two numbers of the year he had finished writing his book – in 1948. But this is not the case, the real reason for the title "1984" is the Fabian Society – which was formed in 1884, "1984" was the one hundred year anniversary of the Fabian Society.

"Brave New World" and "1984" are not instruction manuals, they were and still are warnings. It's time we move both of these books from the "fiction" bookshelf to the "non-fiction" bookshelf.

Transhumanism: is the end goal, and the final form of a collectivist utopia (should I say dystopia). The topic of Transhumanism would need to be covered in a separate book, which is the reason I will not dwell on it for too long. Transhumanism is the goal of the technocratic elite.

The term transhumanism was coined by Julian Huxley (Aldous Huxley's older brother). Julian Huxley was the first director of UNESCO and a prominent eugenicist – like all the Huxley family members.

David Icke, by no means a person who is against the LGBT community, said some interesting stuff about the topic at hand. In 2017 in Belgrade Serbia, he held a 13-hour long lecture on various topics. He said that the government wants to destroy the nuclear family and take away kids from their biological parents in order to take the role of parenthood. In regards to this, he rightfully said that the gay laws and legislation in the U.S. are not there to protect gay people but rather to silence anyone who has a different opinion. When it comes to transsexuality he said that the transsexual/transgender movement is being pushed to confuse kids, he also said something that never occurred to me. He added that transsexuality/transgenderism is a stepping stone towards transhumanism.

These are the three of the most sinister organizations on planet Earth (known in the public arena):

- Monsanto: the Big Pharma Complex promotes genetically modified organisms (GMO food / Frankenstein food / cancer food) through the implementation of Codex Alimentarius
- Planned Parenthood: designed to destroy the family and promote abortion
- DARPA (Defense Advanced Research Project Agency): leading technocratic organization for the transhumanist agenda

CULTURAL MARXISM:

Difference between Classical Marxism and Cultural Marxism:

Classical Marxism, Communism, Socialism (call it what you want): in the simplest terms it is a social conflict or struggle between the "have not's" and the "have's", the oppressed and the oppressors, the exploited and the ones who are supposedly doing the exploitation, the proletariats and the bourgeoisie usually personified by some sort of revolution and fast pace changes in society.

Cultural Marxism: is the conflict between the oppressed (or better yet the ones who want to be presented as the oppressed – LGBT in the west) and the alleged oppressors (anyone who disagrees with them). Sometimes Cultural Marxism is referred to as Gradual Marxism because unlike Classical Marxism, it has a more gradual, methodic approach to changing society. This is done, not by one single revolution, but by decades and throughout multiple generations of people.

Cultural Marxism relies on Karl Marx's Critical Theory which says that the majority is by definition privileged and the oppressor, while the minority is at a disadvantage and is oppressed. According to this theory in order to reach equality between the majority and the minority in society, the minority must gain in numbers. Translated in today's world this looks something like this: if heterosexuals are the majority in society the solution/answer is to increase other forms of sexuality, if cisgender (cisgender is a person who identifies as the gender they were born) people are the majority the solution/answer is to increase transgenderism, if white people are the majority in white native countries the solution/answer is racial diversity (multiculturalism/ forced uncontrolled migration). This principle can be applied to virtually anything, you only need to have some minority that may or may not be oppressed (if the minority isn't oppressed like the LGBT population in the west, make it seem as they are oppressed) and the majority who will be presented as the oppressor – Divide et impera.

Marxism had 3 goals:

- Destroy national sovereignty and national identity
- Destroy the family
- Destroy religion

Why am I talking about this you might ask yourselves. Cultural Marxism comes from the Frankfurt school (a Socialist school of thought), it gained in popularity in the 1920s. The Frankfurt school is preceded by the Fabian Society in London (known for their gradual, slow approach to changing society from within, hence why their logo is a tortoise – slow and steady wins the race). Many of the members of the Frankfurt School have infiltrated the west as intellectuals and academics. This is what led some to say that Universities have become Marxist churches. Marxism and churches – a true oxymoron.

Here are a few things that came out of the Frankfurt school through Cultural Marxism and have infiltrated our society:

-Political correctness, though presented as something to ensure that feelings of no one would be hurt, in reality, it is a powerful weapon people use to shut down any political or social discourse. In practice, political correctness ends a debate as soon as someone's feelings get hurt. Somehow to these "special snowflakes" their feelings are more important than an honest/objective debate and yet they are the same people who supposedly preach tolerance of ideas and opinions.

-Social Justice Warriors (SJW), presented as a sort of freedom fighters, yet they always resort to violent rhetoric once their theories are challenged or opposed. The modern-day Left generally uses violence and intimidation tactics once their arguments fail (example: the group ANTIFA-meaning anti-Fascist, yet they are renown for using classic Fascist tactics). The easiest job in the world is being a social justice warrior or human rights activists because there is no limit to the number of things that could be added to the human rights bandwagon. Things have gotten so out of hand that now there are people that make a living by arguing that pedophiles should be given rights to satisfy their sexual degeneracy.

-Moral relativism, one of the more iconic theories that came out of Cultural Marxism. Remember what I said in an earlier chapter – to these nut-jobs everything is a social construct. This ideology also stems from the postmodernist movement. Postmodernism, just like the name suggests, came after modernism. The aim of postmodernism is the deconstruction of society, the deconstruction of everything known to humans, something on par with nihilism. These people say morality is a social construct or is relative yet they call you immoral if you disagree with LGBT ideology. The elite wants to make morals relative (practically arbitrary) because this way they are the ones who can define what is moral and what isn't, what was moral will be immoral and what was considered immoral shall be moral at the whim of the elite. This will result in that the elite, and not the societal moral compass, will decide what is wrong and what is right (another thing Dr. Lawrence Dunegan talks about in his tapes).

Postmodernism is the deconstruction of everything and I do mean everything. Long gone are the days of the search for objective truths, enter postmodernism which promoted relativism or better yet absolute relativism. According to these nuts, there is no such thing as objective truth and we should not waste our time trying to find it, instead of that they promote the idea of relative truth. This is an extreme version of humanism, where it is no longer humanity that is at the center of things but rather the world revolves around each and every human (Sound familiar? The "me, me, me" or the "mine, mine, mine" millennial generation.). Postmodernism argues that everything is relative, including reality itself. Since reality is relative/subjective to every person and not objective there are as many realities as there are humans. In this case, all of these realities are equal and are equally valid since no one can disprove the existence and validity of one of the realities because objective truth does not exist. Objective truth does not exist and all realities are true – this means one can not infringe on another person's reality. This leaves us in a precarious situation if there is a reality that exists only in my head the rest of the population has no right to refute that reality. This is one of the bases for transsexual teachings. If I, a born male start identifying as a female you have no right to argue against my reality and must accept me as a female. This is how Socialists from the Fabian society started changes in society.

Communism, Socialism (including National Socialism), Marxism, Bolshevism or Stalinism, call it whatever you want, they are all the same only with a different mask, they all are forms of collectivism and they all exist on the left side of the political spectrum. They all are movements that resulted from postmodernism. In the "Manifesto of the Communist Party" by Karl Marx and Frederick Engels under the section "Proletarians and Communists" it states page 26: *"But Communism abolishes eternal truths, it abolishes all religion, and all morality, it therefore acts in contradiction to all past historical experiences."*

Cultural Marxism in its essence aims to destroy the values on which Europe and North America are built on, and that includes the traditional family unit. The "free love/hippie movement" is actually a Communist movement or its subsidiary, go back and read again what happened to Russia once Communists took over. Polyamory, which is going to be one of the next "free love" movements, is nothing more than hippie crap.

Was Cultural Marxism (and not Classical Marxism/Communism) what Joseph McCarthy was referring to during the "McCarthyism" era, an era of Communistic paranoia?

FREEDOM OF SPEECH IS DEAD:

Another quote from Eric Kaiser: *"you got freedom of speech until you speak against their policies"*. Even though this is something that can be applied to nearly any situation, there are not many groups that are protected so vehemently as the LGBT. Just look at how vigorously anyone (including those in the scientific community) gets attacked for challenging and/or disproving their queer theories, whether it is the myth of innate homosexuality, born in the wrong body theory, theories about infinite numbers of sexual identities and sexual orientations. So let me get this straight, proponents of queer theories get promoted and financed to spread their opinions (even though they have yet to be proven correct) and those who argue against those theories (again, scientists included, with research to back their claims) get fired from their jobs and labeled as homophobes/transphobes – the leftists definition of equality I presume. After all, if you can't win a debate with arguments you might as well "handicap" your opponent by cutting his right to disagree. So you end up with three types of people, the ones who agree with the popular notion that the Gay Agenda is pushing, those who for whatever reason don't agree but are in most cases unwillingly "forced" to stay silent knowing all too well what are the repercussions of exposing this agenda, and finally the agnostics, so too say, of the debate – those who simply don't care claiming that this doesn't concern them (how wrong they are). If you agree with the gay movement you get a platform from which to voice your opinion, but if you don't agree with the movement you get silenced under the guise of hate speech. The funniest part of the whole situation is the fact that the same people who supposedly grant us the right of free speech are the same people who decide what is considered hate speech thus branding any usage of free speech with which they don't agree with as hate speech. This is nothing more than the intolerance of the so-called "tolerant" Left. Take into consideration that nowadays everyone is so easily offended, any criticism towards any group regarding anything can be defined as hate speech. Like I said feelings are more important than truth – the truth hurts. Freedom of speech is a right to offend someone, sorry but words can't hurt people.

THE HYPOCRISY OF THE LEFT:

If hypothetically speaking a father decided to take his 13-year-old son to a striptease bar (note: I am not advocating for fathers to take their sons to striptease bars, I'm merely using it as an example) the Leftists (Left-wingers) would be outraged at how could this father dare take his son to such a degrading place (fair enough I agree). But if that same father were to take his son to a gay pride parade to show his support, Leftists would uphold the father and hail him as a morally exalted human being. According to leftists, a father who takes his son to a striptease bar is barbaric but parents who take their kids to gay pride parades are great parents. I mean what's the harm? They aren't going to see anything unusual at those parades, right? Wrong, what they will see is a hedonistic, nihilistic, vapid culture, they will see gay men dressed as dogs pretending to be animals, they will see kids dressed in bondage or close to butt-naked, they will see people dressed in costumes that depict reproductive organs (female and male), they will see half-naked people performing what can only be described as almost sex on the streets, they will see a multiplicity of destructive lifestyles. So apparently a father taking his son to a striptease bar to see a pair of boobs is worse than parents who take their kids to participate in gay parades where they will be exposed to far worse stuff than in the striptease bar. Please explain to me how that works, then again in a previous chapter I mentioned real-life scenarios in which schools don't need the parent's consent to take their children to partake in gay parades.

Supposedly we live in a secular western world, the church and state are separate. The church can't influence the state and vice versa. This is not the case. We have accepted the notion that the definition of today's marriage derives from Christian theology (even though previously I discussed that heterosexual marriage as an institution existed who knows how many thousands of years before Christianity) but yet it's the state that defines marriage in reality. We get the situation where the church can't influence the state in defining marriage but the state can influence/force its definition of marriage on the church (not so secular if you ask me). What if the church doesn't want to accept the state's definition of marriage (i.e. doesn't want to change the definition of marriage). In that case, the state, a benevolent all caring behemoth, will force the church to adhere to the new definition of marriage. First churches, synagogues, mosques will have their tax-exempt status removed and in the future, if they don't comply with the state's definition of marriage they will have their license to marry revoked. The same thing will happen if churches refuse to cater to a gay wedding (so much for religious freedom).

It's mainly leftists that say that the planet is overpopulated and that we need to lower the human population, while at the same time advocating for artificial insemination for those who can't conceive naturally – mostly aimed towards homosexuals. Please tell me how this makes sense. Kill heterosexuals so that fewer people could procreate but give gay people the right to have children of their own.

FIRST THEY CAME FOR RELIGIOUS PEOPLE:

Why do I, a non-religious person, care about religious rights? To explain this I'm going to use a quote by Voltaire: *"I disapprove of what you say, but I will defend to the death your right to say it."*

Why are they targeting religion and religious people first? It simple, religious arguments against gay marriage don't hold weight. For a religious argument to be taken into consideration it requires for all parties involved to be religious – otherwise, if a person is not religious a religious argument won't convince him. This is why religious people hinging on religious arguments against gay marriage have lost the debate. That is why in recent years religious people (Ben Shapiro, Henry Makow, Michael Savage, Alex Jones) no longer use religious arguments to oppose gay marriage since they know those arguments are fruitless, rather they use logic and evidence.

The war on religion is the first but most certainly not the last step on the path to silence people with opposing opinion.

Let's put it this way, yesterday they took away religious rights, today they infiltrated science rendering it bias, tomorrow anyone who for whatever reason doesn't agree with their agenda will be silenced. It's only a matter of time before my right to disagree is taken away. So, instead of waiting for the inquisition to knock on my door (by which point it will be too late since there will not be anyone else willing to protect my right to voice an opinion) I might as well protect other people rights to disagree before I regret staying silent. Albert Einstein said it best *"The world will not be destroyed by those who do evil, but by those who watch them without doing anything."* This is why I despise passive pacifism.

FORMAL EDUCATION A.K.A. INDOCTRINATION:

Why are they targeting kids? The younger the better (go read the Dunegan tapes again). Because kids are more impressionable, their minds are not formed and can be molded into whatever the elite want. And what the elite want is an obedient society that won't challenge their stances. If they condition the young ones into accepting the LGBT narrative, when those kids become adults they are far more likely to have a positive view of the LGBT movement. Those same adults are then far more likely to educate their kids into accepting and promoting LGBT-like behavior, and the cycle continues. I have already covered the horrors that are school sex-educational programs. In the U.S. and Canada, they now have Gay-history classes where kids who don't know how to read yet are being taught about prominent gay activists. Kids who don't yet grasp the concept of gender are taught about the LGBTQRPSAA (insert new language). And if you are a parent who, for whatever reason disagrees with this, your kid gets expelled and you get reported to social services. They are now proposing that the government should have the right to take your child away if you don't agree with the gay movement. Don't believe me?

"Ontario passes 'totalitarian' bill allowing gov't to take kids from Christian homes. TORONTO, June 1, 2017 — Ontario's Kathleen Wynne Liberals have passed what critics describe as "totalitarian" Bill 89 by a vote of 63 to 23 on the last day before Queen's Park adjourns for the summer. Pro-family advocates warn Bill 89 gives the state more power to seize children from families that oppose the LGBTQI and gender ideology agenda, and allows government agencies to effectively ban couples who disagree with that agenda from fostering or adopting children. But the "same activists who cried discrimination in 1995 [are] now actively legislating the same discrimination upon Bible-believing Christians. Will the left never feel ashamed of its hypocrisy?" (source: lifesitenews.com) Simple answer NO.

This bill is now valid only in Ontario, though there are talks about it regulating the whole of Canada in the future.

The bill says that if a child's parents denied the child's preferred identity (they mean gender identity here, one of infinite gender identities) that could be considered child abuse and the state can take the child away and place them in foster care.

The headline *"Canada's New Law Lets Government Take Children Away If Parents Don't Accept Their Gender Identity"* (source: heatst.com) This should not come as a surprise since Canada has a liberal government.

This is only the beginning. Expect more laws to come under some kind of false pretence. This is being pushed under the guise of "tolerance", "anti-discrimination", "positive discrimination", "equality", "some kind of reparation" and the ones who are pushing it are one of the most intolerant and discriminatory groups there are.

There is another reason they are targeting kids. The more people have LGBT friends and family members who are homosexuals and the more people have homosexual experiences (which are an ever-growing number of people, especially amongst the younger crowd and amongst women) the higher chance is that they will be tolerant and accepting towards any and all LGBT propaganda. The earlier they start the faster the elite will achieve their goal.

Across the western world, parents are opting for homeschooling, a system where one parent works and the other stays home with the kids and acts as an educator. There are numerous reasons as to why this is gaining in popularity, one of them being the fact that parents are slowly rebelling against the gay agenda which is evident by them not wanting for their kids to be indoctrinated with LGBT ideology by the state. Parents are the first educators of children, but of course, the state has other plans. In the last few years, there has been a push from the top echelons of the U.S. government to ban homeschooling. The reason is quite simple, the state wants to eradicate parents from the child raising picture so it can control the flow of information children get on a daily basis and they do this through formal education.

THE TRANSGENDER ISSUE:

I would like to start by saying I don't believe in the "born in the wrong body" theory. That being said I would also like to add that in the grand scheme of things I do think that there is a higher chance of transsexuality being closer to normal than homosexuality. On one hand, there is no biological reason for the existence of homosexuality, and on the other, I could see transsexuality being valid, though I don't think it is.

Pro-transgender activists say that transgender people are born in the wrong body, yet it's the transgender crowd and feminists that say gender is a social construct. On the one hand, they say that people are born male or female (sometimes in the wrong body) but they also claim that genders (both female and male) are social conventions and don't truly exists outside of enforced social norms. If gender is a social construct than one can't be born in the wrong body since gender is not predetermined. Which one is it? These two notions completely contradict each other, but both are being pushed as valid theories.

Was Camille Paglia (transgender herself) perhaps right when she said that transsexual phenomena are normal in very small numbers, but that the modern day transsexual movement is blown way out of proportion?

When it comes to scientific research and studies, they are conflicting. There is research pointing that transsexual behavior is normal (in some cases) and there is research denouncing the validity of transsexual behavior.

In one of the previous chapters, I mentioned that the suicide rate in the transsexual community does not change pre and post-sex-change operation (it stays around 40 percent). Another thing, depending on which study you look at around 20-25 percent of transsexuals that go through the sex-change operation start identifying as the gender they were born as and end up regretting the sex-change operation.

So, after all this transsexual indoctrination in schools, media, brainwashed parents, is there any surprise that we now see the aftermath of the LGBT movement on the kids?

The title *"SEX-CHANGE treatments for kids on the rise", the article continues "A small but growing number of teens and even younger children who think they were born the wrong sex are getting support from parents and from doctors who give them sex-changing treatments, according to reports in the medical journal Pediatrics. It's an issue that raises ethical questions, and some experts urge caution in treating children with puberty-blocking drugs and hormones. An 8-year-old second-grader in Los Angeles is a typical patient. Born a girl, the child announced at 18 months, "I a boy" and has stuck with that belief. The family was shocked but now refers to the child as a boy."* (source: CBS News)

"Rise in Transgender Children in UK Fuels Identity Fears" (source: nbcnews)

"Rise in transgender children puts British primary schools under pressure" the article says the following "UK primary schools are attempting to enforce "trans-inclusive environments and curricula" as the number of British children who want to change their gender is at an all-time high. England's only center for trans children and adolescents, the Tavistock Clinic, says the number of British children who want to change their gender has doubled in six months. According to the Guardian, the clinic says it is under huge pressure, with many of the referrals involving children under the

age of 10, including one three-year-old and 12 four-year-olds, the Guardian reports." (source rt.com)

"Reckless, profit-driven doctors prescribing children as young as 12 sex-change hormones. Doctors at British "gender identity clinics" are prescribing sex-change hormones for children as young as 12 years old, according to recent U.K. media reports. One Welsh GP, Dr. Helen Webberley, admitted that she is treating a "handful" of patients under 16 with cross-sex hormones, one of whom is a 12-year-old living as a boy. The child in question has been taking puberty blockers since the age of nine and wants to begin testosterone treatments, which are not provided by the NHS until the age of 16." (source: davidicke.com)

"Sweden's feminizing boys with genderless schools - Did you just assume my gender?" (source: politiek.tpo.nl) Then again this is Sweden, a country that will soon cease to exist thanks to their liberal policies.

"Number of children wanting to become opposite sex doubling each year in Sweden" (source: Breitbart.com)

"Parents furious over school's plan to teach gender spectrum, fluidity - One of the nation's largest public school systems is preparing to include gender identity to its classroom curriculum, including lessons on sexual fluidity and spectrum – the idea that there's no such thing as 100 percent boys or 100 percent girls. "Human beings are created male and female. But the current transgender ideology goes way beyond that. They're telling us you can be both genders, you can be no gender, you can be a gender that you make up for yourself. And we're supposed to affirm all of it."" (source: beforeitsnews.com / fox.news)

"School Told to Call Kids 'Purple Penguins' Because 'Boys and Girls' Is Not Inclusive to Transgender - Nebraska school district has instructed its teachers to stop referring to students by "gendered expressions" such as "boys and girls," and use "gender inclusive" ones such as "purple penguins" instead." (source: thenationalreview.com)

"Lesbian Couple Gives Son Hormone Blockers, Says The Child Is Transgender" "Pauline Moreno and Debra Lobel, a lesbian couple from California, claimed their 11-year-old son Thomas didn't want to be a boy. Thomas, who prefers to go by "Tammy," wanted to be a girl. So his mothers gave him hormone treatments to delay puberty so that he could fully "transition" into a female through surgery when he is old enough." The boy was pushed into taking hormone blockers preventing his body to go thru puberty." (source: mrconservative.com) Where are the social services

now? Why is this being tolerated? Why is this not considered child abuse? If this isn't child abuse nothing is.

"Top London private school to allow boys to wear skirts as part of new 'mix and match' uniform rules for children questioning their gender identity - Highgate School plans to bring in uniform rules allowing boys to wear skirts. Children are already allowed to request that staff address them by a name of the opposite gender. The headteacher, Mr. Pettitt, added that addressing gender identity was mainly occurring in the sixth form, but said he guesses 'that will change over time' and parents will start seeing primary school children asking similar questions. Pettit also said: "In common with all other schools and youth organizations we are seeing greater numbers of pupils questioning gender identity that in the past. Having said that, in years gone by absolutely no young people were raising it at all and it seems inconceivable that these sorts of questions didn't exist." (source: dailymail.co.uk)

"Insanity is Hereditary: Transgender Parents Raising 'Gender-Fluid' Child – Transgender and Pansexual Parents are raising their child as gender-fluid: This is Britain's first gender-fluid family. They are raising four-year-old Star Cloud as a 'person' and are telling him to 'not get hung up' on being a boy. Parents Nikki and Louise Draven say they are 'just ordinary' and are being 'who they want to be'. Star calls Louise, 31, his mummy, but she is in fact his biological father and is transitioning to become a woman with hormone treatment. Nikki will dress as a woman on some days and will dress as a man on others. The parents want Star to be free to wear make-up, paint his nails, wear girls or boys clothes and play with dolls if he wants to. In September, he will go to school for the first time and will wear a boy's uniform, but with a pink vest and socks. Nikki said: 'We don't want our child constrained by that either. We're just an ordinary family being who we want to be. 'We never tell Star he's a boy, we tell him he can be whatever he wants. We don't buy gender specific toys or clothes and we let him choose what he wears. Pink is one of his favorite colour.' " (source: theothermccain.com) Just like Bruce Jenner said: "*I am the new normal*". This is perfectly normal, nothing wrong with this, this is definitely not a sign of a decadent society that is on the verge of total collapse, definitely.

"Judge orders boy, seven, to live with father after his mother raised him as her daughter and even registered him with his GP as a girl. Seven-year-old boy 'living life entirely as girl' removed from mother's care. Social workers let a mother raise her young son as a girl because they were in thrall to 'transgender equality'. The boy, who was made to wear a pink

hairband, dresses and nail varnish, lived 'entirely as a girl'. He was registered as a girl with his doctor's surgery and was referred to as 'she' in official documentation from the age of just four." (source: dailymail.com)

"School Told to Call Kids 'Purple Penguins' Because 'Boys and Girls' Is Not Inclusive to Transgender – A Nebraska school district has instructed its teachers to stop referring to students by "gendered expressions" such as "boys and girls," and use "gender inclusive" ones such as "purple penguins" instead. Furthermore, it instructs teachers to interfere and interrupt if they ever hear a student talking about gender in terms of "boys and girls" so the student can learn that this is wrong." (source: Nationalreview.com) Dr. Lawrence Dunegan, who I mentioned previously, said that in the future boys and girls will be the same. The goal of the elite is to eliminate/supersede men and women and to create one gender. This gender will be either a mixture of male and female (androgyny) or a third gender so to say. Nevertheless, the main feature of this new gender will be that it can't reproduce. The reproductive capabilities will be in the hands of the ruling elite, who will, just like Aldous Huxley wrote nearly 100 years ago, make children in laboratories and state hatcheries.

"Sweden's 'confusing' gender-neutral preschool - What is Egalia? Egalia is a taxpayer-funded school in the Sodermalm district of Stockholm, Sweden. The school has incorporated a gender-free pedagogy, operating under the theory that by eliminating any reference to gender, the students won't fall prey to the stereotyping of gender roles. "Society expects girls to be girlie, nice and pretty, and boys to be manly, rough and outgoing," says one of the school's teacher's, Jenny Johnson,as quoted by Britain's Daily Mail. "Egalia gives them a fantastic opportunity to be whoever they want to be."How do the kids talk to each other? For starters, there are no boys and girls in Egalia, just "friends." That's the term teachers in the school use to address all students. In addition, the staff refrains from using the pronouns "him" or "her." Instead, the gender labels, which are "han" and "hon" in Swedish, are replaced by the "genderless" pronoun "hen" — a word that doesn't actually exist in the Swedish language. They use a made-up word? Yep. For example, when a doctor or plumber is coming into the classroom, "we don't know if it's a he or a she, so we just say, 'Hen is coming around 2 p.m.," says director Lotta Rajalin,as quoted by the Associated Press. "Then the children can imagine both a man or a woman. This widens their view." What about playtime? Lego blocks are stored directly next to kitchen and cooking toys, so as not to encourage gender preference through toy storage and organization. There are no squabbles over who gets to play mommy in

a game of house, either. If one girl has already claimed the role, "then we suggest two moms or three moms and so on," says Rajalin. And don't expect to find gender-promoting fairy tales on the bookshelves, either. Snow White and Cinderella are nixed in favor of books featuring gay and lesbian couples, single parents, and adopted children, says CNN." (source theweek.com) This is nothing more than unadulterated, pure brainwashing MK Ultra-style.

BBC's show for children called "Just a girl" is aimed at 6-year-olds. This show is a fictional transgender story about a boy formerly called Ben, now called Amy, who takes hormone blockers while transitioning to a girl and talks about these experiences in video diaries. Parents have complained that this show has confused their children, but as yet this show is still airing. This is no surprise since the BBC is as Left-wing as you could possibly get. Then again, this is the same BBC that is still embroiled in a giant pedophile scandal due to their connection with Jimmy Savile which I have covered earlier.

How is gender reassignment surgery performed on kids seen as tolerant, progressive and not something akin to child abuse is beyond me.

Correct me if I'm wrong, but I remember the LGBT community saying it will not go after kids and they would leave them alone. Why is there an ever-growing push to force transsexual teachings in schools then? I know that they are presenting it as an anti-bullying campaign, but the true reason is much more sinister. None of these kids would question their gender identity if it wasn't for the brainwashing that they are bombarded from the day they are born. When are they going to leave the kids alone?

Transsexuality is still classified as a mental disorder called "gender dysphoria" or "gender identity disorder", though there is no doubt in my mind that it's only a matter of time before they change the definition of transsexuality to suit their future goals. This will, most certainly, be done the same way with homosexuality – without objective research.

"Dr. Paul R. McHugh, the former psychiatrist-in-chief for Johns Hopkins Hospital and its current Distinguished Service Professor of Psychiatry, said that transgenderism is a "mental disorder" that merits treatment, that sex change is "biologically impossible," and that people who promote sexual reassignment surgery are collaborating with and promoting a mental disorder. Dr. McHugh also reported that there are "misguided doctors" who, working with very young children who seem to imitate the opposite sex, will administer "puberty-delaying hormones to render later sex-change

surgeries less onerous – even though the drugs stunt the children's growth and risk causing sterility." The pro-transgender advocates do not want to know, said McHugh, that studies show between 70% and 80% of children who express transgender feelings "spontaneously lose those feelings" over time. He also reported on a new study showing that the suicide rate among transgendered people who had reassignment surgery is 20 times higher than the suicide rate among non-transgender people. Dr. McHugh further noted studies from Vanderbilt University and London's Portman Clinic of children who had expressed transgender feelings but for whom, over time, 70%-80% "spontaneously lost those feelings."While the Obama administration, Hollywood, and major media such as Time magazine *promote transgenderism as normal, said Dr. McHugh, these "policy makers and the media are doing no favors either to the public or the transgendered by treating their confusions as a right in need of defending rather than as a mental disorder that deserves understanding, treatment and prevention." Such action comes "close to child abuse," said Dr. McHugh, given that close to 80% of those kids will "abandon their confusion and grow naturally into adult life if untreated ...." "'Sex change' is biologically impossible," said McHugh. "People who undergo sex-reassignment surgery do not change from men to women or vice versa. Rather, they become feminized men or masculinized women. Claiming that this is civil-rights matter and encouraging surgical intervention is in reality to collaborate with and promote a mental disorder."* (source cnsnews.com)

Let's go a step further. In recent years America has been a hotbed of transsexual bathroom bills. These bills allow people who identify as transsexual or claim to identify to use the bathrooms, restrooms, changing rooms, locker rooms of the gender they identify as regardless of their biological sex. This was supposedly done so to stop "bullying" transsexual people. How is this done, like all civil rights - for someone to get rights someone else must lose their rights. These bills, when implemented, allow people to use any bathroom they choose hinging on their gender identity. Proponents of these bills say that this is done to help the transsexual community and that it will not infringe on the rights of anyone else. Let's put their claims to the test.

"Convicted Sex Offender Leads Transgender Rights Effort in North Carolina - The homosexual leader of efforts in North Carolina to allow men to use women's bathrooms is a convicted and registered sex offender, according to documents made available to Breitbart News. Chad

Sevearance is president of the Charlotte Business Guild, which describes itself as "a network of LGBT professionals, business owners, employees. Sevearance and his group have taken a lead role in seeking the right to allow males to use the restrooms and showers of females, including those of little girls, which is described by advocates as nothing more than nondiscrimination measures." (source: Breitbart)

"A Seattle man, citing transgender bathrooms laws, was able to gain access to a women's locker-room at a public recreational center while little girls were changing for swim practice. In February, The Daily Wire reported that a Seattle man who walked into the women's locker-room—on two occasions—and began undressing, cited the "new state rule that allows people to choose a bathroom based on gender identity. Subsequent to this new rule, no one called the police on this man who reportedly came back a second time when young girls were changing into their swimsuits for swim practice."

"A Toronto man claiming to be transgender was arrested and sentenced to jail for sexually assaulting several women in a women's shelter after he gained access to the shelter and its shower facilitates as "Jessica." As Life Site notes, "A biological man claiming to be 'transgender' so as to gain access to and prey on women at two Toronto shelters was jailed in early March. Christopher Hambrook, 37, using the name "Jessica," was able to gain access to Toronto women's shelters."

"A Virginia man was caught and arrested for peeping on and filming two women and a 5-year-old child in a women's restroom after receiving entry. "Richard Rodriguez, 30, filmed a woman in a bathroom stall at the Potomac Mills Mall, Prince William County Police said," reported NBC Washington. His victim was a 35-year-old woman who was in a bathroom stall when "she saw a bag moved toward her under the stall divider." According to police, Rodriguez had been filming her."

"Los Angeles man dressed in drag, entered a Macy's department store bathroom and videotaped women under bathroom stalls. Charges were filed against Jason Pomare, 33, for allegedly disguising himself as a woman, sneaking in to the women's restroom at a Macy's department store and secretly videotaping hours of footage of women in bathroom stalls. Pomare reportedly disguised himself with a wig and fake breasts; he kept his video camera with him in a small purse. Reports NBC4 News."

"Two male students were caught at the University of Toronto exploiting "gender-neutral" facilities to peep on women in the shower with their cellphone cameras. The University of Toronto had to change their gender-

neutral bathrooms back to bathrooms separated based on biology "after two separate incidents of 'voyeurism' were reported on campus September 15 and 19. Male students within the University's Whitney Hall student residence were caught holding their cellphones over female students' shower stalls and filming them as they showered." (source for the previous five stories: dailywire.com)

A man in a Los Angeles shopping mall was arrested after women realized that he was secretly videotaping them. The man was able to get in the women's bathroom because he was dressed as a woman and thanks to the bathroom bill. (source: SouthernCalifornia.com)

How bigoted of these women, how dare they assume that their rights to privacy are greater than the rights of delusional men to use women's bathrooms.

The list just goes on and on, and yet the mainstream media is not reporting it. These and other similar incidents are becoming more common as people are forced into accepting the notion that men should be able to use women's bathrooms.

These bills allow men and boys to enter girl showers and locker rooms just because they claim to identify as female and no one sees the problem? No one sees the possibility of this being abused? So let me get this straight, the rights of the transsexual community (which in the U.S. is roughly 0.3 percent of the total population) overrides the rights of women and girls (which are around 50 percent of the population).

The transsexual community is not forbidden from using bathrooms, they should just use the bathrooms of their corresponding biological sex, otherwise, the rights of women and girls are violated. Before you call me a hateful, intolerant, bigot let me ask you a few questions. Hypothetically speaking (a real life scenario), would you be okay with a 50-year-old man, who puts on a wig and makeup, using the same bathroom as your 5,6,7-year-old daughter. Would you ladies be okay with biological men/boys using the same bathrooms, showers, and locker rooms as you at the same time? Yeah, I didn't think so. Believe it or not, there is an even worse side to the whole story. If sexually assaulting women in bathrooms wasn't enough, these bills (some implemented, some yet to be in the future) would open doors to sexual predators and pedophiles preying on kids. Again and again we see this pattern, that rights of a tiny minority are used to trample rights of the majority – in this case, the right of women/girls to privacy in bathrooms and rights of kids to be safe from child molesters are put on a backburner.

The insanity doesn't end here. Since the theory that there are an infinite number of genders is being pushed, does this mean every one of these gender identities needs special treatment with getting a bathroom of their own in every facility in the country?

Science is not even settled on the simplest transsexual theories (transsexual men and transsexual women), yet almost every day there are new movements that derived from the original transsexual movement:

An infinite number of genders (gender identities):

At this day and age, there is a prevailing theory that there are more than two genders (male and female), an infinite number of genders to be more precise. Let the insanity begin:

"Here's a List of 58 Gender Options for Facebook Users. Facebook introduced dozens of options for users to identify their gender. Previously, users had to identify themselves as male or female. Users can now select a "custom" gender option. Facebook will also allow users to select between three pronouns: "him," "her" or "their."

The following are the 58 gender options identified by ABC News:
Agender, Androgyne, Androgynous, Bigender, Cis, Cisgender, Cis Female, Cis Male, Cis Man, Cis Woman, Cisgender Female, Cisgender Male, Cisgender Man, Cisgender Woman, Female to Male, FTM, Gender Fluid, Gender Nonconforming, Gende, Questioning, Gender Variant, Genderqueer, Intersex, Male to Female, MTF, Neither, Neutrois, Non-binary, Other, Pangender, Trans, Trans, Trans Female, Trans* Female, Trans Male, Trans* Male, Trans Man, Trans* Man, Trans Person, Trans* Person,*
Trans Woman, Trans Woman, Transfeminine, Transgender, Transgender Female, Transgender Male, Transgender Man, Transgender Person, Transgender Woman, Transmasculine, Transsexual, Transsexual Female, Transsexual Male, Transsexual, Man, Transsexual Person, Transsexual Woman, Two-Spirit"* (source: abcnews.com)

"According to the New York City Commission on Human Rights, there are more than two genders. There are 31, to be exact.
Here's the complete list:
Bi-gendered, Cross-dresser, Drag King, Drag Queen, Femme Queen, Female-to-Male, FTM, Gender Bender, Genderqueer, Male-to-Female, MTF, Non-Op, HIJRA, Pangender, Transsexual, Trans Person, Woman, Man, Butch, Two-Spirit, Trans, Agender, Third Sex, Gender Fluid, Non-Binary

Transgender, Androgyne, Gender Gifted, Gender Blender, Femme, Person of Transgender Experience, Androgynous" (source: RebelMedia and capoliticalreview.com)

Let's take a look at some of the definitions for these made-up genders: -
- Non-binary: "any gender identity which does not fit in the male and female binary"
- Genderfluid: "is a gender identity which refers to a gender which varies over time" or "is a gender identity best described as a dynamic mix of boy and girl."
- Genderqueer: "relating to or having a gender identity that is other than male or female"

If I had a dollar for every gender that exists, I would have 2 dollars and a pile of counterfeits.

We now have people who identify as 1/3 male and 2/3 female, or 2/5 woman and 3/5 man, or who change their gender identity on a daily basis.

Canada passed bill C-16 in 2017 colloquially known as the "Transgender Bill". The bill is intended to protect individuals from discrimination on the basis of gender identity or gender expression. It also adds that evidence that an offense was motivated by bias, prejudice or hate based on a person's gender identity or expression constitutes an aggravating circumstance for a court to consider when imposing a criminal sentence. Thanks to this great work of art if you refuse to address someone according to their preferred pronouns (keep in mind that there are an infinite number of genders) you could end up in jail. This bill also says that homosexuality is innate while heterosexuality is an imposed social norm. (Let me get it straight, gay people are born gay while heterosexuality is a social construct, please do explain how this is not discrimination towards heterosexual people)

"Canadians Could Be Jailed or Fined for Using Incorrect Gender Pronouns. Canada passed a law Thursday making it illegal to use the wrong gender pronouns. Critics say that Canadians who do not subscribe to progressive gender theory could be accused of hate crimes, jailed, fined, and made to take anti-bias training." (source: dailysignal.com)

"Canadians Could Face Hate Crimes Over Using The Wrong Gender Pronouns" (source: dailycaller.com)

"ORWELLIAN: Canadians Can Now Be Fined Or JAILED For Using Wrong Gender Pronouns. Taking a page out of George Orwell's Nineteen Eighty-Four, Canada passed a new law that opens Canadians up to fines and even jail time if they use gender pronouns that do not correspond to a person's subjectively determined "gender identity. Critics of the legislation say the bill will target conservatives who cling to reality and science and refuse to adhere to progressives' gender theory, which is rooted in mere feelings. Canada's Prime Minister Justin Trudeau was predictably overcome with joy over the progressive crackdown on free speech." (source: dailywire.com) Of course, Justin Trudeau is involved in this – the champion of LGBT rights, this Hillary Clinton of Canada, the idiot who still believes in man-made global warming. So if I "misgender" someone I might get fined or even end up in jail, keep in mind that there are an ever growing number of genders and gender identities. Who can possibly keep track of this insanity anymore?

"Canadian gender-neutral pronoun bill is a warning for Americans. If you are wondering, reasonably, why any of this might be relevant to Americans, you might note that legislation very similar to Bill C-16 has already been passed in New York City. Authorities there now fine citizens up to $250,000 for the novel crime of "mis-gendering" — referring to people by any words other than their pronouns of choice (including newly constructed words such as zie/hir, ey/em/eir and co). First, most simply, are the practical problems. The Big Apple now legally protects a non-exhaustive list of 31 gender identities. Facebook offers a choice of 58. *Bill C-16, and its legislative sisters, are particularly insidious constructions. So, a note from a Canadian friend. The citizens of your great country, and ours — and of our allies across the Western world — are at risk."* (source: thehill.com)

"Not using transgender pronouns could get you fined. Employers and landlords who intentionally and consistently ignore using pronouns such as "ze/hir" to refer to transgender workers and tenants who request them — may be subject to fines as high as $250,000. Penalties of up to $250,000 can be imposed for violations that are deemed to be the result of malicious intent. The idea of using pronouns other than "he/she" has come to light in the past decade as more people are identifying with "non-binary" gender roles, meaning not traditional male/female. The Obama administration last week issued a decree mandating that every US public-school district allow transgender students to use the bathroom that matches their gender identities." (source: nypost.com) Yes, free speech is dead

"NYC Will Fine You $250,000 For 'Misgendering' A Transsexual. Did you call a transsexual person "he" or "she" when they preferred to be called "zhe?" According to a newly updated anti-discrimination law in New York City, you could be fined an eye-watering $250,000." (source: Breitbart.com) Note: They are referring to American dollars, not Canadian.

"California Law Allows Jail For Using Wrong Gender Pronoun - Violations can be punishable by a fine of up to $1,000 or 'by imprisonment in the county jail for a period not to exceed one year.' Under a new California law, those who work in health care who use the wrong gender pronoun when referring to a transgender patient could face prison time. The law states that violations can be punishable by a fine 'not to exceed one thousand dollars' or 'by imprisonment in the county jail for a period not to exceed one year' " (source: dailywire.com) This was one out of two changes California made to its law in the same month in regards to their gay and transgender policy at the tail end of 2017. The second change was "knowingly infecting someone with HIV became a misdemeanor instead of a felony with a maximum penalty of 6 months". Let that sink in, if you knowingly infect someone with HIV, a life-altering and detrimental disease effectively ruining someone's life, you get a maximum of 6 months jail time, but if you, God forbid, use the wrong pronoun (keep in mind there are an infinite number of pronouns) when addressing some lunatic you can be imprisoned up to 1 year. If this isn't insanity I don't know what is. Then again, by this point I shouldn't be surprised, this is California after all – a major breeding ground for mentally insane degeneracy.

In the University of Toronto in 2016, the LGBT community held a protest named "gender is over." The protest was used to silence Dr. Jordan Peterson. He is a Canadian clinical psychology and professor of psychology at the University of Toronto. Peterson was attacked and silenced for refusing to use gender-neutral pronouns like "they", "them", "zir", "hir", "sie", "em" when addressing his students. He didn't want to submit to the insane political correctness ideology. So much for free speech, I assume.

There is no scientific evidence that there are more than 2 genders, sorry to inform but there are only two genders: female and male. I don't care how you identify, you can identify as a chair for all I care. I don't care if you identify as any of the made-up genders in your make-believe fictional world that only exist in your delusional head. As I said, free speech is dead, the LGBT will force you to use the "correct" pronouns under the threat of imprisonment. This is classical "1984" language policing through political correctness.

If you think the saga ends here, think again:

Trans-age:

"'I've gone back to being a child': Husband and father-of-seven, age 52, leaves his wife and kids to live as a transgender SIX-YEAR-OLD girl named Stefonknee. A Canadian man who was married, with seven kids, has left his family in order to fulfill his true identity - as a six-year-old girl. Now, Stefonknee lives with friends who she calls her 'adoptive mommy and daddy' as a six-year-old girl, dressing in children's clothing and spending her time playing and coloring with her adoptive parents' grandchildren. Stefonknee says her 'adoptive' family, which consists of an older couple and their children and young grandchildren, are completely accepting of her identifying as a little girl." (source: Dialymail) A grown man leaves his WIFE and SEVEN KIDS because one day he decided that he is a 6-year-old girl and now lives with his "adoptive" parents? Would you let this delusional 52-year-old man play with your kids? If not, then you are a hateful, intolerant bigot. They call this "Trans-age" the notion that someone can change their age by free will and that rest of society has to accept that.

Trans-species / otherkin :

"Trans-species? Woman claims she is actually a cat. A girl in Norway claims to be "trans-species" and is actually a cat. Much like transgender people, she believes she was born this way and was assigned the wrong species at birth. Nano finally came to terms with the mistake when she was 16 and has lived as a cat ever since. Nano expects people to treat her like a cat, whatever that means." (source: naturalnews) I am deeply sorry to inform you, but this is not a hoax, this in fact is a true story of a woman who identifies as a cat. This is peeeerfectly normal in this day and age.

"Trans-Species? Meet the Grown Men Who Identify as Dogs. In the midst of national discussion on transgender issues, the trend of men dressing up and behaving like dogs, known as "pup play," was recently discussed in a new documentary on "The Secret Life of Human Pups." The documentary, produced by Britain's Channel 4, features a variety of English men who live like dogs in their private lives—a movement that often involves living with a handler, dressing in a rubber canine suit, barking to communicate, fetching

balls, having your belly rubbed and other dog-like behavior. "In the U.K., there are estimated to be 10,000 human pups: men who dress in elaborate dog suits and behave like dogs. This remarkable documentary explores their hidden world." (source: LouderwithCrowder.com , MarkDice, Christiannews.net) Still not fake news. No one should be surprised that these real-life chimeras are mostly homosexual men. This identity was, for the first time, introduced during the 2016 gay pride parade in Seattle where around 70 homosexual men alongside their partners, who are also their "owners", paraded in the streets.

"Transgender woman 'Dragon Lady' chops ears off to look like a reptile." (source: mirror.co.uk) A born woman now identifies as a dragon made possible "thanks to" plastic surgery.

Trans-racial :

Rachel Dolezal, a Caucasian woman, with white parents and a white ethnic origin identifies as an African-American. People are actually convinced that she is black even though she is as white as mayo on white bread.

"Dove's new 'Real Moms' commercial features transgender parent. Dove, trying to appeal to a younger audience, has a new "Real Moms" ad campaign, and it features a transgender woman. The ad showcases a diverse spectrum of mothers — parents of all races, with differing careers, and sexual orientations — and begins with the text: "Moms are redefining what it means to be a 'good mom.' " After introducing a stay-at-home mother and a mom who works as a cattle rancher, the soap brand featured a couple, both of whom identify as mothers, raising their biological newborn son. We are both his biological parents," Shea, a transgender woman, says. "You get people that are like, 'What do you mean? You're the mom?' We're like, 'Yep. We're both gonna be moms." (source: Mikedice, Theblaze,) A commercial that features a biological mother and father, but the father identifies as a mother in that family, apparently, they both are mothers

Do you know what the best part of this is? Sex-change operations are taxpayer funded (in America). Yes, that's right hard-working women and men who need to feed their kids now have to separate a portion of their salary and give it to the state so it can pay people to "transition" into the opposite sex. Britain is one of the countries where plastic/cosmetic surgeries are paid by the government thanks to tax collected from its citizens. Now the British people, for example, have to give up a portion of their salary so that women can get breast implants. Thanks, but no thanks. No way. I'm not giving these delusional oafs my money. I'm not going to reinforce the notion that this is normal behavior, I'm not going to endorse a mental disorder.

The lunatics have truly taken over the mental asylum.

Just a few examples of the top of my head. What's next? What is the next great big push in the trans movement? Will I be able to identify as an innocent person after I have committed a murder? In this new liberal age, you can literally be whatever you want and the rest of society has to conform to how you feel inside. So now our gender/sex, age, race, and species are dependent on our feelings and have nothing to do with biology and psychology. This is the classical postmodernist ideology – skepticism towards everything and the deconstruction of everything known to humankind.

SIMONE DE BEAUVOIR:

A French feminist (shocker). One of the founders of the Second wave of feminism, in 1949 wrote "The second sex." In this book she said *"One is not born but becomes a woman"* and *"every female human being is not necessarily a woman"*. More of this notion that sex is a social construct rather than it being rooted in biology. Simone is one of the most influential feminists, and as a result of her teachings one of the most popular courses for young women across colleges in the U.S. is "gender studies" – the most useless college degree a woman could ever get, in no small part due to the fact that it revolves around man-hating and feminist myths that have been debunked more times than I could possibly count. De Beauvoir is the matriarch of LGBT and feminist beliefs of gender fluidity and non-binary theories.

As I stated at the very beginning of this study there is not only an attack on gender identity but also on sexual orientation.

ALFRED KINSEY:

Was an American biologist, professor of entomology, zoology, and sexology. A bisexual himself, he and his wife had an open marriage and had multiple sexual partners. Kinsey also believed in the superiority of homosexuality over heterosexuality. He is the so-called father of the sexual revolution. His research was founded by the Rockefeller Foundation (what a surprise). Hue Hefner, inspired by Alfred Kinsey, was instrumental in legalizing pornography. The porn and prostitution industry were and still continue to be pushed by the Rockefeller dynasty. Porn and prostitution are implemented in order to distance men from women, marriage, and commitment while at the same time feminism aims to distance women from motherhood, femininity, and to destabilize the family (so that the state can be the "parent"). One of Kinsey's acquaintances was the infamous Aleister Crowley (a name that should send shivers down peoples spine), an admitted Satanist, founder of various Masonic lodges, alleged pedophile which is why Mussolini ordered his execution, unfortunately, Crowley left Italy for France and remained unpunished.

Alfred Kinsey is one of the pioneers of the pansexual theory, a theory that advocates the attraction to people regardless of their gender, similar to bisexuality.

This is the "Kinsey scale." also called the Heterosexual-Homosexual Scale, it is used in research to describe a person's sexual orientation based on their experience or response at a given time. The scale typically ranges from 0, meaning exclusively heterosexual, to 6, meaning exclusively homosexual. This scale was later expanded to 10 sexual orientations. Today it's probably close to infinite.

Rating	Description
0	Exclusively heterosexual
1	Predominantly heterosexual, only incidentally homosexual
2	Predominantly heterosexual, but more than incidentally homosexual
3	Equally heterosexual and homosexual.
4	Predominantly homosexual, but more than incidentally heterosexual
5	Predominantly homosexual, only incidentally heterosexual
6	Exclusively homosexual
X	Asexual, Non-Sexual

First, we had the deconstruction of biological sex by Simone de Beauvoir and then deconstruction of sexuality (innate sexual attraction to the opposite sex) by Kinsey.
Kinsey's research is compiled in his two works:

- Sexual Behavior in the Human Male (1948), in which he said that around 1/3 of American males have had a homosexual experience. This is based on interviews and analysis that he did on the male population. A few problems that I have with this number being so high. First, the interviews were conducted on the prison population (including many sex offenders), also in prisons homosexuality is present in much greater numbers than in the general population precisely because there is an absence of the opposite sex. Second, he also based his research on prostitutes (both male and female). Third, there were other, unwilling participants to his experiments – kids. In recent decades the Kinsey experiments have come to the public arena. It is now, more than ever, clear that he conducted his experiments on kids as well. Kinsey, or one of his henchmen, would sexually abuse kids, which would later report having homosexual experiences as a result of these assaults. Kinsey himself said that there is a link between sexual molestation and sexual deviancy. And lastly, Kinsey based his claims after conducting interviews with members of homosexual clubs.
- Sexual Behavior in the Human Female (1953), where Kinsey, according to the research he conducted, claimed that a bit over 30 percent (let's just say 1/3) of American women had committed adultery (in other words had an illicit sexual partner outside of marriage). To anyone with half a brain (which by today's standards is too much to ask for anyway) it is easy to conclude that this percent is too high even in our contemporary promiscuous society, let alone in the 1950s more conservative America. Thanks to Judith Reisman (who spent decades exposing the flawed research on which Kinsey based his two books) and many others it is now concluded what was suspected for many years and that is that Kinsey's research is anti-scientific. This percentage Kinsey got by interviewing women of America. There are things that Kinsey's books won't tell you, but people like Judith Reisman and others who went to the Kinsey Institute (which to this day is funded at the taxpayer's expense) archives and checked the credibility of his research will. As was expected for many years Kinsey's research was ripe with subjectivity, confirmation bias, cherry-

picking and selective data gathering. When it comes to the 30 percent Kinsey augmented this number artificially. After interviewing women of America he quite literally threw in the trashcan the data and research that wasn't to his liking, thus violated any objectivity. Kinsey cherry-picked those interviews in which women admitted to committing adultery while throwing the majority of cases (thousands of them) in which women said that they were faithful to their husbands. This way he got the desired result by artificially increasing the numbers of adulteries by comparison because he threw data that showed that the majority of women didn't commit adultery in marriage. Is this kind of "research and science" alongside the "objective research" that resulted in the declassification of homosexuality from the list of mental illnesses and the mythical gay gene what we now call objective science?

It's because of Kinsey's experiments that the "10 percent homosexual population theory" was born. According to Kinsey at any given time homosexuals account for 10 percent of the population, a percentage that has never since been able to be replicated in later experiments, not even in our sexual free-for-all society.

After Kinsey's books came out (they both go by the name the "Kinsey's reports"), as the sexual revolution slowly crept in, cases of homosexuality, adultery, and prostitution rose up.

There are those that refute Kinsey's research. Dr. Judith Reisman dedicated decades to exposing Kinsey's research. According to her, Kinsey's research became the foundation for major changes in our sex laws and are still present globally. Based on her accounts and traveling she noticed the impact of Kinsey's research is present in many countries, a few countries that she mentioned were: China, Serbia, Switzerland, Holland. She concluded that modern sex-educational curriculums and sex-laws are based on Kinsey's research.

According to Kinsey, sexual orientation is a spectrum that can change during one's life. He stated that sexuality can change, that sexuality (sexual orientation) is fluid and not confined only to heterosexuality or homosexuality. Of course, this contradicts the notion that one is born gay or that there is a gay gene. This sexual fluidity concept is the basis for the pansexual theory, a theory that one is not attracted to another person because of their gender (biological sex) but rather because of the person in that body. Pansexuality says that people are attracted to what is on the inside. This has never (and will never) been scientifically proven. Regardless of which scientific field you look at, whether it be biology, psychology, evolutionary psychology, anatomy, anthropology and so one, the only sexuality that is proven to exist for a reason is the attraction to the opposite sex, mainly due to the biological need to procreate. Of course, they are trying to split sex and reproduction. By splitting sex from reproduction they can say that every sexual orientation is on par with heterosexuality. Pansexuality is one step further from bisexuality.

Kinsey was very much interested in the sexual behavior in children on whom he conducted his experiments, that's why he and his entourage were heavily linked with pedophilia. Kinsey's research and date are based on one of his helpers - Dr. Fritz von Balluseck – a former Nazi pedophile. According to Kinsey *"a child molester may have contributed favorably to their later socio-sexual development."* (remember what I said about sexual experiences in early childhood being linked with sexual deviancy later on in life and how pedophilia and homosexuality are linked?). He also was one of the biggest proponents of the idea that children are sexual from birth and that they can be unharmed by sex with adults. Kinsey was heavily influenced by Sigmund Freud (or better yet fraud), another pseudo-scientific quack-theorist. Kinsey and his pedophile entourage are responsible for hundreds if not thousands of rapes, the majority perpetrated on little boys and girls.

According to Kinsey's research around 95 percent of men have done crimes that would make them sex offenders, he also claimed that neither women nor children were seriously harmed by rape or incest (this claim came after he interviewed 4441 women). He, just like Freud, said that children are sexual from birth and that 5-month-old babies can have orgasms. In his personal diary, Kinsey said that in one of his experiments a 4-year-old boy had 26 orgasms in the space of 24 hours. Kinsey also said: *"the only abnormal sex is no sex, the earlier boys and girls have orgasms the better for them."* Kinsey claimed that children could, with the assistance of an experienced adult, enjoy sexual activity from the moment they were born.

We had heterosexuality and homosexuality as its alternative, then came bisexuality (with the bisexual gene I presume?), now we have pansexuality where sexuality is one infinite spectrum with an infinite number of sexual orientations that are all equal or superior to heterosexuality. As I previously stated the most numerous members of the LGBT community are bisexuals, bisexuality has been on the rise. By the passing generation, fewer people identify as exclusively heterosexual and more people identify somewhere on the infinite scale of part heterosexual part homosexual (bisexual). Now we are on the verge of not only having an infinite number of gender identities (genders) but also an infinite number of sexual orientations. The Kinsey scale and the pansexual theory (some call it the "queer theory" though that is a much broader term in my opinion) have paved the path to the concept that sexuality is fluid and can be changed during one's life. It also laid the foundation for the concept of an infinite number of sexual orientations (which are constantly increasing) that can all be put somewhere between heterosexuality and homosexuality in an infinite number of combinations. First, they said that homosexuality is innate and rooted in biology (meaning one can't change being gay), now sexuality is fluid and ever-changing.

Years ago I said that the goal is to turn all people into bisexuals and from that turn them into asexual/non-sexual (not attracted to any sex) so procreation would not occur.

Kinsey was a chronic mastrubator, a masochist, he used to put objects into his private parts. He eventually died of a slow and painful disease called Orchitis – a lethal infection of the testicles due to years of brutal masochistic masturbation and other sexual acts, which is no surprise considering his sexual lifestyle. Oh the irony, the father of the sexual revolution and the preacher of sexual liberation died from following his own message.

Kinsey's so-called "objective" and "scientific" research is the foundation for sex-educational programs implemented all over the world. Is there really any surprise then, that this is happening:

"Nearly half of young people don't think they are exclusively heterosexual. YouGov survey reveals 49 per cent of people aged between 18 and 24 identify as something other than 100 per cent heterosexual.
A total of 49 percent of 18-24 year olds who took part in the survey defined themselves as something other than totally heterosexual. Every generation sees sexuality as something which is slightly less set in stone, according to the report. People of all ages have become more accepting of sexual fluidity, with 60 per cent of heterosexuals and 73 per cent of homosexuals thinking sexualities other than homosexual and heterosexual exist. This could be due to cultural figures such as Miley Cyrus and Cara Delevingne being more open about the fact that they like both genders or it could be indicative of a shift in the general culture." (source: telegraph.co.uk.)

"Study: Same-sex experiences are on the rise, and Americans are increasingly chill about it. A rise in bisexuality is driving a sharp increase in same-sex experiences in the United States, according to a new study — and Americans are increasingly open to the shift. Using data from the General Social Survey (GSS), a nationally representative survey of U.S. adults conducted since 1972 including a total of 33,728 participants, a team of social scientists found that the percentage of men reporting male sexual partners had nearly doubled from 1990 to 2014, and the percentage of women reporting same-sex experiences had more than doubled during the same period. Their study, published Wednesday in the journal Archives of Sexual Behavior, also shows a dramatic increase in the percentage of Americans who find these sexual interactions acceptable." (source: Washington post)

"A new national survey shows a rise in women using the label, and finds that more ladies report same-sex sexual contact than in years past. But make no mistake, the report also found an increase among men, although it was much smaller. The report, based on data collected between 2011 and 2013, found that 5.5 percent of women and 2 percent of men identify as bisexual. Compare that to the CDC's last report on the topic, published in 2011, which found that 3.5 percent of women and 1.1 percent of men claim the sexual identity. Far more women and men report having had same-sex sexual contact—17.4 and 6.2 percent, respectively—than identify as bisexual. That means almost one-fifth of women have fooled around with another woman. These numbers have also risen since the last survey, which found same-sex nookie reported by 12.5 percent of women and 5.2 percent of men." (source: vocative.com)

"More young people now identify as bisexual than gay or lesbian in UK - The number of young people identifying as bisexual has overtaken the number of those who consider themselves gay or lesbian for the first time, new figures have revealed. Figures for 2015 released by the Office for National Statistic (ONS) indicate that 1.8 percent of people aged 16-24 identify as bisexual, up from 1 percent in 2012. Meanwhile, 1.5 percent of people in this age bracket identified as gay or lesbian, a 0.1 percent drop over four years. The figures, collected as part of the Annual Population Survey, also show that overall, one in 30 young people in UK now identify as lesbian, gay or bisexual (LGB), compared with one in 38 in 2012. The national average across all age groups is one in 60. In every age group except the 16 to 24s, the number of individuals identifying as lesbian or gay was greater than that of those who identified as bisexual, according to the

survey, which polled some 320,000 people. Young people were far more likely to identify as LGB than older people. While 3.3 percent of people within the 16- to 24-year-old bracket consider themselves LGB, just 0.6 percent of those aged 65 and over identify as LGB." (source: www.rt.com)

Yet when I talked about this many years ago people dismissed it as a conspiracy theory.

HOMOSEXUAL LIFESTYLE:

Data resulting from research done in Canada and the U.S.
Facts the media will never tell you about the homosexual lifestyle:

-while an average heterosexual male has around 7,8 sexual partners in a lifetime, an average homosexual male has between 20 and 106 sexual partners in a year

-42 percent of homosexuals have admitted to having over 500 sexual partners over a lifetime, homosexuals (especially gay men) are far more promiscuous than heterosexual people

-78 percent of homosexuals are infected with STD's which is not a surprise considering their promiscuous lifestyle and the fact that homosexuality is statistically much more unhealthier than heterosexuality (could it be because nature intended for sexual intercourse to occur between members of the opposite sex and not between ones of the same sex)

-homosexuals are 100 percent more likely to be murdered than an average heterosexual, and those murders are committed by another homosexual – thanks to AIDS and other sexually transmitted diseases, further proof that homosexuality is unhealthy

-the average age for death for homosexuals is 42, again – the lifestyle (in the Dunegan tapes it is said that the reason as to why they are promoting homosexuality is to get rid of those who are dumb enough to indulge in it)

-homosexuals account for more than 50 percent of AIDS cases, again their lifestyle (just take into consideration that the gay population in the U.S. is between 1 and 2 percent of the total population), 2 percent of the population account for more than 50 percent of AIDS cases, in the U.S. it costs around 300.000 dollars a year to care for each AIDS patient – jest let that sink in for a moment.

According to the U.S. Gay and Lesbian Medical Association: *"homosexuals are at risk of HIV, AIDS, depression, substance and alcohol abuse, hepatitis, anxiety, syphilis, gonorrhea, chlamydia, papillomavirus, anal papilloma, pubic lice, testicular cancer."* Before you say anything, these and many other diseases are much more common in homosexuals than in heterosexuals.

Tell me again why we should promote and encourage this destructive lifestyle. Who is going to pay for the treatment of homosexuals that have contracted any of these or other diseases? The general population will, thanks to taxes (just like in the U.S.). So now heterosexuals raising children in an ever grimmer economy also need to pay for the treatment of homosexuals because of the lifestyle that they have chosen. Why is homosexuality, a lifestyle that is so destructive to the individual and society later down the line, being promoted and encouraged?

There is a link between homosexuality and mental illnesses. The homosexual community accounts for around 2 percent of the population, yet their members are over-represented in the mental illness department. Practically all studies show that people who identify as LGBT are far more likely to suffer from all sorts of mental illnesses (and that doesn't count in homosexuality itself, regardless of whether homosexuality is or isn't a mental illness). The usual and highly predictable "argument" to justify this, coming from apologists, is to cry out "homophobe" or "discrimination" insinuating that the reason for such high number of mental illnesses in the LGBT community is because of the lack of tolerance. But this is simply a cover tactic, research done in countries that were the first ones to legalize gay marriage (Denmark, Holland) shows the same thing – mental illnesses of all kinds are present in the LGBT community in much higher numbers than in the rest of the population, so clearly it's not the rest of society that is causing this. Yet despite this unhealthy and destructive lifestyle we are forced to accept the notion that homosexuality and other forms of sexual deviancy are on par or superior to heterosexuality.

ADOPTION:

Adoption is proof that the whole "legalize gay marriage because it won't affect anyone outside the marriage" argument is wrong. Legalizing gay marriage is one thing, but bringing children into that conversation is a completely different topic. Years before gay marriage became legal in the U.S. I said that they will make the argument that gay "parents" are as good as heterosexual biological parents which would eventually lead to them claiming gay people are better parents than actual heterosexual parents. Let's take America as an example. As well as having a right to marry, in 2015 gay couples have been granted the right to adopt children. The reasoning behind this was the supposed stance of science back at the time. Scientists claimed that there were no differences between a child being raised by heterosexuals or homosexuals. Gay people have been given the right to adopt even though there is research to indicate the opposite. Studies done by Professor Mark Regnerus, a sociology professor indicates that children raised by gay couples are at a disadvantage compared to those raised by heterosexuals in 24 out of 40 categories listed in his research. Another study done by a pro-gay organization published research that found that children raised by gay couples are more likely to identify as homosexuals themselves (no surprise since children naturally mimic their parent's actions, kids raised by homosexuals will see homosexuality as something normal and accepting or even encouraged in society). Milo Yiannopoulos (a homosexual) said that he would rather be straight because he wants kids but is unsure if he wants to raise them in a homosexual household. Not to mention the ever-growing number of people raised by gay parents who are advocating against gay people adopting kids. Clearly, science is unclear in regards to this topic, yet gay adoption was rushed through without taking into consideration the most impressionable members of society – the children.

To be honest, I never understood gay people wanting kids, we all know what is the natural way of bringing kids into this world and raising them. Kids are a result of a heterosexual union, not a homosexual one. How can someone defend the normality of gay people raising kids if they can't create life – it's unnatural, it's against the laws of nature for them to raise children.

To make things even stranger, recently I came upon scientific research that claims that "science supports gay parents." The publication actually claims that gay parents are better than biological heterosexual parents. I guess I was right all those years ago. For a few years they were equal and now gay parents are better than heterosexual parents. This is why I said that every civil rights movement is a strive for supremacy, not equality. I would say that gay people wanting to adopt is selfish because they are only thinking about themselves and not the child's natural innate need for a mother and a father. To claim that a child doesn't need a mother or father refutes all scientific research. Two homosexuals, whether two men or two women, cannot supersede the fact that a child needs a father and a mother. I don't care what you believe in: God, mother nature, evolution, aliens, letting gay people adopt is selfish since it doesn't take into consideration the needs of that child. A child never asked to be raised in a homosexual household. Your argument I am sure will be to say that a child also never asked to be born and raised in a heterosexual environment. The problem with that so-called argument is that a child doesn't have a choice but to be born from a heterosexual union. It's only in a heterosexual union that any child can be born, no child can result from a homosexual union anyway. If mother nature wanted gay people to raise kids it would have given them the ability to procreate. Correct me if I'm wrong but last time I checked gay people can't procreate so it's illogical to let them raise kids. An increasing number of people raised by gay couples are speaking out against gay adoption. Are we just going to ignore all the people that were raised in a gay household that say that they missed out on not having a mother or a father?

"Adults Raised by Gay Couples Speak Out Against Gay 'Marriage' in Federal Court" (source: cnsnews.com)

"Gay Parents Study Suggesting Downside For Kids Draws Fire From Social Scientists - A new study claiming to find disadvantages for children raised by same-sex parents is attracting criticism from social scientists, who say that the research does not actually address how well gay and lesbians parent." (source: huffingtonpost.com)

I'm sorry but to claim that heterosexual and homosexual relationships are equal is intellectually dishonest. Heterosexual relationship brings life and ensures the continuation of our species, homosexual relationship does not.

Statistically speaking gay marriages are far more likely to result in separation. Where does this leave their adopted kids? Every study on the face of Planet Earth shows that the best environment for raising kids is in a household where parents (mother and father) are married, research after research shows that kids from divorced/separated parents are at a disadvantage (in numerous parameters) compared to those who were raised by parents who are married. Since gay people are more likely to get separated/divorced this would leave the adopted kids at an even bigger disadvantage. I can only guess that this is because gay people (especially homosexual men) are far more promiscuous thus are unable or unwilling to stay monogamous so why should the kids suffer further. Unlike with some animals (like frogs) and some other amphibians who use the "spray and pray" mating tactic (impregnate as many females as possible to ensure the best chance of the continuation of the species, quantity over quality), when it comes to humans things are different. Again and again, research shows that the best tactic for raising human babies is the "pair bonding" tactic, where the mother and father co-exist (example: marriage) and raise the kids together, this way the kids have a father and a mother.

Gay adopted parents are also much more likely to abuse their adopted children (in chapter 6 I quoted a research that said *"the highest chance of a child being abused is if it is living with a single parent and the single parents partner who is not the child's biological parent"*), because from an evolutionary perspective most child abuses and molestations are carried out by non-blood related "parents". In a gay marriage, at least one parent is not related by blood to the child (or both parents in case of adoption), the same thing applies to step-fathers and step-mothers.

People who are more open to a non-monogamous relationship are usually LGBT members (in the west), again kids are the ones that end up with the short stick in this situation.

Monogamous heterosexual relationship (marriage being the most prominent one) actually works unlike other set-ups (homosexuality, polygamy, polyandry, polyamory). There is a reason as to why monogamous heterosexual relationships stood the test of time unlike others, and I would argue it's because it's the only one that has been proven to work, in no small part because it's the best for raising kids.

There is a reason as to why they are targeting the monogamous heterosexual traditional/nuclear family, it's because they know that once the nuclear family (the bedrock of all civilizations) falls the rest of society will collapse like a deck of cards. Then they (the true elite) can begin their process of rebuilding society, but rebuild it into what since the nuclear family is the only family set-up that has ever been proven to work.

GRADUAL TOLERANCE:

Probably the most important way this agenda is being pushed is gradual tolerance. David Icke calls is Totalitarian tip-toe. Basically, it's a gradual approach to a certain goal. This can be applied to a multitude of topics but let's stick to the topic at hand. Let me give you an example, but first, remember that one of the goals of this agenda is to normalize/legalize pedophilia. The current civil right being pushed is the push for tolerance towards pedophiles. In the 1950's U.S., there was no way in hell someone would still have their head standing on their shoulders if they dared mention rights for child molesters. Why? Because the social conventions would never allow for such a thing, today on the other hand pedophilia is (yet) one of the rare taboos that is still not accepted. So, how will the social perception towards pedophilia change – thanks to gradual tolerance.

You see, the elite knew that in 1950s society would never have accepted pedophilia outright, so they had to mask their true goal (legalizing pedophilia) with less drastic changes. Let me show you how they operate, just a simple example in steps:

1) don't kill homosexuals
2) tolerate homosexuals
3) out-of-wedlock homosexual cohabitation rights
4) gay marriage rights
5) adoption rights
6) transsexual rights
7) polygamy, polyandry, polyamory
8) incest
9) zoophilia
10) necrophilia
11) normalize pedophilia
12) legalize pedophilia (the end goal)

Remember what Dunegan said, this will be pushed on the younger generations because the old generation is set in their "archaic" ways and will not change.

In 1950s U.S. gay marriage would have never been accepted had it not been for gradual tolerance. Every new generation is bombarded with something new – slowly inching towards their true goal.

Most of today's younger generations either support gay marriage or is impartial (agnostic so to say). Let me show you how gradual tolerance works. For example, you support gay marriage, but maybe you don't support transsexual rights. Your kids will almost certainly support gay marriage (due to two things, your support as their parent and the fact that they are bombarded with propaganda) but they will also support transsexual rights because they will be exposed to transsexual ideology for a longer period of time compared to their parents. The subsequent generation will maybe be unsure over incest or zoophilia but later down the line, their kids or grandkids will have a more positive view on that as well. Step by step until they get to the desired goal. Milo Yiannopoulos (a homosexual) said that the next rights movement, after the transsexual movement, is going to be the push to normalize pedophilia.

You probably think that I'm joking.

"Cosmo Posts Story Normalizing Incest, Twitter Reacts. "It's a rare condition called genetic sexual attraction." (source: chicksontheright.com)

"Sibling incest should be legal, says Danish professor for criminal justice ethics" (source: thewashingtonpost.com)

"What's it like to date your father" (source: scienceofus)

"Swedish Liberal Party Youth Wing Calls for Legalization of Necrophilia, Incest. The Swedish Liberal party's youth wing proposed legalizing necrophilia and incest Sunday during the group's annual meeting in Stockholm. According to the motion filed, two consenting siblings 15 years of age and older should be allowed to engage in sexual intercourse while sex with a human corpse should also be legalized so long as the deceased gave written permission prior to passing." (source: prisonplanet.com) Exactly what we need, more liberalism, since it turned out so great for Sweden, or should I say Swedistan.

"German ethics council calls for incest between siblings to be legalized by Government. Germany's national ethics council has called for an end to the criminalization of incest between siblings after examining the case of a man who had four children with his sister." (source: independent.com) I am sure that you all know the argument for gay marriage over pedophilia was that gay marriage is consensual between two adults. The same argument is now being used to normalize incest, it's okay if it's between two consensual adults. What about the aftermath of that kind of union? What about the fact that children that result from incest are far more likely to have a physical or psychological defect or deformity?

"Bestiality brothels are 'spreading through Germany' warns campaigner as abusers turn to sex with animals as 'lifestyle choice. Bestiality brothels are spreading through Germany faster than ever thanks to a law that makes animal porn illegal but sex with animals legal, a livestock protection officer has warned." (source: dailymail.com)

"Denmark's Bestiality Problem: It's Legal. Amazingly, the Danes, Finns, Hungarians and Swedes currently say it's legal to have sex with animals as

long as the animals are not hurt." (source: thedailybeast.com) *"Canada's Ridiculous Ruling That Oral Sex with Animals Is Legal Shows Need for New Bestiality Laws. The Supreme Court of Canada ruled today that only penetrative sex with animals is a crime, not oral sex. The Supreme Court of Canada has ruled that a person must actually penetrate an animal or vice versa in order for the act to be considered bestiality."* (source: vice.com) How intolerant of me, these people must have a gene that determines their sexual orientation towards animals.

People are delusional if they think this will stop once gay marriage is achieved. Why? Because it's not meant to stop there, that is only the beginning. Every new generation will either accept something new, something further down the line (something more insidious) or will be more tolerant/accepting of a particular lifestyle. All that until the true goal is reached. If you are one of those that think that pedophilia could never become legal, just think that in the 1950s no one could have ever predicted that gay marriage would become legal (let alone the other stuff). Just because you deem something as unacceptable doesn't mean that generations to come will share your view. Think about it, you are most certainly more accepting of the homosexual lifestyle than your parents, your kids will surely be more open to the idea of legalizing polygamy or incest than you are right now. People would have never accepted the stuff they have accepted had there not been a push (from the very top) to do so. They will use incest, zoophilia just like they used gay marriage – to soften up the public in preparation for the finish line, and that's a line that I never want to come close to, let alone cross.

In Brave New World – Revisited, Huxley said: *"If the first half of the twentieth century was the era of the technical engineers, the second half may well be the era of the social engineers"*

This is social engineering on a global scale, changing the public's opinion to suit their purpose. People would have never become so tolerant and accepting of lifestyles like these if it weren't for the brainwashing and propaganda.

DE-EVOLUTION OF HUMANITY:

For as long as humans existed our brains grew larger and our intelligence increased. Now, for the first time in recorded human history our civilization is dumber than ever before (here I am not including the Middle East since its drop in IQ is a result of practicing incest, there is a direct correlation between civilizations that practice incest and loss of IQ in future generations). For the first time, mankind (especially the western world) is artificially getting dumber. Studies show that people in North America and Western Europe are, or better yet, have been losing IQ for a significant period of time. Westerners now have less IQ than back in the Victorian days.

"Western IQs drop by 14 points in last century, study says - Research published online in the journal Intelligence on Thursday claims the IQ of people in Western nations has fallen by an average of 14.1 points over the past century. Scientists in Europe used visual response times recorded in Western studies from 1889 to 2004. Their findings *showed a decline in general intelligence of 1.23 points per decade."* (source: pri.org)

"Researchers say Western IQs dropped 14 points over last century - A new study from researchers in Europe claims that the average IQ in Western nations dropped by a staggering 14.1 points over the past century." (source: Prisonplnet.com)

To quote Dr. W. H. Sheldon *"nobody knows just how far the average IQ in this country [the U.S.A.] has declined since 1916"*

The reason, they say, is our way of life, unhealthy food to be more precise. Our brains are literally shrinking. The areas of the brain that are affected by this tissue loss relate to critical thinking, long-term memory, and cognitive functioning. This drop has mainly affected the western world (America and Western Europe). For the first time in human history, there is a drop in average IQ. In pretty much the same time frame, in those areas where there is a drop of IQ, there is an increase of acceptance and tolerance of sexual liberation. Is there a link between lower intelligence and acceptance of unregulated sexual freedom (LGBT) or is it all just a coincidence?

Another thing I would like to touch upon only briefly is overpopulation. Speaking purely statistically and based on my own research it would seem that LGBT-like phenomena tend to be present (in much larger numbers) in big cities (which are more often left-liberal wing anyway). There are far more LGBT members, percentage-wise, in cities than in the suburbs, villages or small towns compared to the overall population in each of these categories. To that I have this to say: in the book "Between two ages: Americas role in the technetronic era" the writer Zbigniew Brzezinski reflects on the overcrowding and I quote *"Julian Huxley*[Aldous Huxley's brother] *was perhaps guilty of only slight exaggeration when he warned that overcrowding in animals leads to distorted neurotic and downright pathological behavior. We can be sure that the same is true in principle of people. City life today is definitely leading to mass mental disease, to growing vandalism and possible eruptions of mass violence."* To explain, human beings are not meant to live in over-populated, over-crowded metropolises, it's devastating to our mental health. Human beings are not completely social, they are only moderately gregarious.

PLAYING GOD WITH REPRODUCTION:

There are those (advocates for gay parenting, feminists and men rights activists/MGTOW) who believe that the nuclear family (mother and father living together and raising their offspring) is either obsolete or draconian in some shape or form, but nothing could be further from the truth.

In the human and animal world, there are two main reproduction strategies: the R selection strategy and the K selection strategy.

The R strategy (also known as "spray and pray") is present in harsh environments where resources are scarce. It is something similar to polygamy where members of a particular species tend to procreate as much as possible to ensure the best possible chance that at least some of their many offspring will continue the lineage of that species. This strategy involves having many young ones but spending little time rearing them which results in many young ones dying early on in their lives.

The K strategy (also known as dual-parenting / pair-bonding) occurs in stable environments where life isn't as harsh and resources aren't as scarce. In this strategy, fewer young ones are born but they get more parental investment. It's thanks to this higher parental attention that the young ones get that gives them a higher chance to survive and prosper. This method also allows the connection between the parents and the young ones to grow stronger through natural chemicals released in the body (at least with humans) which include: vasopressin, oxytocin, and prolactin.

Humans are one of the species that throughout their history used the K strategy, fewer children are born (compared to animals), high level of parental investment in the young ones which means more young ones will reach adulthood. On the other hand you have the R strategy (frogs, turtles, fish are just a few examples that use this strategy) more young ones are born but the majority of them die early, soon after birth (most tadpoles die early in their lifespan), a relative minority (minority compared to the original number of the ones that were born) reaches adulthood, all this because of very small or in some cases the complete absence of parental investment from biological parents (note: human young ones need parental investment for the longest period of time out of any living beings on this planet). In California there are two species of mice, one species after impregnating the female sometimes leaves or sometimes stays until the young ones are born and leaves after the gestation period. This type of mouse is prone to killing its own offspring if there is no food around if he even stays around that long. The other species of mouse, some refer to it as one of the best fathers in the animal kingdom, is monogamous and stays with the young ones for a long time and it is exactly because of this parental investment (and the fact that they don't kill their young) more young ones from this second species of mice reach adulthood than those from the first species in comparison to the number of born young ones. It's not uncommon to for gorillas, who practice polygamy since they have harems, to kill their young ones or to kill young ones that are not related to them by blood, female gorillas can rarely protect their young from male gorillas (fathers or not) since they are physically weaker than males.

It's no surprise that human beings have become the most dominant beings on the planet. There is a direct correlation between human progress and the amount of parental investment in the young. Sorry to say to all the social engineers that want to restructure society but when it comes to child rearing, biological parents (father and mother) are not and never will be superfluous.

Reproduction is the epitome of a natural right. Reproduction is not a right to be controlled by the government.

Even reproduction – one of the most basic human rights is under attack. This natural right, the right of people to have a family, to reproduce, to continue our species, the right of children to have parents is being assaulted. In natural conditions (I am not taking into account laboratory settings) every single child has two parents. No matter what you do and how you create a child one child is always made by two people of the opposite sex and those who "made" the child are morally obliged to raise it. But since we are hurtling towards a technocratic-nightmarish society the powers that be want to control reproduction.

"Genetically modified children: Baby born with DNA from three different people - U.S. scientists recently announced the birth of a baby containing DNA from three different people in an article in New Scientist. The procedure, which is illegal in the United States, was performed in Mexico. It is not the first time that scientists have used biotechnology to produce a child with DNA from three separate people, but the researchers claim that their new technique is significantly more precise, and has major implications for the prevention of genetic disease." (source: naturalnews.com)

"World's first GM babies born - The world's first genetically modified humans have been created, it was revealed last night. The babies have been tested and have been found to contain genes from three 'parents" (source: Dailymail.co.uk)

"Exclusive: World's first baby born with new "3 parent" technique - It's a boy! A five-month-old boy is the first baby to be born using a new technique that incorporates DNA from three people, New Scientist can reveal." (source: newscientist.com) Before you say anything I know that this seems noble, the mother (woman that gave birth) was suffering from a genetic disease present in her DNA and in order for the disease not to pass on to her offspring the doctors switched that particular part of the DNA that had had the hereditary disease present with DNA of another woman, but you are missing the bigger picture. This has major ethical red flags. Could, in the future, two men have a child together by mixing their DNA, could three women have a child of their own that has their genetic structure? What about 5 men and 3 women mixing their DNA to create a baby? Creating real life chimeras. I guess nowadays as long as it's liberal and trendy there is nothing wrong with it. Almost the entire scientific community is celebrating this as a "great leap for mankind" yet they are blissfully unaware of the ramifications this can have. For example, if there is a disease present in people's DNA, but doctors know how to switch that part of the DNA with DNA that is not infected, what if some people can't afford the medical procedure? What if the rich and powerful elite want a baby that will grow up to be tall, above average IQ, or good at a particular

sport, should they have the ability to create their "perfect" baby just because they are wealthy? Should anyone, regardless of the amount of money they have be allowed to literally order what kind of baby they want? In the future, rather than creating babies the old fashion way, couples or better yet people (any number of people) that want to have a baby will go to the local laboratory-marketplace and place an order for a baby with particular traits that they find desirable. Eugenics anyone? You will be able to create a baby with specific physical and mental traits using DNA of any number of people. That baby might end up having the genetic structure that is more similar to that of the DNA-donors than its parents (than again in this scenario who is considered a parent?). If a baby was created by combining the DNA of a large number of people will all of these people have a right to raise the child, does the child belong to the entire community then?

In February of 2015, Britain became the first country in the world to vote in the favor of 3-person IVF (In Vitro Fertilization). This involves taking a fertilized or unfertilized egg from the mother and using a donor's egg to replace parts that are damaged or unhealthy. Supporters of this procedure argue that only 0.1 percent of the donors DNA will be used. They claim that due to this procedure all kinds of genetic diseases will be eradicated. But the 0.1 percent DNA from a donor won't cure everything. What if they, in the future, decide to increase the donor's share of DNA to more than 0.1 percent to cure more diseases (if so then their current argument of the "only 0.1 percent of donors DNA" automatically goes out the window)? What if you increased it to an equal share from three people? What if you can take the DNA from more than three people? Or maybe you could cure more diseases if you take the DNA from an entirely different species and mix it with human DNA to create babies. Where do you draw the line?

In western countries like the UK, IVF is taxpayer funded even for single women and same-sex couples, this is nothing more than a violation of natural rights. What we see here is the state stepping out of line and enabling people who can't conceive naturally to conceive (the state acts as a friend/ally). Since reproduction is a natural right and natural rights are by definition inalienable, this means that they can't be transferred to others, which rules out any form of surrogacy, donation of gametes or sperm to another person, or other similar procedures. In the natural/normal world only those who procreate (who can conceive naturally) should have the right to raise that child. No matter how you put it, in a natural environment (without scientific assistance) a child is made by two parents (one female/mother and one male/father) thus they are the ones who have parental rights. If we let the state define natural rights (reproduction in this case) this will ultimately lead to a totalitarian society. Gay parenting and gay marriage are at a forefront of the present push towards totalitarianism where the state/government, and not nature, defines parenthood. This is based on the attempt to make you accept the notion that authority should, as opposed to nature, define reproduction. Marriage has always been about reproduction first and foremost, mothers and fathers pulling their resources (monetary or otherwise) together for the goal of maximizing the chance of success for their offspring. Marriage has always been and still is a constant target for totalitarian ideologies because it allows the authority to control reproduction (in a different way to how nature intended). Reproduction as a natural right belongs to those who can conceive naturally, not to those who have been granted reproduction rights by the state outside the boundaries of nature. Reproduction is a biological imperative, anything else is opposite to what nature intended.

The IVF procedure was supposed to be reserved only for married couples that couldn't conceive by natural means (note: marriage in Britain is defined as a union between a woman and a man). But now it is available to absolutely anyone who wants a child whether it be a gay couple (keep in mind that Britain doesn't recognize gay marriage) or single parent. This way, children are turned into commodities to be bought and sold to "parents" (I didn't know children have become the property of the state). Nothing could be more dystopian than the idea that social engineers can manufacture methods to conceive and raise children on par or superior to biological parenting. Gay couples, no matter how feminine and masculine who "make" a child through IVF, surrogacy, sperm donors will leave that child without a mother or father (depending what kind of gay couple is in question), thus depriving that child of its parental needs. When it comes to single parents being able to have a child through IVF we get the same situation – a child is left without one parent either a father or a mother. The selfish acts of these "parents" neglect the child's biological need for both biological parents. So let me get this right, a woman that doesn't have a man (boyfriend, husband) in her life can now order a baby and raise it by herself. That child is left without a father. Again, where is the right of a child to be raised by its parents (both of them)? This selfish act should never be allowed, it's not the child's fault that the woman spent her childbearing years doing something else that she deemed more important.

When she hits a wall (her biological clock starts winding down) and realizes she wants a child, no man is willing to help her conceive by conventional means due to her age, and now the government can help her through IVF, surrogacy, sperm donors and other methods. Again we see the state acting as though it were a friend to women. The states grants rights, or better yet entitlements, to those who don't have those rights in natural settings (single people, gay couples). Natural rights (reproduction and parental rights) should not be given (by the state or anyone/anything else) to those who don't possess those rights in natural circumstances (i.e. without the aid of science and/or technology).

IVF itself poses potential complications for the conceived child. The most obvious reason for this is many people decide to have IVF because their gametes are of such poor quality that the odds of natural conception is far too low. But artificial insemination doesn't change the quality of the gametes. While this procedure makes it more likely that fertilization will take place it does nothing to change the fact that the gametes themselves are of low quality. This leads to complications in the development of the fetus that can manifest long after birth. But now those with weak gametes are given an option to use the DNA of a third party during IVF. If only women didn't wait until their late 30s or early 40s to have children. Of course, this is not the only reason but is most certainly one of them.

Thanks to IVF the government has yet again taken more power when it comes to defining parents and parental responsibilities. This way, natural parental rights are ignored.

The leftists that are promoting IFV are nothing more than hypocrites. They claim that they are concerned that the planet is overpopulated while stating that artificial insemination is something that should be encouraged for those who can't conceive naturally (gay couples included).

"GMO babies now being engineered in labs under guise of preventing incurable disease - Life, whether human or otherwise, is no longer sacred to many of today's scientists, who actually believe that tampering with the genetic blueprints of living beings will somehow improve humanity and create a better world. And this disturbing reality became ever more apparent recently when genetic butchers at Oregon Health & Sciences University (OHSU) announced their discovery of a way to manipulate the DNA of human embryos to obstruct normal gene transfer and create genetically "superior" babies that are supposedly less prone to disease. According to the Chicago Tribune, these genetically-modified (GM) embryos are not yet intended to actually produce real, living children -- although it is

only a matter of time before this nightmare becomes a reality (remember the movie Gattaca?) -- but they will be used in the present to investigate how babies of the future might avoid certain inherited diseases. By combining the genes of one man with those of two women, OHSU researchers claim they have devised a way to effectively replace "defective" genes with normal ones. There are two types of genes contained in cells -- those found inside the nucleus of cells, which influence visible traits such as eye color and height, and those found outside the nucleus in energy-generating mitochondria, which do not influence visible traits, and are only passed along by the mother rather than the father. It is these exterior genes that OHSU scientists have learned to alter, reprogram, and literally block from being passed down from mother to child, which they claim could one day unveil ways by which inherited diseases might be avoided. But is this genetic manipulation of the human genome safe and ethical? The answer to this, just like to all genetically-modified organisms (GMOs), is a resounding no, as nobody knows for sure what the long-term effects of vandalizing human genes really are until after the irreversible process has been set into motion. And yet this has not stopped OHSU researchers nor their British predecessors who conducted similar experiments back in 2008 from engaging in the abominable practice under the guise of supposedly preventing incurable diseases. According to reports, the OHSU team that worked on the study, which was published in the journal Nature, is currently trying to gain federal approval to test the development of its GMO babies in actual women rather than in petri dishes, which will take such experiments to a whole new level of reality. It will presumably not be long after, should these "Frankenscientists" receive such approval, before GMO babies are normalized throughout society, and eventually perceived as genetically superior to normal babies with genetic "defects. The U.K.'s Daily Mail; however, reported recently that similar GMO babies are already in existence, having been created using similar techniques in women with fertility problems. According to that particular report, at least two babies born using gene-splicing techniques have already been confirmed to possess genes from three different parents, one father and two mothers."The fact that the children have inherited the extra genes and incorporated them into their 'germline' means that they will, in turn, be able to pass them on to their own offspring," wrote Michael Hanlon about the issue. "Altering the human germline -- in effect tinkering with the very make-up of our species ... could be used to create new races of humans with extra, desired characteristics such as strength or high intelligence." (source: davidicke.com)

"Life-threatening risks arise from new DNA-modified "three parent" babies - A controversial new biotechnology technique to produce children with three genetic parents might not actually cure the congenital diseases it's designed to target, experts have warned — most recently, in a study conducted by researchers from Oregon Health and Science University and published in the journal Nature. The technique in question, popularly known as three-person (or "three-parent") in vitro fertilization (IVF), is designed to produce babies free of inherited defects in their mitochondria, the organelles that provide cells with energy. Mitochondria have their own DNA, separate from the DNA in the nucleus that is believed to control nearly all our bodily processes and traits. Because mitochondrial DNA is inherited only from the mother, three-person IVF takes the nucleus of a zygote produced via IVF and implants it into the donor egg, resulting in a cell with nuclear DNA from the two parents and mitochondrial DNA from a third person. In September, U.S. scientists announced the birth of a baby produced using three-person IVF. The procedure had been performed in Mexico, because it is not legal in the United States. In 2002, the FDA actually banned a previous incarnation of three-person IVF, called cytoplasmic transfer, due to concerns over possible side effects. Following the September announcement, another three-person IVF child was born in China. The United Kingdom followed by formally approving the procedure and setting up a protocol by which fertility labs could apply for approval to perform it. But unbridled enthusiasm over the technique may be premature, mitochondrial experts have warned. That's because the separation between mitochondrial and nuclear DNA isn't as simple as it sounds. The mitochondrial genome is so stripped down that 99 percent of mitochondrial proteins are actually synthesized by the nucleus. That means that mitochondrial and nuclear DNA must work in tight coordination with each other. Swapping out mitochondria from a completely different mother might produce unforeseen health complications. Additionally, three-person IVF cannot completely remove 100 percent of the original mitochondria. Studies suggest that around 2 percent of the original mitochondria migrate to the new cell along with the nucleus. Is that 2 percent enough to matter? The Nature study provides an overwhelming "yes."The researchers performed three-parent IVF in mice, then modified the embryos produced so that they could live indefinitely and be multiplied over and over again. The researchers found that in about 15 percent of cases, the original

mother's mitochondria eventually reasserted itself and eradicated the donor mitochondria. This process could occur at any time during fetal development, or perhaps even during the adult life of a child produced by three-parent IVF. Other studies suggest that if the nuclear and mitochondrial DNA fail to recognize each other properly, the organism can suffer from poor health and infertility. This can occur if researchers change as little as 0.2 percent of an organism's mitochondrial DNA." (source: naturalnews.com) Again, science is unclear about the possible negative side-effects and instead of researching them IVF is being pushed as though there is no cause for alarm.

"Infertility time bomb: IVF (in vitro fertilization) children have higher risk of infertility, obesity and diabetes - Britain faces an infertility time-bomb because a generation of IVF babies may have inherited their parents' inability to conceive, a leading doctor has warned. More than 260,000 children born from IVF treatment in the UK are at greater risk of health problems than naturally conceived youngsters, a conference heard yesterday. And as the generation of IVF children reaches adulthood, many will discover they too are unable to have babies naturally." (source: DailyMailOnline.com) This is only a part of the whole plan, which I will address at the very end of this chapter.

"COMMON CORE EDUCATION: SURVEILLANCE AND SEXUALIZATION OF CHILDREN - Common core is the set of educational standards for American children funded by Bill Gates, the very same man who is pushing GMOs, vaccines and other New World Order (NWO) Agenda 21-style schemes. In another example of blatant dublespeak, the curricula are named "Common Core State Standards", despite the fact they were forced onto the states with bribes, came top-down from the US Federal Government and were written by the international elite. Common Core first came onto the scene in 2009, after Obama took office, using money from the $350 million stimulus package. Common Core is another manifestation of a long-held dream of the NWO manipulators to replace the family with the State, a plan laid out in novels such as Brave New World by Aldous Huxley, which included reference to State hatcheries (i.e. State control of reproduction). Did you know Common Core is actually a private set of standards. It's of the manipulators (since it's owned by them), written by the manipulators, but it's for the masses – all the "common" people not wealthy enough to go to rich schools where the future leaders of the New World Order will learn an entirely different curriculum ... one which probably trains them to become creative thinkers rather than the "obedient

workers" John D. Rockefeller wanted common Americans to become. Is Common Core helping the school to replace the family as a surrogate parent? Is Common Core promoting the idea of collectivism, that the individual is subservient to the group, institution, system and State? It would appear so, but that's not all it's doing. Common Core is now being used in 47 out of 50 US states – in almost all public schools. This is all bad enough, but hold on, because now it starts to get really Orwellian. Children are being spied upon more and more under Common Core. Some of the ways are stealthy, such as through devices like iPads. The NWO manipulators also have plans to introduce all sorts of devices into the classroom which intrude upon the basic privacy of children, including a "facial expression camera", "posture analysis seat", "pressure mouse" and "wireless skin conductance sensor". Introducing kids to sex, including sexual education, at too young of an age, can be confusing and detrimental. A core theme of the worldwide conspiracy is the increasing sexualization of children, which is being fueled by the NWO manipulators' indulgence in widespread pedophilia. Children are being encouraged to have sex and be sexual at an early age, which may well be developmentally inappropriate and harmful, given that amount of emotional maturity that is necessary to be involved in a sexual relationship. Now it's going one step further. Some American public schools under Common Core are already giving advanced forms of birth control to children without parental knowledge. According to Duke, under Common Core, schools now have legal capacity to take teenage girls off campus to an abortion clinic to get an abortion – without informing or consulting parents! The word "common" in common core really means "lowest common denominator". Essentially, Common Core is a form of socialism, Marxism or communism that brings everyone down to an equal level. The bottom line is this: if you want your child to have your values, don't throw him or her away to the State. Avoid Common Core all you can! Homeschool or find a private school that doesn't do Common Core curriculum." (SOURCE: VIKINGTIMES.COM) This is the same Bill Gates that admitted (with video evidence on multiple occasions) that vaccines will be used for depopulation of humanity, just something for those who think that mandatory vaccines are a good idea.

All of this, babies without parents being made in test tubes and raised by the state, was predicted by Aldous Huxley back in 1932 in "Brave New World", which he confirmed both in 1958 in "Brave New World – Revisited" and in 1962 while giving a speech at Berkeley University of California, but don't worry it's all just a conspiracy theory, right...?

CHEMICAL WARFARE:

"Gay bomb" – in 1994 the US government proposed to create the "gay bomb" to use it against their enemy. This was named the "make love not war" plan. It was supposed to discharge female sex pheromones on enemy male soldiers in order to make them sexually attracted to each other. This non-lethal weapon was supposed to chemically alter the state of mind of enemy male troops and make them want to have sex with each other rather than fight. The experiment ended in being unsuccessful. The mastermind behind this idea was the Pentagon. Though not successful this doesn't mean they didn't try again.

"Pesticide atrazine can turn male frogs into females. Atrazine, one of the world's most widely used pesticides, wreaks havoc with the sex lives of adult male frogs, emasculating three-quarters of them and turning one in 10 into females, according to a new study by University of California, Berkeley, biologists. The 75 percent that are chemically castrated are essentially "dead" because of their inability to reproduce in the wild, reports UC Berkeley's Tyrone B. Hayes, professor of integrative biology. These male frogs are missing testosterone and all the things that testosterone controls, including sperm. So their fertility is as low as 10 percent in some cases, and that is only if we isolate those animals and pair them with females. In an environment where they are competing with unexposed animals, they have zero chance of reproducing. The 10 percent or more that turn from males into females – something not known to occur under natural conditions in amphibians. Though the experiments were performed on a common laboratory frog, the African clawed frog (Xenopus laevis), field studies indicate that atrazine, a potent endocrine disruptor, similarly affects frogs in the wild, and could possibly be one of the causes of amphibian declines around the globe. In exposed populations, it looks like there are frogs breeding but, in fact, the population is being very slowly degraded by the introduction of these altered animals. More and more research, however, is showing that atrazine interferes with endocrine hormones, such as estrogen and testosterone – in fish, amphibians, birds, reptiles, laboratory rodents

and even human cell lines at levels of parts per billion. Recent studies also found a possible link between human birth defects and low birth weight and atrazine exposure in the womb. Hayes's studies in the early 2000s were the first to show that the hormonal effects of atrazine disrupt sexual development in amphibians. Working with the African clawed frog, Hayes and his colleagues showed in 2002 that tadpoles raised in atrazine-contaminated water become hermaphrodites – they develop both female (ovaries) and male (testes) gonads. This occurred at atrazine levels as low as 0.1 parts per billion (ppb), 30 times lower than levels allowed in drinking water by the EPA (3 ppb). Subsequent studies showed that native leopard frogs (Rana pipiens) collected from atrazine-contaminated streams in the Midwest, including from areas up to 1,000 miles from where atrazine is applied, often had eggs in their testes. And many males had lower testosterone levels than normal females and smaller than normal voice boxes, presumably limiting their ability to call mates. Hayes' research also established that many frogs in Midwestern streams contaminated by atrazine and other pesticides have compromised immune systems, leading to increased mortality from bacterial disease. Before, we knew we got fewer males than we should have, and we got hermaphrodites. Now, we have clearly shown that many of these animals are sex-reversed males," Hayes said. "We have animals that are females, in the sense that they behave like females. Atrazine has caused a hormonal imbalance that has made them develop into the wrong sex, in terms of their genetic constitution." (source: barkeley.edu)

"ATRAZINE: IT -IS- TURNING THE FROGS GAY - THEY REALLY ARE TURNING THE FREAKING FROGS GAY, Of course, the effects of xenoestrogens certainly aren't limited to frogs and certainly are present in humans. The impact of xenoestrogen exposure on humans is starting to be understood more clearly, and the picture isn't pretty. Xenoestrogens can cause: breast cancer, infertility, disturbance of insulin production, birth defects, reduction in testicle tissue and efficacy, depression caused by testosterone suppression, premature aging and obesity. This all comes at a time when men's sperm production is declining worldwide, as the "scientific community is struggling to find an explanation". Unfortunately, the mainstream does not seem to fully understand or appreciate the huge risks we are getting ourselves into by carelessly spraying Atrazine and using other xenoestrogenic chemicals in our daily lives. I'm sure this has

absolutely nothing to do with recent trends in human sexuality. Sure." (source thewholestory.com)

Endocrine Disruptors: A Case Study on Atrazine, a scientific study says:
page 400: "As an endocrine disruptor, atrazine is thought to have both serious human health and ecological effects. The EPA's (Environmental Protection Agency) recent risk assessment states that the EPA suspects that endocrine disruptors may be responsible for adverse effects on the following bodily systems in humans: 1) female reproductive and development; 2) male reproductive"

"Common chemicals destroying humanity, suggests prominent journalist - They are literally all around us, yet most people are unaware of their invasive presence: chemicals, and especially the hormone-mimicking variety. Everything from plastic bottles and receipts to clothing and furniture is silently teeming with them, and one prominent New York Times (NYT) journalist suggests that they could be humanity's undoing. Also known as endocrine-disrupting chemicals (EDCs), these hormone-mimicking compounds are increasingly turning up in scientific studies as a leading cause of many common conditions, including infertility, diabetes, obesity and cancer. Both males and females throughout the animal kingdom appear to be suffering genital deformities and other sex-related problems because of them, and males in particular are losing, well, their maleness. "Endocrine disruptors are everywhere," writes Nicholas D. Kristof for the NYT. "They're in thermal receipts that come out of gas pumps and ATMs. They're in canned foods, cosmetics, plastics and food packaging. Test your blood or urine, and you'll surely find them there, as well as in human breast milk and in cord blood of newborn babies." Many have also expressed concerns that the FDA has repeatedly refused to evaluate the long-term effects of EDCs, which can take decades to emerge. The synthetic estrogen drug DES, for instance, which is now banned, was once routinely given to pregnant women to help prevent morning sickness and miscarriage. The drug appeared to cause no harm initially but was later determined to cause both vaginal and breast cancer many years down the road." (source: natural news)

"Synthetic female hormones causing mass feminization of men, warns scientist - Estrogen-mimicking chemicals in plastics, industrial products and soy-based foods may be "feminizing" men and driving increases in male

obesity rates, according to a study conducted by researchers from the University of Adelaide, South Australia, and published in the journal PLOS ONE. The researchers compared male and female obesity rates in several countries worldwide. They found that less developed countries, as measured by variables such as Gross Domestic Product, tend to have significantly higher rates of obesity among women than among men. This pattern is considered normal, in part because the sex hormone estrogen (present in much higher levels in women than in men) has been linked to weight gain. The authors attribute part of the cause to the "feminizing" effect of synthetic estrogens, part of a larger category of chemicals known as endocrine disruptors. "We are concerned that in societies with a high dietary saturation of soy, such as the United States, this could be working to 'feminise' the males," researcher Maciej Henneberg said. Other known sources of estrogen mimics include flame retardants, dioxins, PCBs and the plastics chemicals bisphenol A (BPA) and phthalates." (source: davidicke.com)

"MORE WILDLIFE FISH ARE EXPERIENCING 'INTERSEX' – WHAT COULD BE CAUSING THIS? Endocrine disruptors threaten reproduction in fish and frogs - More wildlife are experiencing strange reproductive abnormalities, but why? In a study released last year, the U.S. Geological Survey and U.S. Fish and Wildlife Service (USFW) tested male smallmouth and largemouth bass from 19 National Wildlife Refuges. The research found that 85% of the smallmouth bass "had signs of female reproductive parts." Of the largemouth bass, 27% were intersex. What could be causing this?" (source: infowars.com)

"Fish becoming transgender from contraceptive pill chemicals being flushed down household drains - fifth of male fish are now transgender because of chemicals from the contraceptive pill being flushed down household drains, a study by has suggested. Male river fish are displaying feminised traits and even producing eggs, the study found. Some have reduced sperm quality and display less aggressive and competitive behaviour, which makes them less likely to breed successfully. The chemicals causing these effects include ingredients in the contraceptive pill, by-products of cleaning agents, plastics and cosmetics, according to the findings. Professor Charles Tyler, of the University of Exeter, is to present his findings in a key-note lecture at a symposium this week. He will explain that the offspring of such "transgender" or "intersex" fish can also be more sensitive to the

effects of these chemicals in subsequent exposures. Professor Tyler said: "We are showing that some of these chemicals can have much wider health effects on fish that we expected." (source: thetelegraph.com)

"Study: GMO toxins found in nearly all pregnant women, unborn babies - A recent study published in the journal Reproductive Toxicology debunks yet another lie of the biotechnology industry concerning genetically-modified organisms (GMOs). According to an analysis conducted by researchers from the University of Sherbrooke Hospital Centre in Quebec, Canada, 100 percent of pregnant women and their unborn babies tested positive for GMO toxins in their blood, proving that transgenic materials are not effectively broken down and eliminated during digestion as we have all been told. The study, which is featured in the new Jeffrey Smith documentary Genetic Roulette examined the blood of 30 pregnant women and 39 non-pregnant women. The research team, led by Aziz Aris and Samuel Leblanc, looked for glyphosate (Roundup); gluphosinate, an active ingredient in various broad-spectrum herbicides; Cry1Ab, the Bt toxin of gluphosinate; and several metabolites of both glyphosate and gluphosinate. Upon observation, they noticed that the non-pregnant women all had high levels of both glyphosate and gluphosinate in their blood, while none of the pregnant women had either of the two chemicals in their blood, illustrating that some type of metabolic change takes place when women become pregnant. As far as the other chemicals were concerned; however, 100 percent of the pregnanr women and their unborn babies tested positive for 3-methylphosphinico propionic acid (3-MMPA), a metabolite of gluphosinate, while 93 percent of maternal blood and 80 percent of fetal cord blood tested positive for the Bt toxin Cry1Ab. This is highly concerning, as it shows not only that these two untested chemicals are effectively bypassing the digestive systems of pregnant women, but that they are also persisting in their bloodstreams for an untold amount of time, where they proceed to infect the bloodstreams of unborn children. The long-term health effects of such exposure are largely unknown, as few formative safety studies have ever been conducted on either Bt toxin or the pesticide and herbicide chemicals used on GMO crops. Existing studies do suggest; however, that gluphosinate, the precursor to 3-MMPA, can cause cancer, DNA damage, and reproductive toxicity." (source: alternet.org) Nothing is sicker and more morally depraved than targeting pregnant women and their unborn children

"How sexually confusing moths could save your clothes from holes - Museum tricks male moths into thinking other males are females in bid to stop them reproducing as it wages gender warfare on cloth-eating insects. Now they are using a system which tricks male moths into thinking that other male moths are actually females in a bid to stop them mating and producing eggs and larvae. And it does not involve killing any moths, merely confusing males into fruitlessly chasing members of their own sex and overwhelming their senses so they can no longer smell the females. "It's called the Pheromone Destruction System and in simplistic terms, it makes male moth attracted to other male moths," said Armando Mendex, quarantine facility manager at the museum, who is heading the project. "They only live for a couple of weeks and during that time there is only a small window in which they can reproduce."If they spend this unknowingly attempting to attract and fertilize male moths, then it reduces the offspring we are up against." "It's like birth control for moths," said Georgina Donovan of Exosect. Over time, less mating means less eggs are laid, less larvae hatch." (source: thetelegraph.com / independent.com)

"Sex-Changing Chemicals Can Wipe Out Fish, Study Shows - Tiny amounts of the estrogen used in birth control pills can cause wild fish populations to collapse, according to a new study. The finding raises concern about even low levels of estrogen in municipal wastewater, said study leader Karen Kidd, a biologist with the Canadian Rivers Institute at the University of New Brunswick. "Women excrete estrogen naturally, and women on birth control pills also secrete the synthetic estrogen in those pills," she explained."And these estrogens, depending on the level of wastewater treatment, may not be completely broken down during sewage treatment, so they get discharged into rivers and streams." Male fish exposed to the hormone become feminized—they produce the same proteins that female fish do to develop eggs. Some males even develop eggs in their testes. "It doesn't take a lot of estrogen to feminize male fish and, based on the results of our experiment, to impact fish populations," Kidd said. Several studies have shown that exposure to estrogen and related compounds feminizes male fish, but until now the impact on wild fish populations was unknown. Kidd and colleagues from Canada's federal fisheries agency added the synthetic estrogen found in birth control pills to a remote, isolated lake set aside for such experiments in northwestern Ontario, Canada. For three summers the researchers added estrogen at levels found in untreated municipal wastewaters. Several fish species live in the lake,

including the short-lived fathead minnow. After the first summer, male minnows were producing egg proteins. By the second year their sperm cells were undeveloped. Shortly after that they produced eggs as well. In addition, females were producing more egg protein than normal, and their sexual development was also delayed, Kidd said. The result was an impaired ability of the minnows to reproduce, which caused the population to collapse in the second year of the study, the researchers found. The population even failed to recover in the two years after the researchers stopped adding estrogen, indicating the effects were quite persistent, according to Kidd." (source: nationalgeographic.com)

"Sex-Changing Chemicals Found in Potomac River - Ever since the discovery of gender-bending fish in the Potomac River, scientists have wondered what could be changing the sex of large numbers of fish in the waterway outside Washington D.C. They may not have to wonder much longer. A recent U.S. government study has found large quantities of chemicals in the river and its tributaries—pollutants that are known to cause sex change in animals. "In 2002 we were looking at stream-water chemistry to understand the large fish die-offs at these sites. It was then that we found smallmouth bass with intersex, a condition where male fish develop premature egg cells." Once absorbed by the body, these chemicals—known as endocrine disruptors—interfere with normal bodily functions either by mimicking or blocking the production of hormones. Scientists have also found reproductive problems in fish and birds in habitats along the U.S. Great Lakes. Kolpin said."We need to understand the cocktail of compounds that are in the environment and whether there are certain bad actors that are causing feminization of males—and what it means for humans [who use this water]."" (source: nationalgeographic.com)

"Animals' Sexual Changes Linked to Waste, Chemicals - Animals throughout the world are undergoing unnatural sexual changes in response to environmental pollution, according to a group of scientists. The scientists warn that the gender-bending effects of certain man-made substances and human sewage seriously threaten polar bears, alligators, frogs, mollusks, and other wildlife. The report suggests endocrine disruptors are now widespread in many animals and can seriously harm populations. Endocrine disruptors interfere with animals' endocrine systems, leading to adverse health effects that can be passed to offspring. EASs mimic naturally produced hormones, setting off chemical reactions in the body. Endocrine

disruptors can also block the action of hormones and alter their concentrations. The masculization of female polar bears in the Norwegian Arctic was linked to polychlorinated biphenyls (PCBs), an industrial pollutant that accumulates along food chains, according to a study published in 1998 in the Journal of Wildlife Diseases. The following year, a WWF report associated spontaneous abortions and declining seal populations along the Wadden Sea coast of the Neatherlands, Germany, and Denmark with low female hormone levels due to PCB contamination. Studies undertaken in Lake Apopka, Florida, blame pesticide pollution for sex-organ abnormalities in Florida alligators, which researchers say have resulted in significant population losses. Females were having difficulty creating viable eggs, while males experienced premature sperm production and reductions in penis size, among other effects." (source: infowars.com)

"Study: Science Can Change the Sexual Orientations of Mice - By altering serotonin in their brains, researchers caused female mice to prefer to mount and sniff the genitals of other females. Researchers led by Shasha Zhang at Peking University in Beijing and reviewed by Dr. Catherine Dulac at Harvard bred certain female mice that lacked either serotonin or certain neurons that release serotonin in parts of their brains. They then compared their behaviors to the typical non-mutant mice. Those mice with the mutations showed preferences for sniffing the head and genital areas of other female mice, as well as "try[ing] to grasp ... females by the waist before mounting on their back. ... Females displayed strong mounting preference toward the females, mounted female targets with shorter latency, higher frequency, and longer duration." "Mutant females lacking serotonergic neurons" showed preferences for females over males. Zhang and company concluded that not having certain neurons that release serotonin "cause[d] a reversal of sexual preference, revealing a role for [serotonin] in regulating sexual preference."" (source: theatlantic.com)

"Scientists shocked as common pesticides are confirmed to accelerate puberty in boys by drastically altering hormone production - Environmental exposure to common pesticides speeds up the onset of puberty in boys, a new study found. Researchers at the Zhejiang University in Hangzhou, China found that a class of pesticide called pyrethroid accounted for more than 30% of pesticide use around the world. Pyrethroids are commonly used both indoors and outdoors to kill mosquitoes and other bugs. The chemical is also sprayed on crops. Residential use and food intake were associated with

pyrethroid in humans. Lead researcher Dr. Jing Liu said residues of this pesticide are most commonly found in milk, baby food, and vegetables. The chemical is a known endocrine-disruptor that affects the body's hormones. Pyrethroid exposure in humans can be detected in urine as a metabolite, or molecule, called 3-phenoxybenzoic acid (3-PBA).For the study, researchers examined 463 Chinese boys ages nine to 16 years, and found that each 10% increase in 3-PBA was tied to a 4% increase in the levels of luteinizing hormones and follicle-stimulating hormones in participants. Both hormones are responsible for stimulating testosterone production in males. According to the study, higher urinary 3-PBA levels increased the odds of early puberty by 73 to 110%." (source: natural.news)

"Early Puberty in Girls Is Becoming Epidemic and Getting Worse - Girls with early onset puberty face a number of mental and physical health risks. Padded bras for kindergarteners with growing breasts to make them more comfortable? Sixteen percent of U.S. girls experiencing breast development by the age of 7? Thirty percent by the age of 8? Clearly something is affecting the hormones of U.S. girls—a phenomenon also seen in other developed countries. Girls in poorer countries seem to be spared—until they move to developed countries." (source: alternet.org)

"Girls now reaching puberty at age nine, thanks to chemicals in the food supply (milk and plastics) - The average age of puberty in girls is now nine, in a phenomenon increasingly being blamed on rising obesity and exposure to hormone-disrupting pollutants in the food supply. The study was conducted in 2006 by researchers from the world-renowned Department of Growth and Reproduction at University Hospital in Copenhagen, Denmark. The researchers found that among 1,000 girls, the average age of breast development was nine years and 10 months, a full year earlier than when a similar study was conducted in 1991. "We were very surprised that there had been such a change in a period of just 15 years," researcher Anders Juul said. Although the study was conducted in Denmark, experts believe that it applies to other parts of the First World, including Europe and the United States. This earlier age of maturation is even more striking when compared with the 19th century, when girls reached puberty at an average age of 15, and boys reached it at 17. Since then, the age of puberty has moved back steadily, until age 14 for boys and age 12 for girls were formally declared "normal" in the 1960s. These numbers were based on the average age of first period for girls and of voices breaking for boys. It's not just scientific

studies suggesting these figures are now obsolete; anecdotal reports of boys dropping out of choir schools when their voices break at age 12 or 13 are now widespread. According to Richard Stanhope, an expert in childhood hormonal disorders, specialists are now convinced that early puberty is a real phenomenon. Early puberty can be hard on children who are mature physically but still young emotionally, experts warn. "All the things we experience as teenagers are difficult enough to cope with, but when it happens at 10 or 11 it is much worse," Stanhope said. "These children are also at a much higher risk of being sexually abused, because it is hard for some adults to understand and behave appropriately towards them." The biological risks can also be dire. Earlier menarche in girls means a longer lifetime exposure to estrogen, which has been linked to an increased risk of breast cancer and heart disease. "If girls mature early, they run into teenage problems at an early age and they're more prone to diseases later on," Juul said. "We should be worried about this regardless of what we think the underlying reasons might be. It's a clear sign that something is affecting our children, whether it's junk food, environmental chemical or lack of physical activity." "We don't know if this is the result of better nutrition or environmental factors, but it does create social problems for girls who are already living in a sexualized society," agreed Richard Sharpe, head of the human reproductive sciences unit for the United Kingdom's Medical Research Council." (source: naturalnews.com) Again, something Dr. Lawrence Dunegan said. Why are children, both girls, and boys, reaching puberty at an earlier age than ever before? Why are most people silent? Could it be – pedophilia?

"Research Proves 'Gender-Bending' Chemicals Affect Reproduction - New research proves that 'gender-bending' chemicals, which leach from human products into rivers and oceans, can have a significant impact on the ability of fish to breed. The study has important implications for understanding the impacts of these chemicals. Endocrine-disrupting chemicals (EDCs) affect hormones. They are found in products ranging from contraceptive drugs to liquid detergents. They have been seeping into rivers through the sewage system for decades and alter the biology of fish, changing male fish to make them more female. Intersex fish contain both sperm and eggs, and this new study found that their reproductive abilities may be reduced by up to 76 percent. How did these fish end up "intersex"? Through exposure to endocrine-disrupting chemicals (EDCs) that are polluting the environment -- a finding that raises serious implications for humans as well because all

vertebrates have similar sex hormone receptors. Already these chemicals, nicknamed "gender-benders," are causing the males in many species to become feminized. In some rivers in Britain, up to 50 percent of male fish are now growing eggs along with sperm in their testes. Hermaphrodite polar bears have also been found. The more a pregnant woman is exposed to high levels of one type of endocrine-disrupter known as phthalates, the greater the risk her son will have smaller genitals and incomplete testicular descent, leading to impaired reproductive development. The chemical also appears to make the overall genital tracts of boys slightly more feminine. It is believed that phthalates have these adverse effects because they reduce testosterone synthesis by interfering with an enzyme needed to produce the male hormone. They also affect women's endocrine systems and reproductive health although the effects are different between the genders. For instance, girls are also reaching puberty earlier than ever before, and these chemicals may be culprits. These chemicals are virtually everywhere in the modern world, lurking in personal care products, food containers, medical tubing, toys and more. Some of the top offenders you should be aware of, and watch out for, include: Phthalates, Bisphenol A (BPA), Perfluorooctanoic acid (PFOA), Methoxychlor and Vinclozin, Nonylphenol ethoxylates (NPEs), Bovine growth hormones, Non-fermented soy products, MSG, Fluoride." (source: Mercola.com) Interesting facts: fluoride was invented by the Nazis and was used on prisoners and captured enemy troops to make them more docile. Fluoride, amongst other adverse repercussions, diminishes female fertility.

"The New Zealand government's bio engineering facility, AgResearch, has succeeded in genetically engineering androgynous goats. This expertise could give the Illuminati the means to neuter mankind and take control of reproduction. Ominously, they have dubbed the androgynous goats "goys," which is supposedly an amalgam of "girls" and "boys." But they could have used the term, "mems" (from males-females.)" (source: henrymakow.com)

"How ibuprofen damages the fertility of unborn girls: Painkiller can halve the number of eggs in their ovaries - Women taking ibuprofen while pregnant may be damaging daughter's fertility. Study found the painkiller can halve the number of egg cells in girls' ovaries. Meaning girls exposed to ibuprofen in the womb may struggle to have a family. Women who take ibuprofen in the first six months of pregnancy may harm their daughters'

future fertility, a study suggests. Scientists found the common painkiller can halve the number of egg cells in girls' ovaries. This suggests girls exposed to ibuprofen in the womb may struggle to have a family, as their body makes fewer eggs. Women are born with all the eggs they will ever have, unlike men who increasingly produce sperm. It means females could go through menopause earlier, running out of time to have a child, or struggle with infertility in later life." (source: DailyMailOnline.com)

"FACT: There is no Gay gene, but there ARE chemicals that turn people gay - First let me show you evidence there is no such thing as a Gay gene. "There's No Gay Gene, Says Scientists In The Quarterly Review of Biology, *researchers at UC Santa Barbara and Uppsala University in Sweden have concluded through their research that sexual orientation can be decided through epi-marks, which are temporary switches in a fetus' DNA that exist while in the womb and shortly after birth...."Genes are basically the instruction book, while epi-marks direct* how *those instructions get carried out. For example, they can determine when, where, and how much of a gene gets expressed." "As a press release explains in almost comprehensible terms, the study finds "sex-specific epi-marks, which normally do not pass between generations and are thus 'erased,' can lead to homosexuality when they escape erasure and are transmitted from father to daughter or mother to son."" Now let me show you evidence of the* NWO actively trying to turn people gay. *Gay people didn't need help to become that way 2,000 years ago and they sure don't need to be forced to become that way. Why would the NWO want to do that. It's a variation of eugenics. If a population does not breed it eventually dies. For more information on eugenics see my other blog: Pro abortion = Pro eugenics So, what can turn people "gay"? Actually In my opinion I don't think "Gay" or "homosexual" is the right term. This stuff literally turn animals and people into hermaphrodites. Lowering testosterone levels alters males to females. Getting to the point high estrogen levels feminizes males. What is estrogen? The definition of estrogen is: "any of a group of steroid hormones that* promote the development and maintenance of female characteristics of the body. *Such hormones are also produced artificially for use in oral contraceptives or to treat menopausal and menstrual disorders." How can testosterone be lowered? Well the proper amount can be disrupted with endocrine disruptors. The definition of endocrine disruptor is:*
"Endocrine disruptors are chemicals that at certain doses, can interfere with the endocrine in mammals. These disruptions can cause cancerous tumors,

birth defects, and other developmental disorders. Any system in the body controlled by hormones, can be derailed by hormone disruptors." What chemical can be used to do this? BPA. BPA is a Endocrine disruptor. "Bisphenol A (BPA) is an estrogenic endocrine disruptor widely used in the production of plastics. Increasing evidence indicates that in utero BPA exposure affects sexual differentiation and behavior…We hypothesized that BPA may disrupt epigenetic programming of gene expression in the brain…BPA exposure induced persistent, largely sex-specific effects on social and anxiety-like behavior, leading to disruption of sexually dimorphic behaviors." "If a mother is ingesting BPA while carrying her fetus sex-related genes are turned on and off in response to fluctuating levels of hormones in the womb. Although a child may become male in the womb the fetus is being bathed in estrogen [Blogger comment: This could lead to the male having a female brain] and subsequently nursed on BPA bottles which consistently causes estrogen to metabolize in the infant's body. Is this what is causing male children to gravitate toward the nature of a female?" Below is proof that Gay people are used as a weapon by the elite. LBGT folks should be in a uproar about this. The NWO wants to use your cause to promote their sick evil eugenics program. "Air Force Considered Gay 'Love Bomb' Against Enemies The Air Force on Tuesday confirmed a report that in 1994 a military researcher requested $7.5 million to develop a non-lethal "love bomb" that would chemically alter the state of mind of enemy troops and make them want to have sex with each other rather than fight." There are multiple chemicals that are endocrine disruptors. I don't know them all but I wanted to highlight BPA because this stuff is used in making things we eat and drink out of. "BPA is used to make certain plastics and epoxy resins; it has been in commercial use since 1957 and around 3.6 million tons (8 billion pounds) of BPA are used by manufacturers yearly. BPA-based plastic is clear and tough, and is used to make a variety of common consumer goods (such as baby and water bottles, sports equipment, and CDs and DVDs) and for industrial purposes, like lining water pipes. Epoxy resins containing BPA are used as coatings on the inside of many food and beverage cans. It is also used in making thermal paper such as that used in sales receipts." *To use this biological weapon, BPA, on people is so evil! Some of you may be asking why I put this in the religious section. Well for one the gay/straight debate usually ends up as a religious conversation. Also, I'm not posting this to bash LBGT. LBGT folks around the world should be outraged by this. Evil scum is actively trying sexually cripple all of us so we can't procreate as God intended. LBGT don't let the NWO use your* *platform as a base for one of their eugenic programs. Speak out against this."* (gachiyellow.worldpress.com)

"Gender-bending chemicals - Almost 90 per cent of teenagers have gender-bending chemicals from plastic in their bodies, according to a study. Bisphenol A (BPA) is found in plastic containers and water bottles, on the inside of food cans and in till receipts. The chemical, used since the 1960s to make certain types of plastic, mimics the female sex hormone estrogen, and has been linked to low sperm counts and infertility in men, as well as breast and prostate cancer. A study by the University of Exeter, whose researchers tested urine samples from 94 teenagers, found 86 per cent had traces of BPA in their body. Experts fear it is all but impossible to avoid the chemical, given the widespread use of plastic packaging for food. Researchers surmise that people all over the world of all ages are likely to have a measurable amount of BPA in their blood, urine or body tissue. Several government studies have detected BPA in large portions of the population, including 93 per cent of the US population aged six and older, and 99 per cent of the population in Germany aged 3-14. This new study into the high number of teenagers with BPA in their digestive system serves only to underscore that concern." (source: dailymail.co.uk)

"Are we being chemically altered into homosexuality? - It has been shown in numerous studies that (Triazine) Atrazine, an endocrine disrupter, induces hermaphroditism and over time complete feminization and chemical castration in frogs. All Atrazine exposed males in the control groups had greatly reduced testosterone levels and noticeable demasculinization. Atrazine is one of the most widely used pesticides in the world. It is also marketed as Triazine. Approximately 80 million pounds are applied annually in the United States alone, and Atrazine is the most common pesticide contaminant of ground and surface water. I know I am making a leap here (no frog pun intended) but we, as humans, are exposed to pesticides such as Atrazine without knowing it and without our consent many times. This, and many other chemicals end up in our tap water, the water we shower and bathe in. If this chemical is powerful enough to change the actual sex of a frog and it is in water we are exposed to and drink, I have to ask what is it doing to us as humans? I have wondered many times what is happening to our society, as so many men seem to be becoming more and more feminine, softer, and more and more are coming out as transgender or gay. I had assumed that this was their natural state

and they were just coming to a place of self-acceptance. But what if it isn't actually happening naturally at all? What if these feelings and physical changes are being chemically induced without their knowledge or consent? Their very DNA being changed through the water supply. I am going to guess that this plays right into Agenda 21 and the New World Order. Population control becomes easy if you cannot reproduce and are sterile but even easier if you are chemically altering the males to be attracted to males vs. females, as there is no reproduction possible at all in a homosexual relationship. Believe me, I know how crazy this article sounds... please feel free to do your own research and draw your own conclusions on this... my mind is blown." (source: naturalnewsblobs.com) The exact same thing I have been talking about for some 6/7 years.

Two things. If they are capable of doing this to animals, who is to say they aren't doing it to humans? I'm not saying that these examples give an answer as to why homosexuality occurs in all cases but I do think that at least in theory it explains as to why homosexuality and other LGBT-like behavior continues to rise.

The Gay agenda is the precursor to a much wider agenda which is colloquially known as Agenda 21, though some refer to it as Communism 2.0. Agenda 21 is a plan for global depopulation of the human race, and it will be done through the United Nations. To my knowledge, there are two main reasons as to why people refer to the depopulation agenda as Communism 2.0. First of all, the methods that will (are) being used to cull the human race are eerily similar to those implemented in Russia after 1917: anti-family ideology, anti-natal ideology, sexual free-for-all, and sexual liberation, not to mention open unscrupulous genocide. The Second reason is that the United Nations had ties to Communism since its inception. In any case, it boils down to reducing the human population on Earth without the consent of the people. For years I have been talking that abortion and the rise of homosexuality, transgenderism are forms of population control and that the elite are planning for global depopulation of the human race.

There are two ways to reduce the population:

- increasing the death rate (increase of mortality)
- decreasing the birth rate (decrease of natality)

As far as the first one is concerned, increasing the death rate might seem like a good way to reduce the human population. This would involve more conventional means of killing: war, genocide etc. But, in fact, it's not as good as it might seem. History has shown us that anytime there is a great culling of a particular population, birth rates of that population skyrocket afterward. My guess is that this is a survival-type mechanism by which the members of the population that survived compensate for the great loss of population. In a relatively short period of time, they will negate the depopulation effect and the elite are back at square one.

The second method, decreasing the birth rate, is in my opinion much more fruitful for the depopulation goal. This is done through unorthodox methods like eugenics (or better yet the antonym of eugenics a.k.a. - dysgenics since the elite are decreasing and not increasing the quality of the general human population), and its 21st century sister/science eugenics epigenetics (epi-eugenics for short, which unlike classical eugenics doesn't take multiple generations to reach a certain goal but rather focuses on changing the genetic make-up of already developed living beings). One of the ways the elite are doing this is by lowering testosterone levels. Testosterone levels in both men and women have been on a steep decline for many decades. If the testosterone levels are low both sexes suffer from fatigue, exhaustion, weight gain, mood swings, depression, anxiety (amongst other things). Testosterone in men stimulates the sex-drive and sperm production, which have been declining for at least 3 decades (certainly for longer than that). This is done through estrogen mimickers or estrogen disruptors (bisphenol-A, atrazine, etc.) which lower the natural testosterone levels in humans while artificially increasing synthetic estrogen levels. Women are also negatively affected by this. Just some of the adverse implications of estrogen disruptors on women's health are: depression, low libido, weight gain, infertility. They are slowly but steadily, destroying our ability to procreate. The goal of the elite is to create one gender that will not be able to procreate.

For the population of a particular region to survive it needs to replenish its numbers on a consistent basis through a healthy birth rate. In order for any given population to maintain its numbers throughout generations, every married couple needs to have a specific number of kids (depending on which research you look at this number is either 2.1 or 2.2 kids per marriage). This means that, in order for a population of any given region, not to start dying off each married couple (woman and man) needs to have on average 2.1 or 2.2 kids. In more practical terms, for example, out of 10 married couples – 1 or 2 of them would need to have at least 3 kids, while the rest should have at least 2, this way the very minimal birth rate will only ensure that the population stays the same, anything less and the population starts dying off because not enough kids are being born to replace their parents and continue the process. Why 2.1 or 2.2 kids per married couple? The 2.0 kids is quite obvious, those two kids will eventually replace their parents one day, the 0.1 or 0.2 that we have left is to negate unforeseen, unpredictable and unfavorable circumstances like people who don't end up having kids, or kids that die before reaching adulthood thus not having kids of their own. The 0.1 or 0.2 is there to compensate for less than ideal situations. If there are more than 2.2 kids per married couple the population increases, if that number drops below 2.1 or 2.2 the population starts declining, which is exactly what the elite want. The majority of western countries (Europe and North America) and peoples (all except Russia) are dying off. Here I am only including white people, a.k.a. people who are indigenous to Europe (I am not including non-European migrants since their birth rates are skyrocketing). White-countries and their white population are dying off (in all honesty they have been dying off for decades), all white countries (Europe and North America, all except Russia) have birth rates that are below replacement level (in most European countries white Europeans have around 1 point something kids per marriage, which is not enough to maintain the population numbers that are unsurprisingly on a steep decline), meaning if things do not change soon enough there will be no white people left, they are already becoming a minority in their own countries. I'm not insinuating that this is some conspiracy involving the entire world against only white people, I'm sure once white people are wiped off the face of Earth the elite will move on to eradicate non-white people as well. They plan to do this on all continents, in all countries, to all peoples, races, and religions. For one reason or the other, they decided to start this mass genocide first on white people, afterward the rest of Earth's population. They started doing similar things in the U.S. between the two world wars on the black population with Planned Parenthood and people like Margret Sanger. This "white-genocide" or the "great replacement" as it is known, is the greatest genocide in human history, and the elite are conducting it in a number of ways. These ways as I have shown you are all directed at decreasing the birth rate. Whether it's decimating fertility in men and women, destroying the family unit, abortion or increasing homosexuality they all aim to decrease the human population in preparation for the great culling of the human race.

Perhaps homosexuality is normal in a very small number of cases. Personally, I don't think so since there is no reason for the existence of homosexuality nor does society or the human race benefit from homosexuality at all. Maybe homosexuality in some cases occurs naturally, without outside interference. Maybe, just like transsexuality the way Camille Paglia described it, homosexuality is normal is small cases, maybe it represents a normal occurring isotope or an anomaly in nature. That being said, there is no doubt that today homosexual and other LGBT-like phenomena are being artificially increased through sexual liberation, propaganda, early sexual experience and child sexual molestations, social engineering and chemicals in our plastic bottles (BPA), cans, food (GMO's), water (fluoride) and who knows what else, not to mention the ways that they are poisoning pregnant women and their yet unborn children.

The last thing we should do is give the state (the pedophile elites that run this world) control of the reproductive system.

Power corrupts and absolute power corrupts absolutely. We are sliding towards a totalitarian global super-state which will control every aspect of our lives.

Mark Twain *"Truth is stranger than fiction"*

GAY AGENDA 21

CHAPTER 9 "THE OMEN"

There are two main reasons as to why I wrote this book. The first one being the age-old condescending "I told you so". Everything that you have read up until this point I have predicted years ago (approximately 6-7 years ago). Even though it took several months to write all this, it took years to compile all the data and research. Years ago I said that once they legalize gay marriage they will use it as a platform to normalize pedophilia (which is quite evident now), I also said that it's only a matter of time before they start pushing their dogma on impressionable and malleable kids. Back then and now the usual response from people is "conspiracy theory" or "you are paranoid", both coming from people who use emotions and feelings as arguments and evidence. The tipping point which led me to write this was when they attempted to push their ideology across elementary schools in Serbia in early 2017. To anyone who bothered to read the sex-education curriculum they intended to implement in elementary schools in Serbian one thing they will notice is that it is a carbon copy of the one already implemented in Canada which I covered in chapter 5. Same as in Canada they tried to rush it without the consent of parents. Though they failed, mark my words this is just the beginning. The second reason for writing this, as the name of the chapter suggests, is intended for the future.

To anyone who knows history one thing should be apparent, and that is that history constantly repeats itself. It's close to being a loop. What was will come again and what is now once was. Nothing new can happen that hasn't already occurred at some point in history. Meaning one could predict the future by knowing the past.

Rome, the Greek City States, and many other civilizations fell into obscurity because of complete sexual liberation, yet people are doomed to repeat the same mistakes over and over again. Whether you believe in the Sodom and Gomorrah story or not (I personally don't) or you think it is an interpretation of a real story, it's almost irrespective whether it really occurred or not, it is one of many warnings from the ancient world, a warning what happens to civilizations that go down the sexual liberation path.

In chapter 2, I mentioned how sexual liberation and hedonism in Germany after World War One led to the rise of Nazis and Hitler. Though true, that is not the whole story. After World War One there was a real possibility that the Communists would take over Germany. In response to this Communist threat and sexual liberation, right-wing ideology rose up in Germany.

To oppose left-wing ideology (Communism) right-wing ideology gain in popularity. Apart from the rise of conservatism as a natural counterweight to Communism, Germany also witnessed the rise of Nazism. The main reason as to why the German people supported Nazism and voted Hitler into power was because he presented himself as an anti-Communist. Unfortunately for them, as time would show, Nazism was nothing more than Communism with a different name. So Communism (far left wing ideology) led to the rise of Nazism (another far left-wing ideology). This is why some historians say Communism leads to Fascism (Nazism being one of its forms). You can make the argument that there is no fundamental difference between Communism and Fascism/Nazism since both stem from collectivist authoritarian ideologies.

The majority of today's European and American politicians and ruling elite are left-wing liberals which is reflected in their policies. For some, to me inconceivable reason, people think America is great. They actually think that the U.S.A. is doing just fine. For at least 10 years I've been saying that the U.S. is on the brink of civil war (which is quite obvious now). Why? Well, feminism and sexual liberation didn't do it any favors in regards to that. Rome and the Greek City States fell because of it, and now North America (I'm only counting the U.S. and Canada) is suffering the same faith. Let's completely ignore the economic sinkhole that is the U.S.A., the reason as to why America is falling apart is the same reason Rome and the Greek City States fell - the breakdown/destruction of the nuclear family. Due to the decay of the nuclear family America is on the brink of moral and social collapse. No society has ever survived the dissolution of a heterosexual monogamous family where the nuclear/traditional family (mother and father) are raising their own children independent from the state/government. The family is the foundation of a society. Once the elite destroys the family the rest of society will fall like a deck of cards.

Our western society (Europe and North America) is at a crossroads, continue the on-going leftist-liberal approach and suffer the same consequences as our ancestors that warned us about what happens once sexual hedonism and sexual liberation takes precedence, or break the cycle. So many civilizations across the ages were destroyed once the family unit fell apart, America and Europe (predominantly Western Europe) are experiencing exactly that right now, yet they are completely blind to the mistakes of those who came before us. At least the entire 20th and 21st century was one big leftist-liberal experiment that utterly failed, yet despite this, they continue to push policies that have previously failed. This is the literal definition of an idiot – do the same things over and over again and expect a different result.

We are at a juncture, continue and end up like the Western Roman Empire, engulfed in sexual liberation and hedonism while the Empire is burning (the U.S. and Canada are currently experiencing that), or we take a different approach and not make the same mistakes over and over again. So if leftist-liberal policies are destroying society by dissolving the family unit we ought to have a more conservative approach that is going to prevent the destruction of the family thus preserving our civilization. Here, when I'm talking about right-wing/conservative ideology I mean ideology where people have rights that derived from nature and not from the state (example: rights of reproduction and child-rearing belongs to those who can reproduce naturally, i.e. without the assistance of technology). The state has no right to give natural rights or better yet entitlements to those who don't possess those rights naturally. This is applicable to natural rights, reproduction probably being the most notable one.

More and more people across Europe and North America are turning to conservatism seeing how leftist-liberal rhetoric brings nothing good to society. People are realizing that in order to preserve society more conservative policies need to be adopted. Even anarchists are becoming conservatives and are adopting more traditional ideologies.

This is why people like Putin, Nigel Farage, Marine Le Pen, Donald Trump, Orbán (and many more across Europe) have massively gained in popularity, they gained more supporters because of their more conservative viewpoints and political stances. The usual and predictable response from leftist-liberals is to call these people and their supporters hateful bigoted backward thinking right-wing radicals, or just refer to them as a literal embodiment of Hitler because to these intellectuals everyone with whom they disagree with is literally Hitler. To these political handicaps, anyone even slightly right on the political spectrum is a Nazi, even though Nazism is a far left-wing ideology just like Communism. Putin, Nigel Farage, Marine Le Pen, Donald Trump, Orbán are not right wing radicals just for having conservative policies, they at least have something new to say. The last thing we need is more policies from political marionettes and political prostitutes like Angela Merkel, Killary Hilton, Emmanuel Macron, Justin Trudeau, Barack Hussein Obama, Tony Blair, James Cameron, Theresa May. Theresa May, the woman who at first said that she would honor the will of the British people who voted in a democratic referendum to leave the EU, but later on said that regardless of the vote Britain will not leave the EU even if it meant holding a new referendum (presumably until they get the desired result, i.e. Britain staying in the EU) – democracy I presume. People say that Theresa May is a conservative, nonsense, the only thing that makes her a quote conservative is the fact that she claims that she is a Christian and the fact that she is married to a man, that's it, all of her policies are left-wing liberal ones.

As I previously stated white native countries (in all of Europe and North America) are dying off, all except one – Russia. Russia, under Putin's government, is the only country in the western-civilized world (Europe and North America) that is encouraging people to have a heterosexual family, the only nation that is actively (with success) trying to preserve itself. In response to the moral and social decay of the West, Putin said the following: *"The future challenge for the national Russian identity is connected to the processes we observe outside of Russia. They include foreign policy, moral and other aspects. In these countries (in his speech he is referring to the western world) the moral basis and any traditional identities are being denied: national, religious, cultural and even gender identities are being denied or relativized. Their politics treats a family with many children as equal to a homosexual partnership. The excesses and exaggerations of political correctness in the countries indeed lead to serious consideration for the legitimization of parties that promote the propaganda of pedophilia. And these countries try to force this model onto other countries, globally. I am deeply convinced that this is a direct way to the degradation and primitivization of culture. This leads to a deeper demographic and moral crisis in the west. What can be better evidence for the moral crisis of human society in the west than the loss of its reproductive function? And today nearly all developed western countries cannot survive reproductively, not even with the help of migrants. And we think it is right and natural to defend and preserve these moral values. One has to respect the right of every minority to self-determination, but at the same time there cannot and must not be any doubt about the rights of the majority. At the same time as this process at a national level, we observe on an international level the attempts to create a unipolar, unified model of the world, to relativize and remove institutions international right and national sovereignty. In such a unipolar, unified world there is no place for sovereign states. Such a world needs merely vassals."*

While the west is pushing for the normalization of pedophilia as just a normal sexual orientation, Putin said: *"A society that cannot defend its children today has no tomorrow. It has no future."* If the west continues like this it will not have a future.

Nikolai Berdyaev, a Russian philosopher, once said: *"The meaning of conservatism is not that it impedes movement forward and upward, but that it impedes movement backward and downwards—to chaotic darkness and the return to a primitive state."* There will come a time, hopefully not when it's too late, when people will realize that we as a human race need to take one step backward in order to take two steps forward.

From time to time I hear people say things such as "heterosexual monogamy is the best setup/arrangement". Though this is not in itself false, I think I will rephrase it more accurately by saying "heterosexual monogamy is the only setup/arrangement that actually works because it is the only one that has been proven to work" especially when it comes to raising kids. For this very reason, many have stopped using terms like "traditional" or "nuclear" family and have replaced it with terms such as "biological" or "natural" family. The age-old adage *'if it isn't broken don't fix it'* comes to mind, but unfortunately, there are those who are trying to reinvent the wheel. This debauchery needs to be stopped immediately.

Many, many years ago, even before Putin showed up in public arena (before it became widely acknowledged) I was talking about the demonization of Russia by the west (mainly their bias media). Today is no different, the so-called intellectuals jump on every opportunity to demonize Russia and Putin. They say Russia is homophobic because of their recent laws. First of all Russia didn't criminalize homosexuality, second, the bill in question is not anti-gay, it's anti-LGBT propaganda. This bill forbids LGBT propaganda being taught to children – something every sane culture should do. Russia has also banned abortion after 12 weeks and has banned the advertisement of abortion services.

Unless you have been living under a rock for the past several years you would have seen that Putin (and his government) has formed an alliance with the Russian Orthodox Church in order to protect morals and values on which our European civilization is based on. Personally, I doubt that Putin, an ex-KGB officer, is protecting Christianity for the sake of religion, but rather because they have a mutual goal – saving society through the preservation of the nuclear/traditional family. Many non-religious people are turning to conservatism because they and religious people know that society will not survive without the traditional family unit. It's time we acknowledge the separation of conservative ideology and religion, they are not one and the same. They just have the same goal – preserving the nuclear family.

The irony is that Russia, out of all the nations in the world, became the bastion for traditional, conservative ideology. Why am I saying this? Because Russia was meant to be the first country to lose and get rid of its traditional, conservative ideology through the implementation of Communism which seeks to destroy the family unit.

In Chapter 2 I listed the things that happened in Russia after Communism was proclaimed thru the Bolshevist revolution. Ever since World War Two ended the population of Russia didn't increase in numbers ("thanks" to Communism). There has been a reversal. Modern day Russia is not the 20th century Communist state while the West has became a Socialist protectorate. Russia knows what it's like being in a far left-wing ideological state and it survived and after Communism, Russia is thriving while the West is falling apart.

We are left with two options. First continue with the liberal-leftist approach that will ultimately lead us to a totalitarian, collectivist, futurist dystopia where all the power is centralized in a single state/government that controls all aspects of our lives, where the state will force you to conduct and cater to gay weddings, will force your kids to learn about LGBT ideology and if you as a parent disagree your kids are taken away from you, will force you to accept the notion that there are more than 2 genders and so on. The elite have stated their goal, make the population bisexual and then asexual so that procreation can't occur, simultaneously use social engineering and chemicals to make men and women first unwilling to procreate and at the end unable to procreate (look up the studies women are becoming infertile while the testosterone levels in men have been on a steep decline for at least 30 years). The state will slowly take over parental and reproductive rights until it completely supersedes biological parents.

The alternative is to throw away the failed liberal-leftist ideologies and adopt the more conservative ideology in order to stop the breakdown of the family so that society doesn't collapse.

There is a shift in the political spectrum for the first time since (at least) the end of World War Two. For the first time in some 70 years, people are turning to more conservative/right-wing ideas. If you look at history every time a nation adopted leftists policies it could end in two ways. That country/nation would collapse/die off due to those failed leftist policies or it would turn to conservative/right-wing policies and survive. Another thing to note from history is when do conservative/right-wing ideas become popular, they become popular once the collapse of a society is nigh. As a society hurtles to its demise it either does nothing (continues the same failed path, for example, leftists) or it survives by going to the right side of the political spectrum. Leftists policies bring a country to its knees and right-wing/conservative policies have the potential to save a nation – it's a no-brainer which should we implement. Since leftists say that everyone even slightly right of the center on the political spectrum is a Nazi, right-wing/conservative ideas have not been popular for the past 70 years due to World War Two and even now as soon as someone says they are conservative or have a mildly (mildly by today's leftists-liberal standards) conservative stance they are labeled as a "literal Hitler". The reason as to why conservative ideology has been looked down upon for the last 70+ years (since the end of World War Two) is because we have been conditioned to equate conservatism with Nazism, even though Nazism was a left-wing and not a right-wing movement. Now, slowly but surely the tides are turning, conservative/right-wing ideas are getting more popular because people are realizing that those ideas need to be accepted if the western civilization is to survive the leftist-liberal infestation. Yes, I know that conservative/right-wing ideas can and have been in the past abused but that is not the point. Unlike leftist-liberal policies, conservatism has actually been proven to work. You have an ideology that can work (conservatism/right-wing) and an ideology that has never worked out (left wing), choose carefully because for the first time in 70+ years the peoples of Europe and North America are, in droves, turning to conservatism without the fear of being labeled a racist xenophobic Nazi by self-proclaimed morally superior leftists who think morals are a social construct that don't exist outside of forced social conventions. The funniest part is that the leftist don't even realize that to the true ruling elite they are nothing more than scapegoats.

I'm going to use Newton's third law as an analogy to try and explain what awaits us in the very near future. Newton's third law says *"For every action, there is an equal and opposite reaction"*. For every push, every movement, every agenda there is going to be an equal and opposite movement that contravenes it. For example, in the 1920s and 1930s Germany, many Germans flocked to Nazism in a desperate attempt for salvation. A specter was haunting Germany, mainly decadent liberalism and the threat of Communism. Seeing how destructive and anti-family Communism proved to be in the Soviet Union many German folks turned their support towards the Nazi party (don't forget Hitler came to power democratically), most not because they agreed with Nazi policies but because they saw the Nazis as an "alternative" to the already failed Communist utopia. Many Germans saw salvation in Nazism in an effort to combat Communism. Unfortunately for them, Nazism proved to be the same as Communism. For all intents and purposes, they are the same movement. Ever since the end of World War 2, conservative/right-wing ideology has been looked down upon with disdain, while liberal-leftists (the modern equivalent of the once free-for-all Communist hippies) has taken centre stage. For the first time since the end of World War 2 things are changing. Similar to how many Germans saw hope and salvation in Nazism, nowadays people are gradually turning to more conservative ideologies/ideas in a desperate attempt to save Western civilization (Europe and North America). I repeat *"For every action, there is an equal and opposite reaction"*, for the last 70 years the western civilization has accepted and adopted new-Socialist ideologies, cultural Marxism, sexual liberation and sexual free-for-all, legalized all manner of moral depravity, anti-family ideology. Now, for the first time in a long time, we have a reversal. We are now witnessing the rise of conservative/traditional/right-wing ideology (which I welcome with open arms) in a last-ditch attempt to save what's left of this degenerate civilization. Apart from this very positive conservative revolution we have, on the other hand, a rise of a radical ideology, the rise of Nazism as an "alternative" for this new-age Communism is ever more apparent. In order to prevent the rise of either of the two extreme ideologies (Communism and Nazism), what genuinely conservative/right wing people need to understand is that Nazism and Communism are one and the same.

The elite has been pushing a certain ideology (liberal leftism) for 70 years and now we are starting to see a backlash that will, just like Newton described his third law, be an equal and opposite counter-movement, a reactionary movement if you will. Historically Nazism/Fascism was a counter-revolutionary movement to the revolutionary Marxists. Communism leads to Nazism/Fascism, they both feed off each other. While some are trying to open the gates of the Underworld, Cerberus is nowhere to be seen.

As Paul Joseph Watson said: *"Conservatism is the new counter-culture. We are red pilling generation Z."* (Matrix pun intended I presume)

Despite me being a perennial pessimist I might potentially have some good news. The millennial generation (my generation a.k.a. the worst generation that ever walked on the face of Planet Earth) roughly encompasses people born from the mid-80s till the mid-90s. After the millennials, we have generation Z, those born around the mid-90s and onwards. As I said there is a shift in the political spectrum when it comes to the newer generation, conservatism is becoming cool once again.

"They don't like drugs or gay marriage, and they HATE tattoos: Is 'Generation Z' the most conservative since WW2? - Teenagers born after 2000 - the so-called 'Generation Z' - are the most socially conservative generation since the Second World War, a new study has found. The youngsters surveyed had more conservative views on gay marriage, transgender rights and drugs than Baby Boomers, Generation X or Millennials. When asked to comment on same-sex marriage, transgender rights and cannabis legislation, 59 percent of Generation Z teenagers said they had conservative view. Around 85 percent of Millennials and those in Generation X had a 'quite' or 'very liberal' stance overall. When asked for their specific view on each topic only the Silent Generation (those born from the 1920s to 1940s) was more conservative that Generation Z. 14% - of the 14 and 15-year-olds took a 'quite conservative' approach, while only two percent of Millennials and one percent of Generation X. As well as being more socially conservative, more than 10 percent of teenagers were more likely to avoid tattoos. This compared to only two percent of Millennials and six per cent of Generation X. The research, which surveyed more than 2,000 people, forms parallels with recent evidence that young people are less likely to drink and take drugs than their immediate elders." (source: Dailymail.com)

"The Next Generation of Americans (Gen Z) May Be the Most Conservative Since WWII" (source: cnsnews.com) Maybe, just maybe unlike my generation (the millennial generation), generation Z might not be a bunch of completely useless mouth breathers. Before you start blaming conservatives know this, conservatism would have never risen once again if it weren't for the leftist-liberal infestation that has been going on for decades. As I said, conservatism always appears and gains in popularity once a nation is on its knees, and the west is on its last limb. It's because

for decades we were so far left-liberal on the political scale the need arose to counterbalance this with right wing/conservative ideology, that is if we want to preserve our civilization. Liberalism is a mental disorder – welcome to Rome 2.0, there is a justifiable reason as to why people have started referring to the U.S. as "Weimerica" (the Weimar Republic + America).

"ESTONIA AND GEORGIA PUSH BACK AGAINST LGBT PRIDE EVENTS!!!" (Source: bitchute.com)

"The young are regarded as the most tolerant generation. That's why results of this LGBTQ survey are 'alarming' – Young people are growing less tolerant of LGBTQ individuals, a jarring turn for a generation traditionally considered embracing and open, a survey released Monday shows. The number of Americans 18 to 34 who are comfortable interacting with LGBTQ people slipped from 53% in 2017 to 45% in 2018 – the only age group to show a decline, according to the annual Accelerating Acceptance report. And that is down from 63% in 2016. Driving the dilution of acceptance are young women whose overall comfort levels plunged from 64% in 2017 to 52% in 2018, says the survey conducted by The Harris Poll on behalf of LGBTQ advocacy group GLAAD. 'We count on the narrative that young people are more progressive and tolerant," John Gerzema, CEO of The Harris Poll, told USA TODAY. "These numbers are very alarming and signal a looming social crisis in discrimination.' Among the findings: 36% of young people said they were uncomfortable learning a family member was LGBTQ, compared with 29% in 2017. 34% were uncomfortable learning their doctor was LGBTQ vs. 27% a year earlier. 39% were uncomfortable learning their child had a school lesson on LGBTQ history vs. 30% in 2017." (Source: usatoday.com)

"Young adults in Central and Eastern Europe largely oppose gay marriage" (Source: pewforum.org)

For decades conservatives and religious people have been warning us about the slippery slope that is the gay movement. Well, they were right. Though a slippery slope quite accurately describes the gay movement, I think I might have a better analogy. The gay movement is like a snowball that has been thrown off a snowy mountain. It starts relatively small and innocent, but as it hurtles with a downward spiral it gains in mass and momentum pulling together all other movements each more regressive than the last slowly revealing it's true nature and intent.

You can even describe the gay movement as the Pandora's box or the Trojan Horse – people are blissfully unaware of the perils sexual liberation inevitably leads to.

Here I am going to quote a modern day philosopher and social critique. I don't know his real name but you can find his website "RockingPhilosophy" where he, amongst other things, dissected the gay agenda in a series he titled "Queer Totalitarianism". This philosopher is as of yet the only non-religious person (apart from myself) that I know of that is talking about the gay agenda. In the last few years, for as long as I have been reading about him, he predicted the failure of feminism and multiculturalism, the rise and fall of UKIP (he correctly said that the fall of UKIP will occur once Nigel Farage leaves and leftists infiltrate it), he exposed that Theresa May is only presenting herself as a conservative, he predicted Brexit, he also predicted the rise of Putin and Marine Le Pen and the inauguration of Donald Trump. He definitely has proven credibility.

At the very beginning in 2017 he said something relevant to the topic at hand.

According to him, just like there were 3 waves of the feminist movement there will be a total of 3 stages of the conservative revolution.

"The first stage is a rejection of feminism." 2015 and 2016 were the years in which feminism was finally exposed as a movement that aims to separate women and men and not a movement for equal rights.

"The second stage is the rejection of the anti-white identity politics and mass immigration into western countries." We are currently experiencing this wave. Multiculturalism is a failed ideology. In the last several years countries that had a more conservative approach to immigration (Hungary, Russia, Poland and to a lesser extent Austria, Czech Republic) haven't experienced the destructive side effects of multiculturalism and open border policies, while countries that have liberal/leftist stances to immigration (Germany, France, Italy, Greece and most of all Sweden and the rest of Scandinavia) are suffering and collapsing. Coincidence? No.

He thinks that we are on a cusp of the third wave of the conservative revolution – which is a rejection of the gay agenda. He says that the third wave will begin to emerge within the next 5 years (he said this in 2017). According to him the third wave of this revolution will begin once people, especially leftist-liberals, realize two things. The first thing they have to realize is that the "born gay" theory is pseudoscience and the second thing they have to realize is the true nature of the gay agenda.

He described the gay agenda at the end of 2016. He refers to homosexual lifestyles as fetishes, paraphilias or a form of sexual deviancy. He explained the gay agenda like this: *"Whenever anyone alludes to an agenda the instant reaction from low-level thinkers, apologists and enablers is to call it a conspiracy theory, attack the character of the person making the claim and make snide remarks. When it comes to the possibility of an agenda people should keep compartmentalization in mind, where the higher up the pyramid you are the more you are aware of what is going on. It's becoming increasingly difficult to keep up with the growing number of sexualities that are a part of the gay agenda and this is quite deliberate. It is certainly true that fetish lifestyles have basically existed anywhere where civilization has ensued, but it's also true that the more open this becomes the more it coincides with the destruction of civilization which would explain why so many moralists warn against the tolerance of sexual deviancy. If the gay gene did exist then there is no reason to believe that there isn't a gay gene for any number of lifestyles and this is precisely the point. The people consciously pushing the gay agenda know that they are never going to find a gay or any other kind of sexuality gene because it doesn't exist. So they have to gradually push the agenda forward by making sex and reproduction two completely separate things, this allows them to put fetishes on par with sexual intercourse, starting with fetishes that more people would tolerate and working towards the ones more people would not. By the time we get to the latter there will already be a pathway and template in place with hate crime legislation to silence descent and a large number of politicians that are either sexual deviants themselves or are too self-serving to care about the consequences of their actions. This gradual acceptance is the reason why this agenda began as simply the gay movement and has slowly added more labels to its cause first with lesbianism then bisexuality followed by trans-identity and now moving towards more ambiguous fetishes that resemble the ultimate aim of a sexual free-for-all like queerness and pansexuality. Gradualism is how many radicals push for change and it isn't something new. If a radical agenda moves too quickly the backlash will put a stop to it this is why the first step for this agenda was homosexuality, by far the most socially accepted fetish in human history. The gay agenda is also about redefining sexual normality and repressing anyone that doesn't conform to this standard. Ironically this merely confirms the social collapse our ancestors warned about when sexual deviancy is openly tolerated. We increasingly see a society where people are so tolerant of sexual deviancy that even pedophiles are agitating for acceptance and mainstream media outlets are giving a platform to pedophiles. This really does show that there is no limit to what will be openly tolerated once Pandora's box of sexual deviancy is opened. The only limit is normal sexual identity which is why normal sexuality must be repressed because if sexuality is fluid then innate attraction to the opposite sex must be false. This explains why so many academics and social justice warriors argue that being straight is a social construct which is nothing but a projection of the fact that fetish lifestyles are social constructs shaped by experiences. As we can see the true goal of this agenda is the acceptance of all sexual fetishes. Another way this agenda is gradually pushed on society is by inventing endless types of sexualities that are equally valid and true except being straight of course. This begun with fabricating the distinction between social and biological sex. The idea is that sex is just a superficial way to describe our biology and anatomy while gender is what actually shapes our sexual desires but no such distinction exists because for normal people the sexual desire to reproduce is directly linked to their sex. The major part of this wider agenda is social engineering, by promoting sexual behavior as separate from reproduction it allows the engineers to control the birth rate in society. This also allows the state to take control of parenting by using the cover of equality. Rather than parenting and marriage being a natural right it becomes a state sanctioned privilege once we have to be inclusive to couples that can't conceive children naturally. The breakdown of the family then accelerates the more couples aren't pair-bonding thru the act of having children together."*

In 2015, after the death of the U.S. Constitution, as the U.S. Supreme Court forced gay marriage on all 50 states in the country, he had this to say: *"Like Roe v. Wade (the famous abortion adjudication) and other Supreme Court rulings in history each one of these decisions has eroded the U.S. Constitution gradually morphing the U.S. from a republic into an oligarchic dictatorship that hides behind tyranny of the majority. Throughout all the shallow celebrations on social media and in the press where gay flags are displayed like religious symbols the collective increasingly controls everything about human freedom as we continue down this LGBT road towards totalitarianism. Gay marriage has always been about socially engineering society by destroying and subverting the family. Anyone that actually thinks that the fake battle for marriage equality is over now that two men or two women can marry one another is woefully naïve. Some of these useful idiots go along with the 'progressive' agenda because it makes them feel all warm and fuzzy inside while others use equality as a cover to hide their hatred of normality. Then there is the 10 percent or so that know exactly what is going on, people like Masha Gessen (I covered her in chapter 5) who are aware of the true as opposed to the stated agenda. They usually have financial backing, influence of state apparatus and strong support from the media and activists. Then there is also another 10 percent or so people that see how society is being manipulated by self-serving narcissists and sociopaths that have no concern for the long-term future. These people have to fight against impossible odds to keep society from falling apart, they are the unsung heroes of humanity and the ones that oppose gay marriage even when they know it comes with a terrible personal cost. Gay marriage is already proving to be the very leftist repression many feared it would be. Despite leftists repeatedly pretending that freedom of conscience and religion would not be threatened by their intentions people are now being punished if they don't recognize gay marriage. Examples of this repression continue to increase dramatically. 'Ashers bakery' in Northern Ireland was fined 500 pounds for not making a gay wedding cake. The 'Chick-fil-A' COO was publically derided by the left wing press for disagreeing with gay marriage. A family run cake shop in Oregon was put out of business for not baking a gay wedding cake. As we clearly see the left now has a state sanctioned license to severely punish anyone that doesn't agree with their war against the family and they are more than prepared to use this power at any turn. Now that gay marriage has been forced on to the U.S. on a national scale it's widely suspected that any church that does not agree to conduct a gay wedding ceremony will lose its tax-exempt status. This is no doubt one of many new forms of state punishment that will come out of the woodwork now that the pretense of religious tolerance is no longer necessary. Gay marriage has always been about redefining the family so drastically that it provides no legal protection from the state and making marriage so open to interpretation that becomes a farce. Leftists in history could have only dreamed of the opportunity that gay marriage has created. Despite the smoke and mirrors, the lefts foundation is rooted in the eradication of the family, religion and the nation-state (if you want proof for this read the "Manifesto of the Communist Party" by Karl Marx and Frederick Engels). Rather than being the agenda of the past, the modern left is as obsessed with eradicating the family and religion as ever. Gay marriage provides a multi-pronged attack against the family and religion and it's important that people prepare themselves for the next stage of this process. Rather than gay marriage being the full realization of the LGBT agenda to redefine marriage and the family it's barely the beginning. Among other things polyamory will become a major part of the next big push and many leftists have admitted this. Whatever the case, gay marriage is just one small step towards the wider goal of subordinating the privacy and freedom of the individual to the collective. This entails a society where family, private property, parenthood and all formerly unalienable rights of the individual are now controlled by authoritarian decree. One of the most harmful changes that gay marriage has led to is the redefinition of marriage not as a union based on reproduction and selfless child rearing but one based on a narcissistic interpretation of love. This has now opened the floodgates to practically any definition of marriage based on the same arguments. Some counter gay marriage arguments by defining the marital reproductive union between a man and a woman as the natural family. A better term than the natural family would be the biological family since the union of a man and a woman leads to the merging of their biological DNA through their offspring. The left has repeatedly tried to deny that this is the basis for marriage effectively making them DNA deniers. Marriage also predates the state meaning that the left using the state to redefine marriage violates natural law and biological reality. What many people don't understand about tyranny is that it usually comes bearing a gift hence the reason why gay marriage is not what it seems. In practice, it's a mechanism to suppress and control the natural right of the individual to have a family. All sorts of sophistic arguments have been employed to tear down the reproductive basis of marriage, therefore, giving licence to the state to interfere with family life. Thanks to the absurd arguments in defense of so-called marriage equality practically any definition of marriage is now possible from polygamy to polyamory between infinite numbers of people. It might eventually involve objects, children, animals or marrying yourself, it just depends on how nihilistic and amoral society becomes. If there is one thing we can say for sure there is no limit to what the left will push for."* Even Helen Keller (if she were alive) could see the truth.

In 2016 he also said the following: *"LGBT-like lifestyles are incompatible with conservative values. Although gays, in theory, can keep their sexual lifestyle separate from their political beliefs this is basically impossible in practice because it always ends up becoming an issue one way or another. This is a big problem if conservative and traditional values are going to make any kind of comeback in western society. Long-term, fundamental incompatibility issues exist between the right and the gay lifestyle. I'm not going to say that I'm an expert when it comes to the gay agenda but I will say that I've done more research into this than most and I have articles to prove it. As a result, I understand this agenda far more than your average milk-toast commentator that buys into the "born this way" myth or doesn't want to cover the gay agenda because they are afraid of a backlash."*

All the things that have been pushed in North America (here I am mainly referring to the U.S. and Canada) are being or will be pushed in other countries (from west to east). Many countries, including Serbia, will soon experience the same things the Western World first experienced some 70 years ago (immediately after World War 2). It will all start with the gay/feminist movement which are for all intents and purposes the same movement, this will slowly but surely and inevitably morph into what the elite truly want and that is an unscrupulous sexual free for all where everything is acceptable.

The way things are planned, in 2020 Serbia will recognize same-sex out of wedlock cohabitation. This means same-sex out of wedlock cohabitation will be, in the eyes of the law, deemed equal to a heterosexual marital union with all the benefits (but no responsibilities like child rearing) of traditional marriage. This will ultimately lead to the legalization of gay marriage. This will be done using the argument "since out of wedlock cohabitation and marriage are equal (at least in the eyes of the law, in reality, they are not equal since, unlike marriage, out-of-wedlock cohabitation doesn't provide as many benefits for children when it comes to raising them) we should legalize gay marriage". Gay couples, will of course, get the right to adopt or create children in laboratories.

I'll ask the same question I asked many years ago because no one has yet given me an answer. What will it take for heterosexual biological parents to say enough is enough, leave our kids alone? Where do you draw the line because believe me those who are pushing this agenda have no line to be drawn. You must be out of your mind if you think that this will end by legalizing gay marriage, that's only the beginning.

In our western civilization, there is practically no demographic group that is protected with such zeal as the LGBTQ+ group. I guess Voltaire was right by saying *"If you want to know who controls you, look at who you are not allowed to criticize"*.

"Give a man a truth and he will think for a day. Teach a man to reason and he will think for a lifetime." – Phil Plait

Since earlier I quoted Huxley it's only right that I do the same for Orwell by saying:
"The further a society drifts from the truth the more it will hate those who speak it" and
"In a time of universal deceit, telling the truth is a revolutionary act"

The truth is out there

Veritas vos liberabit

POSTSCRIPT

This book is the first in the series I call 'The Eleventh Crusade'. Despite such a provoking name, this series, which will eventually be expanded, has nothing to do with historic Crusades, their fight against the infidels, nor their pillaging and ransacking of foreign lands, so why such a name? Depending on how you define a Crusade, and what military campaign you include into the Crusading family, you will obviously get a different number of Crusades throughout the ages. Most historic experts agree, albeit with a grain of salt, that in the Middle Ages there were a total of 9 crusades. Fast forwards a couple of hundred years, in the aftermath resulting from the demolition of the Twin Towers in a false flag orchestrated operation, some commentators have declared that the wars in the Middle East, led by the U.S. President Bush, were the Tenth Crusade. Hence why I am starting my own Eleventh Crusade, one which is not against some imaginary enemy, but rather against a very real enemy which lurks in the shadows away from the public eyes. The aim of this, and subsequent books is to expose this secret cabal of elites, their goals, and the methods with which they are achieving said goals to the best of my ability and knowledge which I have accumulated over the past decade or so. Other books in this series will cover a different agenda or even perhaps add to this one. This is my official proclamation of war against the New World Order and all of its agendas.

Made in the USA
Coppell, TX
06 July 2022

79634352R00129